Economic Analysis of Law in European Legal Scholarship

Volume 12

The purpose of this book series is to publish high quality volumes in the growing field of law and economics research in Europe, from a comprehensive theoretical and practical vantage point. In particular, the series will place great emphasis on foundational and theoretical aspects of economic analysis of law and on interdisciplinary approaches in European Legal Scholarship. Following Nobel laureate Ronald Coase's famous essay "The Problem of Social Cost" (1960) fifty years ago law and economics has become the lingua franca of American jurisprudence. In recent decades, law and economics has also gained widespread popularity in Europe and its influence on Legal Scholarship is growing significantly.

Therefore, the economic analysis of law in European Legal Scholarship academic book series illustrates how law and economics is developing in Europe and what opportunities and problems – both in general and in specific legal fields – are associated with this approach within the legal traditions of European countries. Rather than further exploring economic analysis as such, the main focus of this series lies on the implementation of economic methods in legislation and legal adjudication from a European perspective. It takes into account the particular challenges the European legal systems face. Volumes will address law and economics research in Europe from a critical and comparative viewpoint. The studies in this series are strong and bold narratives of the development of economic analysis of law in European Legal Scholarship. Some are suitable for a very broad readership.

Contributions in this series primarily come from scholars in Europe. The purpose is to provide the next generation of European lawyers with the models and skills needed to understand and improve the economic analysis of law in their own legal field. The series includes monographs focusing on specific topics as well as collections of essays covering specific themes.

More information about this series at https://link.springer.com/bookseries/11927

Aurelien Portuese
Editor

Algorithmic Antitrust

Springer

Editor
Aurelien Portuese
The Schumpeter Project on Competition
Policy, Information Technology and
Innovation Foundation
Washington, DC, USA

Economic Analysis of Law in European Legal Scholarship
ISBN 978-3-030-85858-2 ISBN 978-3-030-85859-9 (eBook)
https://doi.org/10.1007/978-3-030-85859-9

This Springer imprint is published by the registered company Springer Nature Switzerland AG.
The registered company address is: Gewerbestrasse 11, 6330 Cham, Switzerland

Contents

Prologue: Algorithmic Antitrust—A Primer

Aurelien Portuese

Abstract The impact of algorithms in our daily lives is ubiquitous. And the impact of algorithms in the competitive environment within which firms operate and consumers shop is equally ubiquitous. Indeed, in the age of Big Data and technological disruptions, algorithms rank search results, help process information and steer prices. The application of antitrust policies to algorithm-driven companies has given rise to what can be referred as "algorithmic antitrust." This chapter provides an overview of the key antitrust implications of algorithms with a predominantly European perspective. The approach aims avoiding both excessively negative portrayal of the effects of algorithms on competition—since many antitrust concerns rarely materialize—without overlooking the specific and convincing competition issues raised by enforcing antitrust laws to algorithm-driven companies. Algorithmic antitrust in general, and in Europe in particular, deserves particular scrutiny. Without resorting to slogans and catchy answers, this chapter maps out the field before other authors delve into specific topics in the subsequent chapters of this book.

1 Introduction

Do tech companies use algorithms to rank their search results? Are algorithms black boxes hardly penetrable to regulators? The European Union (EU) has adopted June 20, 2019, the Regulation (EU) 2019/1150 on promoting fairness and transparency for business users of online intermediation services (from now on "PSB Regulation"). To better implement Article 5 on the ranking of the P2B Regulation, the EC issued in December 2020 the "Guidelines on ranking transparency pursuant to Regulation (EU) 2019/1150". In short, algorithm-driven companies who rank products online will be more transparent concerning their algorithms and be more accountable. The regulatory scrutiny reaches its apex—for which benefits and which costs?

A. Portuese (✉)
Present Address: The Schumpeter Project on Competition Policy, Information Technology and Innovation Foundation, Washington, DC, USA
e-mail: aportuese@itif.org

A. Portuese (ed.), *Algorithmic Antitrust*, Economic Analysis of Law in European Legal Scholarship 12, https://doi.org/10.1007/978-3-030-85859-9_1

Why are these author's books better ranked than that author's book on Amazon? Why is this app allegedly "promoted" on the app store of Apple? Why is this website allegedly "demoted" on Google? Why does the Windows store favor Open Office? All these questions, and countless others, will be the sort of questions that not only enforcers will ask these companies, but most importantly, that these companies will need to anticipate; otherwise, the regulatory sanctions may unfold.

Although the headlines always focus on the same few big tech companies—the "GAFA" for Google, Amazon, Facebook, and Apple—the regulatory scrutiny on algorithms will impact every tech company. Of course, small, and medium-sized companies will be more impacted and will experience greater difficulty to comply with these heroic regulatory obligations than large companies, expected to be harmed but not jettisoned. This phenomenon of a regulatory burden costing more for small and medium-sized companies than for large companies has been witnessed with the General Data Protection Regulation (GDPR). Now, the regulatory scrutiny has shifted from data regulation to algorithm regulation. The two notions are interrelated, but the specific regulatory scrutiny on algorithms deserves a specific assessment. This is the purpose of this book.

This book narrows its focus on the impact of algorithms on competition, and more specifically, on antitrust enforcement. Algorithm-driven companies may compete for thanks to algorithmic superiority, a new form of entrepreneurial innovation. Why do people search on Google and not on Microsoft's Bing? Certainly because consumers consider that Google's algorithm is superior. Therefore, Google has a competitive edge over Bing until the latter ever achieve to overcome its algorithmic deficiency. Thus, companies in the digital age compete thanks to algorithms. Algorithms are intellectual engineering aimed at optimizing the processing of data. In the digital age, the raw material is the data. The more, the better—thus the need to operate in the "Big Data." But data without processing worth truly little, if not anything. If data is the new oil according to the over-used moniker, data is the crude oil; the algorithm is the processing service that creates the value. When Amazon ranks its products, when Airbnb ranks its hosts, when Spotify ranks artists, they provide a service—i.e., processing data in a relevant way thanks to algorithms. Consumers assess the quality of rankings, while the tech company constantly improves its algorithm according to consumer preferences and new computational innovations.

But why should antitrust authorities worry about algorithms? After all, antitrust agencies intervene only when issues arise—anticompetitive conducts are suspected, competition is distorted, incentives are thwarted. Algorithms seem to process data in an optimized fashion, at the benefit of consumers, companies, and at the benefit of innovation. Indeed, the potential benefits of algorithms are enormous. Consumers benefit from complex algorithms daily. Many companies make business decisions after having analyzed vast amounts of data. Algorithms help consumers find the most relevant information to their queries in an efficient way. This is the essence of search algorithms, from Google's algorithm to Netflix's algorithm and millions of other search algorithms.

Algorithms also help companies to better optimize their supply chains by reducing informational costs. Supply chain companies such as Dell, Tesco, and Vespa optimize their operations with algorithms. Algorithms gain momentum with the rise of the Internet of Things (IoT)—another step further to the Artificial Intelligence (AI) inception into our daily lives. Connected widgets will help us ease the hustle of our daily routines. Empty fridge? The connected fridge may know what to buy according to the consumer's shopping preferences and may automatically buy some groceries online and get them delivered on the same day at the doorstep. Need a home repair? Algorithms may soon tell us what to repair, how to do it, and contact the most relevant technician to provide the solution. Feeling groggy? Your health algorithm located in your watch (if not under your skin) may tell you what's wrong and shop for you the most relevant medicine, or you may immediately call a doctor in case of emergency. Do you want to sue your neighbor? Algorithms may tell us your chance of winning in courts and may eventually write the judicial decision themselves—welcome algorithmic judges[1,2]. Of course, some deficiencies may arise—but the trend appears inevitable.

Eric L. Loomis, a citizen from Wisconsin, was sentenced to 6 years in prison based on the judge's consideration of a report generated by a secret algorithm—"The Compas".[3] The Compas considered that Mr. Loomis represented a "high risk of violence, high risk of recidivism, high pretrial risk." And then, the judge, based on that algorithm, concluded Mr. Loomis was a threat to society. He told Mr. Loomis that "you're identified, through the Compas assessment, as an individual who is a high risk to the community." The Wisconsin Supreme Court ruled against Mr. Loomis. The judicial decision was made solely based on that algorithm, but that algorithm was entirely secret since it was protected by intellectual property (IP) rights and other trade secrets. One of the company's executives owning The Compas, stated that "the key to our product is the algorithms, and they're proprietary. We've created them, and we don't release them because it's certainly a core piece of our business."

It thus appears that the era of algorithms is already here. Algorithms are ubiquitous in our daily lives, from non-market decisions to market decisions. When we make market decisions as consumers or companies, algorithms shape and alter the competitive environment. Algorithms determine the price of the products we purchase. Algorithms rank products so that the way we shop is primarily determined by intelligent programming. This is the aspect on which this book will most focus on. But we first need to define algorithms before scrutinizing their competition implications.

---

[1] Ray (2020).

[2] Brayne and Christin (2020) and Glaubitz (2020).

[3] Liptak (2020).

2 What Are Algorithms?

The seminal textbook to refer to is Cormen et al. "Introduction to Algorithms" to understand what algorithms are. The authors state one overlooked truth: "before there were computers, there were algorithms." They refer to non-computational algorithms: you do not need a computer to have an algorithm.

But to be sure, computers are the ideal bedrock for algorithms to flourish. And the advances in AI and programming only make the development of computational algorithms easier. For the sake of argument and as the focus of this book, algorithms refer to computational algorithms. How can we define today's algorithms? Cormen et al. suggest that:

> Informally, an ***algorithm*** is any well-defined computational procedure that takes some value, or set of values, as ***input*** and produces some value, or set of values, as ***output***. An algorithm is thus a sequence of computational steps that transform the input into the output. We can also view an algorithm as a tool for solving a well-specific ***computational problem***. The statement of the problem specifies in general terms the desired input/output relationship. The algorithm describes a specific computational procedure for achieving that input/output relationship. (emphasis in original)[4]

Algorithms, therefore, sort problems via elementary instructions intended to accomplish a specific purpose. Algorithm is a corruption of the name of the ninth-century Persian scholar Muhammad ibn Musa al-Khwarizmi. Al-Khwarizmi wrote the treatise Al-Kitab al-mukhtasar fihisab al-gabr wa'l-muqabala, which paved the way for the word algebra. He also described the modern decimal system for writing and manipulating numbers developed in India several centuries earlier. Al-Khwarizmi used a small circle sift to represent the missing quantity of the mathematical problem. His methods were influential and led to what was known in English as *algorism* or *augrym*, and the small circles were referred to as *ciphers*. Algorism has become an algorithm as we know them today through another deviation with the Greek words *arithmos* and *algos*. The scientists using algorithms as arithmetic techniques were called *algorists* or *computators*, or even *computers*.

Algorithms solve real-world problems with mathematical objects—numbers, arrays, lists, graphs, trees, etc. Algorithms are thus abstract mechanical procedures implementable in any programming language that supports the arithmetical operations. Algorithm designers describe the problem that the algorithm is supposed to solve before designing the algorithm. The algorithm is often referred to as a black box that can be used and implemented without necessarily knowing how or why the algorithm works. IP rights may indeed further reinforce the secrecy of the algorithm. We discuss this notion below.

Algorithms flourish with both computers and Big Data–that is why our technological age is so prone to extensive use of algorithms. Big Data functions both as input and output: you need data for the algorithm to operate, but the result of the algorithm creates new findings, which constitute valuable data. After all, an

[4] Ib. 5.

algorithm is an efficient way of processing data. The larger the amount of data, the more the algorithm proves helpful to perform tasks out-of-reach to human capacities. For instance, the Humane Genome Project made significant progress in identifying 100,000 genes in human DNA, "determining the sequences of the three billion chemical base pairs that make up human DNA, storing this information in databases, and developing tools for data analysis. Each of these steps requires sophisticated algorithms".[5] Constant improvements of algorithms are critical to (individual and corporate) success. For instance, in 2006, the then DVD rental service company Netflix offered a $1 million prize to the team that could improve Netflix's movie recommendation algorithm by 10% (Hafner 2006).

This is the most significant value of algorithms: efficiency. Algorithms can process an amount of information (data) at speed unparalleled to any human mind. Because speed in processing data delivers greater efficiencies and greater ambitions, algorithms enable computer scientists to solve ever-increasingly complex issues. Technological capabilities, such as those ushered by the ongoing digital disruption, allow for complex algorithms to achieve ambitious goals. With 3.5 billion individual searches every day, the Google search algorithm is one of the most complex and encompassing algorithms. Google's algorithm enabled Google's website index to contain billions of pages and 100,000,000 gigabytes of data per 2020. Algorithms are inherently complex and secret. This secrecy is further reinforced by IP rights attached to the algorithm developed by a company. This leads some to consider that algorithm-driven companies generate a "black box society."

3 Are Algorithms Inherently Secret?

Algorithms are ubiquitous, and yet they are secret. The formulas, the algebraic calculus they contain, remain undecipherable to external actors, be they citizens, regulators, or even rivals. Decisions are made out of a "black box." In the *Black Box Society: The Secret Algorithms That Control Money and Information*, Frank Pasquale describes what he considers to be at the roots of our society's secrecy: the countless algorithms that govern our daily lives (Pasquale 2015). Pasquale demonstrates how technology has contributed to the growing complexity and opacity of some sectors of our lives. Instead of being the "promised land of transparency," Internet has become a powerful instrument of obfuscation—a type of secrecy, according to Pasquale. The "black box" refers to the fact that we know the inputs, we know the outputs, but we don't know the process and the mechanical logic of that process. In other words, algorithms remain secret.

But algorithms greatly influence our lives. Human decision-making is increasingly replaced with the algorithmic decision-making process. It is increasingly used because of the algorithms' efficiency (although governments massively engage in

[5] Cormen et al. (2009), p. 6.

algorithmic surveillance). Pasquale mobilizes the one-way mirror metaphor to describe our algorithmic society:

> We do not live in a peaceable kingdom of private walled gardens; the contemporary world more closely resembles a one-way mirror. Important corporate actors have unprecedented knowledge of the minutiae of our daily lives, while we know little to nothing about how they use this knowledge to influence the importance decisions that we and they make. (Pasquale 2015, p. 9)

Data-intensive technology keeps spreading, and with it, our ability to rely on the human decision-making process shrink, Pasquale argues. He criticizes both Silicon Valley and Wall Street–two places where companies excessively rely on the innovativeness of algorithms to produce superior efficiency. These two places cultivate what Pasquale refers to as "agnotology"—the structural production of ignorance helped by the secrecy inherent to their algorithms. Using an old expression that "knowledge is power," Pasquale hints that algorithms leave us in ignorance, therefore impotent. As technology advances, we regress and become increasingly ignorant. We increasingly are subject to other's decisions (be they algorithmic or human-based), and we lay in passivity as ignorant consumers at the mercy of secretive corporations. "Secrecy is approaching critical mass, and we are in the dark about crucial decisions. Greater openness is imperative," warns Pasquale.[6] In an attempted wake-up call, Pasquale identifies reputation, search, and finance as the three "areas in which Big Data looms largest in our lives":

> Consider just a few of the issues raised by the innovative technologies of ranking and evaluation:
>
> - Should a credit card company be entitled to raise a couple's interest rate if they seek marriage counseling? If so, should cardholders know this?
> - Should Google, Apple, Twitter, or Facebook be able to shut down websites or books entirely, even when their content is completely legal? And if they do, should they tell us?
> - Should the Federal Reserve be allowed to print unknown sums of money to save banks from their own scandalous behavior? If so, how, and when should citizens get to learn what's going on?
> - Should the hundreds of thousands of American citizens placed on secret "watch lists" be so informed, and should they be given the chance to clear their names? (Pasquale 2015, pp. 5–6).

It is surprising that these various questions that barely relate to algorithms figure at the core of the concerns identified in a book to demonstrate the undesirable effects of algorithms. Indeed, the first question refers to personalized pricing, just like an insurance company would do since they exist. Informational asymmetries increase costs for both consumers and the company –therefore, the sharing of information may mean that consumers get a better price/premium for their chosen services. The second question refers not so much to algorithms but to a company's choice to decide what's on its shelves. And none of the cited companies can "shut down" websites since they are on the Internet—owned by none of these companies. And none of these companies own books. Only Google and Apple may sell books on their

[6]Pasquale (2015), p. 4.

platforms. Still, de-listing some books remains a business decision that certainly does not prevent readers from getting these books from other sellers.

The third question refers to a monetary policy decision that involves sheer political decisions and accountability–not only does it not refer to a corporate decision, but the change of decision and the need for greater transparency pare down to elected officials. The fourth and final question refers to government surveillance, which does not relate to any corporate decision. The use of a "watch list" by governmental authorities may legitimately be concerning, but administrative accountability can be invoked, and judicial process can keep in check these pratices. No algorithm-driven companies' decisions seem involved in Pasquale's concerns; however, legitimate these concerns may appear to be for some citizens.

Therefore, what is the noxiousness of algorithms? The secrecy inherent to algorithms seems to fuel the groupthink's fears about decisions that humans would no longer make in favor of robots' decision-making process. Algorithms are today's robots, and, with them, all the fears conveyed by science-fiction pop culture. In 1956, Harry Harrison pioneered the genre with "War with the Robots", a collection of science fiction stories: robots are more robust and superior to humans who become outcompeted. Perceived as Frankenstein, robots and, more generally, algorithms portray superior traits than the limited humans. Do the lasting fears of humans being replaced by robots or dominated by algorithms materialize today?

The influential book of Frank Pasquale describes three critical strategies for algorithmic black boxes to remain closed—absolute secrecy, legal secrecy, and obfuscation. Absolute secrecy "establishes a barrier between hidden content and unauthorized access to it".[7] Pasquale identifies passwords and locking doors as evidence of absolute secrecy. Legal secrecy "obliges that privy to certain information to keep it secret" (Pasquale 2015, p. 6). Core to the nature of the contract generally, and to non-disclosure agreements specifically, the privacy of contractual obligations enable trade secrets to be shared only because the number of people to which they are communicated remains under the contractual parties' control. Also, the secrecy of patents, trademarks, copyrights are core to innovation incentivizes—absent such legal "secrecies," the entrepreneurs would have little incentives to innovation, and society would be worse off. Obfuscation "involves deliberate attempts at concealment when secrecy has been compromised".[8] Pasquale identifies the willingness of a firm to communicate millions of documents to regulators as a strategy to obfuscate–namely, to increase opacity in the name of secrecy. On the other hand, one may legitimately argue that the lack of sharing information to authorities or consumers may lead to legal sanctions.

Pasquale unsurprisingly advocates for greater transparency-not only in society but also in algorithms. He argues that "more transparency would help outside analysts check 'irrational exuberance' in markets and uncover corporate misconduct that is now too easily hidden. But. . .when companies parry with complexity too

[7]Pasquale (2015), p. 6.

[8]Ib.

great to monitor or understand, disclosure becomes an empty gesture. We need to put an end to the recursive games of 'disclosure' and 'tricks to defeat disclosure' that have plagued regulators. Transactions that are too complex to explain to outsiders may well be too complex to be allowed to exist".[9]

This radical conclusion—transparency is not enough; excessively complex algorithmic transactions should be banned–echo Justice Louis Brandeis's point about bigness. Invoking Brandeis' heritage,[10] Pasquale implicitly endorses Brandeis's argument to which too complex transactions or organizations for the human mind to exist should be prohibited outright.[11] Because algorithmic machine learning is extraordinarily complex and often impenetrable, algorithms are increasingly called for greater transparency in the vein of Pasquale.

But what is transparency? Transparency in society or inside the algorithm itself, or both? Accountability, rather than pure transparency, appear to be a more realistic and reasonable goal:

> Explanations are a starting point for accountability, not a destination. An explanation can describe how an algorithm makes decisions, but it does not with built-in means of redress for when those explanations contradict larger societal values. This problem is not one for computer scientists alone; lawyers and policymakers must join the discussion around explaining algorithmic decisions to decide how and when these explanations can address societal harms (Nicholas 2020, p. 730).

Full transparency of algorithms cannot be achieved since algorithms may remain obscure to designers themselves. However, potential violations of core societal values by algorithms require greater accountability. For instance, racist algorithmic bias may need to be addressed and trigger greater accountability by designers.[12]

We need algorithmic governance, not necessarily algorithmic transparency. Because the need to respect the privacy of contracts and the secrecy of trade secrets implies that algorithms cannot be subject to more significant disclosure requirements than any traditional contract could be, algorithmic transparency is both unattainable and undesirable. Algorithmic governance needs to be defined. The governance of algorithms (or algorithmic governance/governability) refers to both the concerns regarding algorithmic transparency and the idea that there should be algorithmic accountability towards regulators.[13] More widely, algorithmic governance encapsulates a range of heuristic dimensions—from algorithm-specific standards to more generic ethical and economic values in society.[14] Algorithmic governance includes standards that are perceived with substantive differences from the firm's perspective or the regulators' perspective. These presumably irreconcilable perspectives are best

---

[9] Ib, 16.

[10] Ib, 11.

[11] Brandeis (1934).

[12] Garcia (2016).

[13] Citron and Pasquale (2014).

[14] Bracha and Pasquale (2008), Granka (2010).

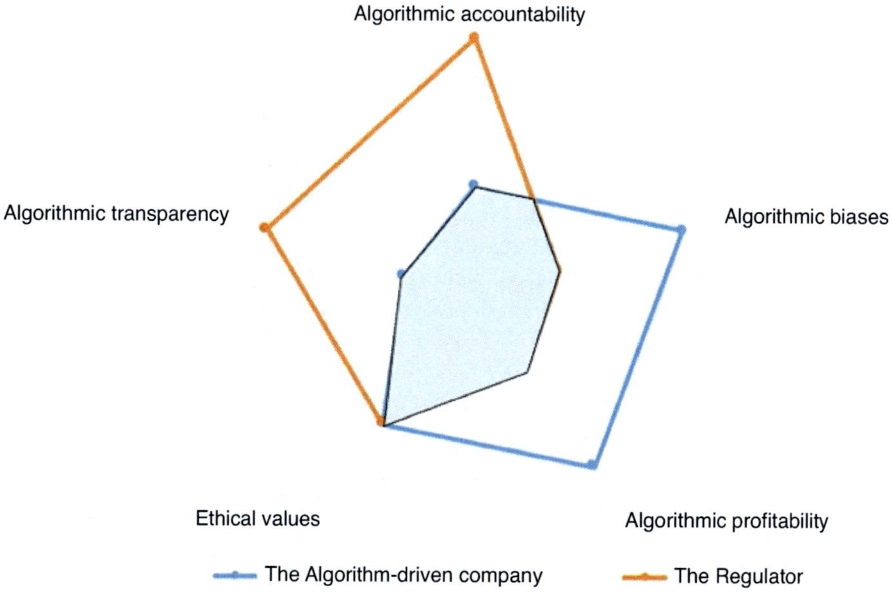

Fig. 1 Perceptions on algorithmic features

sketched out in Fig. 1, where deviations from the center of gravity depict the intensity of one's preferences.

The firm will value most the profitability derived from the complex and innovative algorithms. It will value biases as the best way to price discrimination between customers and devise tailor-made customer services. Algorithmic accountability from the regulator will be willy-nilly accepted as part of the firm's corporate social responsibility, generating societal benefits. Equally, the firm's managers embed their ethical values, which will exist into algorithmic designers and subsequently underpin algorithms. However, transparency concerning IP-intensive algorithms will barely be acceptable by firms, which will legitimately protect trade secrets and confidential information as proprietary assets.

On the other hand, the regulator will most disregard the profitability derived from the algorithms by the rm. and will shun any bias (pricing or non-pricing ones) as unfair practices either for economic reasons (i.e., algorithmic price discrimination) or for ethical reasons (i.e., market partitioning, offensive biases towards minority groups. . .). Algorithmic accountability is considered the paramount goal that any regulatory monitoring is dependent upon, while algorithmic transparency will be sought only to the extent that gross violations of IPRs are precluded. Finally, the regulator (and, more generally, the government) will seek to infuse (and check adherence to) ethical values held dear by the people. Consequently, the shaded area represents the space for acceptable, mutually agreeable areas of algorithmic governance from both the firm and the regulator. This shaded area is thereby space within which algorithmic governance can optimally occur by considering both the firm's and the regulator's subjective preferences. Thereby, optimal algorithmic governance would consider the limits of the inner space of mutually acceptable algorithmic governance to design and enforce regulatory interventions.

However, greater algorithmic accountability is within reach—companies and governments can be explained to consumers, citizens, judges how they design algorithms, how they use the data collected, and how they exploit the algorithmic results in terms of decision-making processes. Both companies and governments can be nevertheless unsure that such accountability may not violate fundamental IP rights associated with the algorithms or with the data used in the algorithms. This approach may deem appropriate concerning how algorithm-driven companies use data in algorithmic decision-making processes to compete and innovate in the markets. Algorithmic governance enters competition policy–or "algorithmic antitrust."

4 "Algorithmic Antitrust": Competition Policy for Algorithm-Driven Decisions

Hence, algorithms impact the competitive environment, hence on the application of competition policy, because they shape consumer choices. In the digital age, firms compete increasingly via innovation: innovation makes them have a competitive advantage or disadvantage. Price competition matters less. Innovation matters more as a viable strategy to gain market shares. Algorithms are part of digital innovation. Thus, the more algorithms are efficient, the better the companies will optimally process the data essential for success in the digital economy. The French Competition Authority and the German Competition Authority have issued a Report on "Algorithms and Competition" in 2019 where, before warning of the potential anticompetitive effects of algorithms, write that:

> There is little doubt that digitalization is revolutionizing many sectors of our economies. Algorithms are among the most important technological drivers of this process and enable firms to be more innovative and efficient.[15]

Algorithms represent strong competitive constraints and therefore deliver considerable advantages for reinvigorating competition in the digital economy. The Organisation for Economic Co-Operation and Development (OECD) published an influential study in 2017 about the role of algorithms in competition policy.[16] Section 3 of the Report outlines the pro-competitive effects of algorithms, and there are many. Indeed, the algorithm's core rationale is to solve problems frequently created by informational asymmetries and high transaction costs. From market analysis, supply and demand do not match, whereas they could under the condition that the information is better lubricated amongst market actors. A textbook example

[15] Autorité de la Concurrence and Bundeskartellamt (2019).

[16] OECD (2017).

is Uber's algorithm: the app allows for consumers and taxi drivers to better be connected thanks to a robust algorithm that ranks the available consumers and available taxi drivers at any given time at any given location.

The pro-competitive effects of algorithms listed by the OECD are numerous. On the supply side, the OECD notes that algorithms "help increasing transparency, improving existing products or developing new ones. . .[M]arket entry has been promoted by the ability of firms to develop new offerings based on algorithms. . .This triggers a virtuous mechanism whereby companies are under constant pressure to innovate, thus promoting dynamic efficiencies. . .The rise of algorithms on the supply side can also promote static efficiencies by reducing the cost of production, improving quality and resource utilization, as well as streamlining business processes".[17] Algorithms can indeed facilitate market entry. TikTok's algorithm enabled the social media app to disrupt market leaders such as Instagram and Facebook.[18] It is also true that the algorithm reduces production costs and optimizes the supply chain.[19] On the demand side, the OECD identifies the dynamics ushered by algorithms as helping consumers to make more informed decisions. The OECD indeed considers that algorithms "better organize information so that it can be accessed more quickly and more effectively, and they provide new information on dimensions of competition other than prices, such as quality and consumers' preferences. Thus, algorithms have the potential to create positive effects on consumers and social welfare".[20] Algorithms can indeed use prices but not only: their complexity enables users to better satisfy their preferences according to their tastes. One seminal example is the algorithms inherent to dating apps: they better match consumer preferences than the old market actors such as marriage bureaus.[21]

Thanks to deep learning techniques–namely, techniques using a multi-layered structure of algorithms called neural networks—can further reduce the transaction costs in complex decision-making processes. Algorithmic decision-making both comes closer to the human brain and surpasses the human brain's limitations. Most importantly, algorithms are ideally suited to perform "dynamic pricing." Dynamic pricing allows consumers and companies to constantly adjust prices according to countless parameters so that price discrimination–namely, the adjustment of prices to each consumer according to their willingness to pay—can be reached. Indeed, pricing algorithms "learn through trial and error and through finding patterns from a great volume and variety of data, leading to optimal pricing".[22]

Pricing algorithms as tools to optimal pricing allow for price discrimination (which is efficiency-enhancing) and leads to better transitory market equilibrium.

[17] OECD (2017), p. 14.

[18] Alexander (2020).

[19] Veinott (2005).

[20] OECD (2017), p. 15.

[21] Courtois and Timmermans (2018).

[22] OECD (2017), p. 16.

The OECD indeed considers that pricing algorithms, enabling dynamic pricing, "not only prevent unsatisfied demand and excess of supply, but under certain competitive conditions it also guarantees that all mutually beneficial transactions between consumers and suppliers are exhausted".[23] In that regard, pricing algorithms help reach "perfect" price discrimination.[24] Indeed, algorithmic pricing has "clear efficiency advantages for companies–it can be cost-reducing, revenue-increasing, or both".[25] Algorithmic pricing takes place in markets where:

- The cost to serve consumers differ considerably from consumer to consumer, in ways which can be approximated using observable data (e.g., credit and insurance markets);
- Demand fluctuates much more rapidly than supply (e.g., hotels and ridesharing); or,
- The price-setter has a wide range of products to price, and algorithmic approaches bring a significant cost advantage (e.g., consumer retail).[26]

The U.K. Competition Authority considers that "algorithmic systems also benefit consumers indirectly by increasing efficiency and effectiveness across many areas; For example, businesses can now use algorithmic systems to reprice portfolios of thousands of products in real-time, and pricing efficiencies can be passed on to customers. As third-party solutions make algorithmic pricing more accessible to smaller businesses, this can lower the barriers to entry and enhance innovation and competition."[27]

Similarly, the French and German competition authorities consider that pricing algorithm "may adapt prices to the company's own cost, capacity, or demand situation but also to competitor's prices, which can be monitored using yet another algorithm." These algorithms may thus have detrimental effects on a competition policy, as discussed below.

On the other hand, consumers benefit from algorithms by more informed purchasing conditions, more substantial competitive constraints exerted on the demand-side thanks to algorithmic advertising and improving equality amongst consumers since less informed consumers may rely on algorithms to gain knowledge. For instance, algorithms for financial trading may help consumers getting into trading without in-depth knowledge of the financial markets.

In his book *The Antitrust Paradigm: Restoring a Competitive Economy*, Jonathan Baker discusses how "algorithmic pricing could promote competition in some cases and harm it in others".[28] He envisages a hypothetical case scenario –the "leader-follower pricing algorithm." In this scenario, rivals' firms use pricing algorithms to mimic leader-follower pricing in the market. In this scenario, the price, he argues, "would be expected to end up at the lowest predetermines maximum established by

[23] OECD (2017), p. 16.

[24] Ib.

[25] Oxera (2018), p. 3.

[26] Ib.

[27] CMA (2021).

[28] Baker (2019), p. 101.

any of the competing firms".[29] But if the predetermined maximum prices "are set above the competitive price, the firms would exercise market power"–thereby suggesting that any price, however algorithmically defined, set above the competitive price could be subject to antitrust scrutiny since this would exhibit market power.[30] Pricing algorithms may also be more "sophisticated," Baker argues, and lead to coordination problems.[31] We scrutinize this possibility in the next section.

Although some reports and studies may allude to the positive effects of algorithms from a competition policy perspective, we have to acknowledge that most of the studies and discussions revolve around the negative impacts—or, more adequately, the risks of harm–posed by algorithms. After all, this is not so surprising: antitrust is all about proscriptive policy. It prohibits undesirable conduct, thereby focusing only on a social phenomenon's negative consequences–be it innovation or algorithms. But there is an undeniable tension in antitrust policy to over-emphasize the negative consequences of these social phenomena: it may alter the regulatory and judicial decision on too much caution and too little on innovation. Indeed, antitrust decisions inherently need to be made through a balancing exercise whereby the positive consequences and weighed out against the negative consequences of the scrutinized conduct. But, given antitrust's focus on the negative aspects of innovative conducts, would the final decision as per the competitiveness of conduct not be biased toward excessive alarmism? The antitrust discussion about algorithms exclusively focusses on the detrimental risks of algorithms and, although little evidence substantiating those fears, the tone of the debate may very well bias antitrust enforcement toward false positives—namely, the risks of over-enforcing antitrust in areas where algorithms may deliver more benefits than costs to society.

The tone of the antitrust debate regarding algorithms has been set by one influential book that, on both sides of the Atlantic, achieved to generate worries amongst antitrust enforcers. This book was published at Harvard University Press in 2016 by Ariel Ezrachi and Maurice E. Stucke, *The Virtual Competition – The Promise and Perils of the Algorithm-Driven Economy*.[32] We discuss the book's central tenets and appraise the risks outlined in light of the experience since the publication of the book.

5 Is The Digital Hand Malicious?

Ezarchi and Stucke recognize how to present algorithms have become in our daily lives. However, the emergence of algorithms, especially in market transactions, the authors warn, comes with considerable risks. These risks are relevant to antitrust

[29] Baker (2019), p. 103.

[30] Baker (2019), p. 103.

[31] Baker (2019), pp. 104–106.

[32] Ezrachi and Stucke (2016).

authorities. The authors identify two categories of risks: (1) the risk of collusion; (2) the risk of price discrimination. Each of these risks corresponds to antitrust concerns–namely, Section 1 of the Sherman or Article 101 of the Treaty on the Functioning of the European Union (TFEU) and Section 2 of the Sherman Act or Article 102 of the TFEU, respectively. We outline the authors' core arguments before discussing them.

First, Ezrachi and Stucke discuss the possible ways algorithms may facilitate cartels and illegal collusive practices.[33] The point is not about sheer cartel agreement among computer and computer scientists. These sorts of agreements may be gross violations of antitrust laws, which may not last long given the ability of antitrust authorities to prosecute them. The point is rather about the "more elusive forms of collusion, achieved through subtler means, which do not amount to a hard-core cartel and are beyond the reach of the law.[34] The authors consider four scenarios where algorithms may subtly collude on prices so that anticompetitive effects may be affected. Here are the four scenarios the authors identified:

(i) The *Messenger* scenario: algorithms are here used to implement humans' desire to collude. Algorithms are nothing but an efficient way of enforcing cartels by colluders. It is clear that "under this scenario, humans collude".[35] This scenario does not revolutionize the conceptual framework of antitrust authorities: they prosecute cartels and collusive practices irrespective of the means chosen by the individuals to make this collusion possible. Therefore, algorithms bring little newness to the antitrust enforcement effort under the Messenger scenario. The authors illustrate this scenario with the Carrefour case in Greece. The French supermarket, Carrefour, has been found that the franchisor could monitor the prices of its franchisees through a complex IT system. In 2010, The Green Hellenic Competition fined Carrefour Marinopoulos €12.5 million for antitrust violations, including the IT-monitored Resale Price Maintenance (RPM) over its network of franchisees. The Commission considered that Carrefour's IT system enabled price monitoring "with the sole purpose of appraising the 'appropriateness' of such retail prices in relation with the total pricing policy of the network".[36] In this scenario, the algorithm may help humans collude. Most specifically, according to the authors, "could weaken the individual's sense of illegality and, in so doing, further facilitate the illegal activity".[37] This scenario is relatively neutral concerning antitrust assessment because "as messengers, algorithms are neither a negative nor positive force; rather, there is a technological extension of the human will";[38]

[33] Ezrachi and Stucke (2016), p. 35.

[34] Ezrachi and Stucke (2016), pp. 35–36.

[35] Ezrachi and Stucke (2016), p. 36.

[36] Ezrachi and Stucke (2016), p. 40.

[37] Ezrachi and Stucke (2016), p. 44.

[38] Ezrachi and Stucke (2016), p. 44.

(ii) The *Hub and Spoke* scenario: under this scenario, the algorithm enables the firms to monitor a wide range of prices through vertical restraints. The algorithm takes advantage of numerous vertical agreements and acts as a hub and "orchestrate industry-wide collusive, leading to higher prices." Here, the centrality of the algorithm allows for coordination across different lines of business, different prices so that algorithmic monitoring of prices leads to collusive practices. The hub and spoke collusion occur because "rivals end up using the same algorithm (the hub), which thereby softens competition and leads to higher prices".[39] The authors refer to the European Commission's prohibition of the LIBOR's manipulation. The London Interbank Offered Rate (LIBOR) is a benchmark interest rate based on the rates at which banks lend unsecured funds to each other on the London interbank market. Multiple rival banks plotted to manipulate these interest rates for profit starting as far back as 2003. The European Commission fined seven banks in December 2013, amounting to €1.49bn.[40] In this scenario, "collusion may be the consequence, but not necessarily the original aim when each competitor opts for the same third-party algorithm".[41] Also, the authors used the case of Uber's alleged hup and spoke algorithmic collusion. They argue that "Uber's algorithm determines for hundreds of competing drivers the base price for the trip when to implement a surge price, for which areas, for how long, and to what extent. Granted, the customer can compare the Uber price to alternatives (such as taxis and other car service platforms like Lyft). Still, as more customers and drivers rely on Uber's platform, one may wonder what effect its algorithm could have on the market price".[42] This speculation may nevertheless materialize given the fierce competitive constraints exerted across platforms and car-hailing services. A more convincing example was the case of *Eturas* on January 21, 2016.[43] The Court of Justice of the European Union (CJEU) considered that travel agents knowingly monitoring price discounts through algorithms can be presumed to have participated in a collusive practice prohibited by Article 101 TFEU. This interesting case is discussed below and in different chapters of the book;

(iii) The *Predictable Agent* scenario: this scenario perhaps most reflects the intuitive idea of algorithms as collusive tools in the marketplace. This scenario refers to the absence of humanly designed collusion: algorithms constantly "monitor and adjust to each other's prices and market data" so that algorithm-powered price parallelism will lead to collusive outcomes.[44] Absent human interventions, algorithms are conducive to a cartelized economy—this is for the authors

[39] Ezrachi and Stucke (2016), p. 51.

[40] European Commission (2013).

[41] Ezrachi and Stucke (2016), p. 48.

[42] Ezrachi and Stucke (2016), p. 51.

[43] C-74/14, Eturas e.a., ECLI:EU:C:2016:42.

[44] Ezrachi and Stucke (2016), p. 36.

"Tacit Collusion on Steroids".[45] The Predictable Agent scenario, together with the Digital Eye scenario, are the two scenarios to be considered by the authors as epitomizing what they consider to be "virtual competition": "industry-wide use of pricing algorithms leads to higher prices, without any clear or implied human anticompetitive agreement".[46] Pricing algorithms may take advantage of market transparency and "quickly access and process key market data, including competitors' prices and sale terms, and respond to market changes".[47] Predictive analytics enables dynamic pricing and, as rivals increasingly using these pricing algorithms, the market "stabilize"—meaning, competition decreases up to the point where it becomes "virtual".[48] In short, the authors speculate that "the industry-wide use of pricing algorithms increases both market transparency and the risk of conscious parallelism".[49] Should antitrust authorities want to investigate and prosecute parallel algorithmic pricing, the absence of collusive agreement or any evidentiary proof of collusion may prove impossible for these authorities to prohibit such tacit collusion. Indeed, the authors recognize that "a rational decision by competitors to market dynamics, in itself, is legal".[50] The authors consider that for a defendant who had used an algorithm exhibiting characteristics of the *Predictable Agent* scenario, the defendant must have developed the algorithm (i) with the intent to achieve an anticompetitive outcome, or (ii) while "aware of their actions' natural and probable anticompetitive consequences".[51] Both requirements refer to the anticompetitive intent rather than the anticompetitive effect: this suggests that the algorithm may be pro-competitive but because the intent was anticompetitive, antitrust authorities may prohibit such an algorithm. We discuss such a problematic outcome. Also, the authors suggest that "another approach may be to consider the use of such algorithms as market manipulation": the law could prohibit excessive algorithmic transparency whenever there is anticompetitive intent from computer designers. Again, the focus on intent may suggest that many pro-competitive algorithms may end up being banned without clear rationale.

(iv) The *Digital Eye* scenario: this scenario is the most subtle, most sophisticated one. The *Digital Eye* refers to the ability of algorithms to self-teach how to maximize profits: deep learning machine learning and progress in AI may reduce informational costs. Increased market transparency thanks to algorithmic-processed monitoring may generate anticompetitive outcomes: competition between firms becomes increasingly less fierce. This paves the

[45] Ezrachi and Stucke (2016), p. 36.
[46] Ezrachi and Stucke (2016), p. 56.
[47] Ezrachi and Stucke (2016), p. 61.
[48] Ezrachi and Stucke (2016), p. 63.
[49] Ezrachi and Stucke (2016), p. 63.
[50] Ezrachi and Stucke (2016), p. 65.
[51] Ezarchi and Stucke (2016), p. 68.

way for a "virtual competition" which benefits no one.[52] The complexity of the algorithm together with Big Data enables companies to "process high volumes of data in real-time to achieve a God-like view of the marketplace".[53] Borrowing from Uber's 'God View' functionality enabling the company to see the location of all Uber vehicles and customers, Ezrachi and Stucke consider that computers can now "anticipate and react to competitive threats well before any pricing change".[54] They explain that "God View enables each algorithm to detect any competitive maneuver quickly, and thus to know when and how to retaliate. By responding quickly, the rivals deprive any would-be mavericks of the benefits of launching competitive initiatives, and thereby diminish the incentive to undertake these initiatives in the first place".[55] The scenario loses any practicality given the strong assumption made from the onset: "our scenario assumes that each firm will have the God View technology".[56] Not only would companies not systematically have the "God View technology," but even if they all have such technology, differences in their algorithms (let alone in their products and services) prevent full similarity, hence homogeneity. Differences in technologies and products prevent collusive practices from arising by the mere fact that companies adopt the self-learning algorithm "God View technology."

The first two scenarios represent nothing new compared to traditional price-fixing collusive practices. They are already present in our lives. Indeed, Ezrachi and Stucke argue that "we are already witnessing the Messenger and Hub and Spoke collusion scenarios".[57] This is true: the cases of *Eturas*, *Libor*, and Asus et al., for instance, illustrate such reality.

But the originality of the two other scenarios—namely the *Predictable Agent* and the *Digital Eye*—are mere speculations as acknowledged by the authors themselves. They argue that the "Predictable Agent will likely be the next scenario we'll see. Our final collusion scenario –Digital Eye –represents the next frontier".[58] Consequently, it appears that the originality of the collusion scenarios is theoretical discussions rather than empirical inductions.

The speculative nature of the two main and original scenarios envisaged in *Virtual Competition* by Ezrachi and Stucke appears to be confirmed by the lack of evidence of the competitive risks exposed in these two scenarios. The risks ascribed to self-learning algorithms referred to in the Digital Eye scenario seem to refer to the very essence of the competitive process rather than to a distortion of such process.

[52] Ezrachi and Stucke (2016), p. 37.

[53] Ezrachi and Stucke (2016), p. 71.

[54] Ezrachi and Stucke (2016), p. 72.

[55] Ezrachi and Stucke (2016), p. 72.

[56] Ezrachi and Stucke (2016), p. 72.

[57] Ezrachi and Stucke (2016), p. 71.

[58] Ezrachi and Stucke (2016), p. 71.

Indeed, the authors note that "rivals without the God View technology and data stream lose sales until they exist the market. Entry barriers increase over time, as weaker firms are eliminated, and the leading firms acquire even more real-time data on the flow of commerce".[59] The authors refer to the God View technology to correspond to a highly sophisticated algorithm (i.e., self-learning algorithm). Therefore, this is a technological innovation, a technical progress, a market improvement for which firms have allegedly spend lots of money researching, developing, and commercializing.

Consequently, it seems that this technological innovation may enable the firms using that algorithm to out-compete rivals. In other words, to effectively compete, firms innovate. Is that illustrative of a lack of competition as suggested by the collusive scenario, or would not it be more illustrative of a fierce competition that takes place based on innovation for the benefits of consumers (i.e., lower prices, better services, higher quality), of the market (i.e., minimization of transaction costs), and producers (i.e., increased profitability through patented algorithms)?

The authors regret that "weaker firms" may exit the market due to the technological innovations of the leading ones. Wouldn't it be the very essence of the competitive process to incentivize such an outcome rather than negating such a process? Thanks to technological innovations, entrants can effectively outcompete incumbents for the benefit of consumers and society. How could Amazon have outcompeted Walmart if not by superior technological efficiency via its algorithms? How could Uber have outcompeted taxi drivers if not by superior technological efficiency via its algorithms? Algorithms are the leverage point by which potential entrants can scale up and effectively compete with laggard incumbents. Thus, it would be ironic for antitrust authorities to prevent the technology and the innovation that benefit consumers and society in general and be the exact route by which entrants can disrupt incumbents. The competitive process takes place based on innovation–to chill innovation would not preserve but rather distort the competitive process.

Ezrachi and Stucke hypothesize that sophisticated algorithms (such as the deep-learning one from the Digital Eye scenario) will lead to potential entrants not entering because of too competitive prices offered by incumbents. They indeed argue that "no one will be tempted to improve their products, lower prices, or enter new markets because others will immediately detect and punish this initiative".[60] This speculation overlooks that prices matter much less than product attributes (quality, features, usage, etc.. . .) in the digital economy. Does the end-user price matter for social media platforms, search engines, etc.? Does it matter even for smartphones, apps, and digital services, given the heterogeneity of services? For instance, do consumers use Uber because they think it is cheaper than Lyft of taxis, or because they favor the service they receive (quality of driving, quality of the car, ease of transportation and feedback, etc.)? To consider that firms may not enter

---

[59] Ezrachi and Stucke (2016), p. 73.

[60] Ezrachi and Stucke (2016), p. 73.

markets because of too competitive prices offered by incumbents willing to retaliate in threat of entry under-estimate the fact that competition takes place based on quality, innovation in the digital economy rather than mere prices.

Additionally, would it not be evidence of significant competitive constraints exerted by potential entrants (hence the ease of entry) if incumbents would immediately react by lowering prices in the threat of entry? Prices would be kept at the lowest (meaning most competitive) level irrespective of entry. Consumers are better off irrespectively of which company offers the service as long as effective competition enables the incumbent to be disciplined by competitive constraints. Rivalry plays out without necessarily market entry—the ease (and threat) of entry suffices for the market to exhibit competitive prices. Antitrust authorities would have difficulty explaining that the incumbents' reactions to competitive constraints not to be disrupted are illegitimate. The very process of competition implies that incumbents cannot rest on their laurels in the potential entry; otherwise, this would be evidence of monopoly power. In other words, the incumbent is placed in a dilemma should antitrust authorities consider, as the authors seem to suggest, that anticipation and retaliation inevitably are anticompetitive: should it react, it would amount to an anticompetitive practice; should it not react, this would demonstrate monopoly power justifying antitrust scrutiny and sanctions. A more realistic (and perhaps reasonable) way to look at these reactions would be to consider that entry barriers are considerably low. Technology, being both an entry barrier and ease of market entry, enables potential entrants to exert competitive constraints on incumbents under the constant pressure of being disrupted. Antitrust concerns should be wary of the unintended consequences on innovation and consumer welfare of hasty conclusions about the companies' use of deep-learning algorithms.

Also, the theoretical example of the Digital Eye seldom refers to the first two scenarios whereby collusive practices made by humans are merely more effective with algorithms. Indeed, the authors argue that:

> Computers are not trusting. But self-learning algorithms and God View could make tacit collusion among more competitors likelier. The stability needed for tacit collusion is enhanced because computer algorithms, while not trusting, are unlikely to exhibit other human biases. Human biases can always be reflected in the programming code, but if some biases are minimized (such as loss aversion, the sunk cost fallacy, and framing effects), the algorithm acts consistently on more deliberative analysis, rather than intuition.[61]

The fear that algorithms may collude because they overcome the human biases seems to relate to the first two scenarios where algorithms are precisely used because they may better enforce collusive practices than humans. To what extent this differs from the first two scenarios may require clarification. And yet, the authors consider that, with the Digital Eye scenario, "we are far removed from the first two scenarios, Messenger and Hub and Spoke, where algorithms helped humans collude. We are

[61] Ezrachi and Stucke (2016), p. 76.

even beyond Predictable Agent, where humans did not expressly collude but knew that tacit collusion was the likely outcome if each adopted profit-maximizing pricing algorithms".[62] This fourth scenario reveals "no evidence of anticompetitive intent".[63] There may also be no evidence of anticompetitive effects. And yet, antitrust authorities should prosecute "an anticompetitive outcome which we may not readily perceive and with no one to blame".[64] To justify a more aggressive antitrust enforcement against this fourth hypothetical scenario, the authors advocate for a change of the law even if, as they contemplate. This may push companies to adopt inefficient behaviors instead of efficient business reactions:

> Can the law credibly ask developers to instruct the algorithm not to react to market changes – to be inefficient? Although conscious parallelism is legal, the question is whether such practices, when implemented by smart machines in a predictable digitalized environment, ought to be condemned.[65]

Suggesting that the law could adopt a presumption of per se illegality, the authors consider that pricing algorithms "instead of representing the end of collusion, potentially mark a new, more durable form of collusion".[66] These risks are merely "potential" risks, and not evidenced risks allude to a precautionary approach by the authors. Although we cannot evidence anticompetitive outcomes by pricing algorithms (in the fourth and most thought-provoking scenario), the authors warn that "competition authorities must be aware of these risks." Despite the absence of evidence, this is precisely what happened after the publication of the book with many competition authorities publishing reports on the impact of algorithms on competition law, thus reiterating the fears expressed in Virtual Competition without nevertheless additional evidence.

Less significantly and less influentially, the authors devote the Part III of their book to discuss the perceived issue of price discrimination by algorithms.[67] Although price discrimination is commonly believed to be pro- and anticompetitive by economists, the fact that pricing algorithms improve, and ease price discrimination (according to each consumer's preferences and traits) generates antitrust concerns for the two authors. The authors are categorical and unapologetically dystopian:

> Perfect price discrimination may be unattainable. But 'almost perfect' behavioral discrimination may be within reach. In the online world where Big Data meets behavioral economics, we are witnessing an emerging category of price discrimination –behavioral discrimination. Here, firms harvest our personal data to identify which emotion (or bias) will prompt us to buy a product and the most we are willing to pay. In tracking us and collecting data about us, sellers can tailor their advertising and marketing to target us at

---

[62] Ezrachi and Stucke (2016), p. 77.

[63] Ezrachi and Stucke (2016), p. 77.

[64] Ezrachi and Stucke (2016), p. 79.

[65] Ezrachi and Stucke (2016), p. 79.

[66] Ezrachi and Stucke (2016), p. 80.

[67] Ezrachi and Stucke (2016), p. 83 et sub.

> critical moments with the right price and emotional pitch. So behavioral discrimination increases profits by increasing overall consumption (by shifting the demand curve to the right and price discriminating) and reducing consumer surplus.[68]

Describing personalized advertising and pricing, the authors consider that these ubiquitous phenomena exacerbated with the digital economy (but existing before it yet) may generate undesirable consequences such as a consumer surplus loss. They are considering erroneously that a shift in the demand curve may mean a reduction of the consumer surplus. In contrast, it precisely exhibits an increase in consumer surplus. The authors rely on textbook models of competition law, which bears little (if not no) relevance to the complexity of the digital economy. Beyond this error on the economic significance of the shift of the demand curve to the right, Ezrachi and Stucke imply that the fact that sellers charge consumers "the right price" and can better personalize advertising contrary to indiscriminate, mass advertising is negative consequences harming consumers and competition. It can be argued precisely the contrary: personalized pricing better takes into consideration each consumer's willingness to pay as opposed to indiscriminate pricing, and personalized advertising better takes into consideration each consumer's preferences and tastes as opposed to annoyingly irrelevant advertising. Thus, it is hard to substantiate the hypothetical claims made by the authors with empirical evidence and economic theory. But what are thus the risks of algorithmic pricing if the main argument–namely, the fourth scenario—proves either unsubstantiated or erroneously analyzed? The risks may be merely hypothetical, but the approach undoubtedly epitomizes a risk-averse, precautionary approach toward technological innovation. Such a precautionary approach may take place at the expense of the pace of innovation and the expense of consumer benefits.

To the authors' perceived problems, competition authorities should intervene: the "competition agency must look beyond the face to see whether competitors are racing to the bottom in finding new ways to exploit us".[69] The solutions proposed by the authors are threefold. First, privacy regulations should be more stringent. The General Data Protection Regulation (GDPR) adopted since the publication of the book appears to follow such recommendation, despite the GDPR's massive unintended consequences.[70]

Second, the authors encourage new entrants to "destabilize algorithm-enhanced tacit collusion or widespread behavioral discrimination".[71] Subsidies, cooperatives, and sponsoring entry are the realistically envisaged solutions advocated by the authors. Third, Ezrachi and Stucki consider that there is a need to reduce price transparency: "careful design of secret bids and sales could help destabilize algorithm-supported tacit collusion".[72] Proposing secret discounts and

[68] Ezrachi and Stucke (2016), p. 101.

[69] Ezrachi and Stucke (2016), p. 218.

[70] Chivot and Castro (2019).

[71] Ezrachi and Stucke (2016), p. 227.

[72] Ezrachi and Stucke (2016), p. 229.

government-enforced reduction of "the speed with which seller can adjust prices," Ezrachi and Stucke aim to return to a period of more significant market opacity where prices were less comparable and where comparisons were not available. Transparency may be reduced; risks of tacit collusion may too be reduced (albeit without certainty). Still, consumers will be harmed with higher prices and innovation chilled with a less efficient way of dynamically adjusting prices. The cost to consumers is apparent when the authors envisage the feasible way to prevent circumvention of the advocated prohibitions:

> This solution has its problems: competitors would so complain that the government is preventing them from discounting. One alternative would be if the government allowed price decreases to be implemented immediately, but imposed a time lag for price increases[73]

Such a radical proposal—i.e., mandatory delay in any price increase—would lead to one obvious, detrimental consequence for consumers: firms will not decrease prices in the first place to avoid being stuck with too low prices when market circumstances change. Costlier price increases will deter firms from decreasing prices, especially the smaller ones who cannot afford to incur transitory losses. Market dynamism will deplete since transaction costs will drastically increase.

Third, Ezrachi and Stucke suggest that the algorithms should be "audited." This popular proposal has nevertheless intractable complications in practice given the rapid technological and market changes in light of the slowness of regulatory interventions. The authors themselves recognized the impracticality of such a proposal: not only evidence of anticompetitive intent may hardly be unearthed by algorithm audits, but also the allegedly tacit collusion may end up being nothing less than legitimate market reactions to price changes.[74] While firms update their algorithms weekly or monthly, regulatory authorities may certainly be completely outpaced by effectively auditing one given algorithm, which may turn out to be obsolete for the company that created it. The enforcement proposals are unclear: they aim to target an unidentified target (i.e., legitimate market reactions) with questionable tools (i.e., privacy, audit, and government subsidies of a thriving market).

Despite the hypothetical risks raised in Virtual Competition, this book has benefited a considerable influence in antitrust authorities. So much so antitrust practice and theory concerning algorithm-driven companies have been shaped by the book's insights and proposals. Since then, a proper "algorithmic antitrust" theory and practice has developed. I now turn to algorithmic antitrust concisely before being addressed more extensively by the contributors of this book.

---

[73] Ezrachi and Stucke (2016), p. 230.

[74] Ezrachi and Stucke (2016), p. 230.

6 Algorithmic Antitrust: A Primer

In a nutshell, we provide an overview of the basic tenets of algorithmic antitrust in the European context. Although some American references may be used throughout this book, the primary focus of analyzing the algorithmic antitrust is the European regulatory framework. This section shall provide broad guidance regarding the competition implications of algorithms concerning the prohibitions of collusive practices, abuse of dominant positions, and anticompetitive mergers.

Article 101 and Algorithms. Pricing algorithms are ubiquitous among retailers. The European Commission found that 53% of the responding retailers track online prices of competitors, 67% of these retailers do the tracking by way of software, and 78% of the responding retailers adjust their prices based on the tracking results.[75] Does EU competition law contain sufficient tools to scrutinize collusive practices involving algorithms?

Contrary to groupthink and shared fears, EU competition law provides sufficient flexibility and effectiveness to tackle collusive practices between algorithms. Under EU law:

> [A] concerted practice refers to a form of coordination between undertakings which, without having been taken to the stage where an agreement properly so-called has been concluded, knowingly substitutes for the risks of competition practical cooperation between them . . .the criteria of coordination and cooperation must be understood in the light of the concept inherent in the provisions of the Treaty relating to competition that each economic operator must determine independently the policy which he intends to adopt on the Common Market.[76]

Parallel conduct does not fall in the scope of Article 101 TFEU because this article requires a type of concertation or coordination. Algorithmic behaviors cannot be categorized as "concerted practice" under the meaning of Article 101 TFEU because such practice requires a knowing or deliberate contact.[77] Algorithms react to the constantly available data and adopt unilateral practices based on their experience. But Article 101 TFEU prohibits anticompetitive agreements both from a horizontal context and from a vertical context.

The competition traditionally sanctions collusive practices irrespective of the means used. Therefore, following the U.S. *Topkins* case where sellers on Amazon conspired with algorithm-based software,[78] the U.S. Department of Justice stated that "We will not tolerate anticompetitive conduct, whether it occurs in a smoke-filled room or over the Internet using complex pricing algorithms".[79] The same holds

[75] European Commission (2016).

[76] Joined cased C-89/85, C-104/85, C-114/85, Ahlström Osakeyhti v Commission, March 31, 1993, §63.

[77] Mandrescu (2018).

[78] US District Court Northern District of California, USA v David Topkins, 6 April 2015.

[79] DOJ (2015).

for EU competition law enforcement. Competition Commissioner Margrethe Vestager stated, shortly after the release of the book Virtual Competition that:

> So far, those cases have dealt with agreements that were put together by humans. The computers only took over when it was time to put them into practice. But no one should imagine they can get away with price-fixing by allowing software to make those agreements for them. It's true that the idea of automated systems getting together and reaching a meeting of minds is still science fiction. But illegal collusion isn't always put together in back rooms. There are many ways that collusion can happen, and some of them are well within the capacity of automated systems... So as competition enforcers, I think we need to make it very clear that companies can't escape responsibility for collusion by hiding behind a computer program.[80]

Collusions decided by humans and implemented through algorithms are constantly prosecuted and fined. Equally, collusions decided by humans and implemented through algorithms where significant efficiencies can be demonstrated may be subject to an antitrust exemption. Indeed, the Competition Authority of Luxembourg has, in the Webtaxi case of 2018, considered that the everyday use of the pricing algorithm by all competing taxi companies did amount to a price agreement between competitors.[81] However, the agreement could be exempted given that it was indispensable to achieve various efficiencies (less waiting time, more rides for drivers, and lower prices for consumers).[82]

Collusive algorithms in a vertical context may take the form of highly efficient resale price maintenance. Regulation 330/2010 considers that resale price maintenance is susceptible to be prohibited by Article 101(1) TFEU and not be justified under Article 101(3) TFEU. A recent example is provided with the four fining decisions issued on November 7, 2018: Asus, Denon & Marantz, Philips, and Pioneer.[83] As of November 2018, the consumer electronics manufacturers sector is the first sector to be fined, totaling €111 million for the companies Asus, Denon & Marantz, Philips, and Pioneer a press release on July 24, 2018. Since the Yamaha decision of 2003, it is the first time the European Commission has fined companies based on resale price maintenance as prohibited by Article 101 TFEU. All decisions concerned vertical restraint instances wherein defendant companies relied upon "fixed or minimum resale price maintenance (RPM)" to restrict "the ability of their online retailers to set their retail prices for widely used consumer electronics products such as kitchen appliances, notebooks, and hi-fi products." (European Commission 2018). One crucial feature of these acknowledged anticompetitive conducts rests upon the fact that these RPMs are algorithm driven.

Indeed, in all four decisions, the European Commission unearthed complex, and innovative RPMs monitored through algorithms. The European Commission notes that "many, including the biggest online retailers, use pricing algorithms which

---

[80] Vestager (2017).

[81] Décision n°2018-FO-01 du seven juin 2018 concernant une procédure au fond mettant en cause Webtaxi S.à.r.l.

[82] Honore and Fabre (2018).

[83] Portuese (2018).

automatically adapt retail prices to those of competitors. In this way, the pricing restrictions imposed on low pricing online retailers typically had a broader impact on overall online prices for the respective consumer electronics products.”.[84] In all decisions, RPMs were deemed to be anticompetitive by the object. More interestingly, it is considered that algorithmic-driven RPMs have more significant harming effects on the competition. Indeed, the European Commission concluded that “price monitoring and adjustment software programs multiply the impact of price interventions”.[85] Suppose the anticompetitive risks of algorithms have indeed been well documented. In that case, algorithms can also yield pro-competitive effects due to the unparalleled price comparison tools they offer algorithm-driven price comparison can therefore be designed and used in pro-or anticompetitive manners. Indeed, the monitoring of prices through algorithms can usher more incredible aggressive reactions to price changes rather than necessarily easier and stable collusive reactions (Portuese 2018).

The application of Article 101 TFEU concerning pricing algorithms demands caution. Given the lack of evidence of anticompetitive effects outside of algorithmically enabled collusions such as in the decisions of Asus et al., there is a need for regulatory humility:

> Competition authorities, in the current state of the law, can do little to sanction tacit collusion on the basis of Article 101 TFEU. This could therefore, from a theoretical point of view, amount to an ‘enforcement gap.’ However, given the imperatives of legal certainty and various risks identified with taking action to close that potential enforcement gap, as well as the benefits flowing from algorithmic pricing in the short term (such as giving the possibility to mavericks to undercut the prices of their competitors), we would favour waiting for a sufficiently certain and convincing body of evidence to show that this risk is not merely a possibility but a reality that needs addressing.[86]

Moreover, the current Article 101 TFEU allows for the application of collusive algorithms as hypothetically envisaged as the fourth scenario in Virtual Competition. Indeed, Van Cleynenbreugel makes that point clearly: without modifying the EU legal framework about Article 101 TFEU. Any collusive algorithm could be caught within the ambit of that article.[87]

The case of *Eturas* illustrates the ability of current EU competition rules to tackle algorithmic collusion.[88] In January 2016, the CJEU issued a preliminary ruling in the Eturas case. Eturas is an online travel booking platform (E-TURAS) for travel agencies. With the platform Eturas, travel agencies have a uniform layout for their online booking services. The Eturas platforms do not set prices. The customers (the travel agencies) have access to Eturas’ mailbox for booking system notifications. In August 2009, an email from Eturas suggested limiting the online discount level from

[84] European Commission (2018).

[85] Case AT.40182 -Pioneer.

[86] Honore and Fabre (2018).

[87] Van Cleynenbreugel (2020).

[88] C-74/14, Eturas, EU:C:2016:42.

4% to 1–3%. Soon after, the platform notified the customers that a new discount cap of 3% had been adopted. Any discount set above the 3% discount rate would automatically be reduced back to the 3% discount rate set by the platform. Travel agencies could still grant more significant discounts on an individual basis but not on an indiscriminate basis. The Supreme Administrative Court of Lithuania, where the case was litigated, referred to the CJEU the following question:

> (1) Should Article 101(1) TFEU be interpreted as meaning that, in a situation in which economic operators participate in a common computerised information system of the type described in this case and the Competition Council has proved that a system notice on the restriction of discounts and a technical restriction on discount rate entry were introduced into that system, it can be presumed that those economic operators were aware, or ought to have been aware, of the system notice introduced into the computerised information system and, by failing to oppose the application of such a discount restriction, expressed their tacit approval of the price discount restriction and for that reason may be held liable for engaging in concerted practices under Article 101(1) TFEU?
>
> (2) If the first question is answered in the negative, what factors should be considered in the determination as to whether economic operators participating in a common computerised information system, in circumstances such as those in the main proceedings, have engaged in concerted practices within the meaning of Article 101(1) TFEU? (para.25).

The Court considered that the undertakings could be seen as having tacitly conspired and engaged in concerted illegal practices. According to the Court, this holds because travel agencies were aware of the content of the message. Eturas acted as a cartel facilitator, thereby facilitating and implementing price-fixing among travel agencies.

The regulatory framework may not necessarily be inadequate to tackle algorithmic collusion.[89] Indeed, agreements of Article 101 TFEU may simply be any "concurrence of the wills" between competitors.[90] Additionally, algorithms used by different rivals—along with the Hub and Spoke scenario of Ezrachi and Stucke—could potentially be designated as "association of undertakings" in the meaning of Article 101 TFEU.[91] Against the judicial reasoning of the CJEU in the case of MasterCard, where it was considered that the company constituted an association of undertakings, Van Cleynenbreugel argues that:

> The liberal, almost open-ended approach relied upon by the Court of Justice in MasterCard thus allows for an interesting inference to be made in relation to platforms that use algorithmic technologies that result in collusive practices, namely, that those platforms, functioning as intermediaries between different undertakings and their clients, may well be characterized as associations of the undertaking... As an intermediary between different economic actors, platform activities typically consist of tailoring the prices of certain products to the demand and preferences voiced by retail customers using the platform. In

---

[89] A contrario, Akman (2019).

[90] C-2/01 P & C-3/01 P, Bundesverband der Arzneimittel-Importeure eV & Commission v. Bayer, EU:C:2004:2.

[91] Van Cleynenbreugel (2020), p. 437.

> doing so, platforms—together with the learning algorithms that they use—can streamline and potentially differentiate the prices of different products offered by multiple businesses offered either within that same platform or on competing platforms. This may very well lead to an alignment of interests between the undertakings that use the platform to access customers and the platform's own decision to use algorithms to deliver greater efficiencies within the platform. Undertakings that rely upon the platform for product distribution, whether exclusively or not, could be considered to have mandated the platform—at least implicitly—to rely on particular algorithms to deliver such results. A platform may thus have a mandate, within the meaning of the MasterCard jurisprudence, to steer the pricing or offering of products in a certain direction.[92]

Therefore, with the existing rules and the current judicial interpretation, Article 101 TFEU is sufficiently flexible to encompass algorithmic collusions; however, these collisions are conducted: the concept of "association of undertakings" encompasses any types of algorithmic collusions.

Consequently, absent the fourth scenario mentioned by Ezrachi and Stucke for which there cannot be demonstrated, nor can there be proof of harm, the three other scenarios they mention can very well—and are, with the most recent decisions—prosecuted and sanctioned by the European Commission and the CJEU. Therefore, it does not seem that algorithmic collusions present a risk of under-enforcement since competition authorities are well aware of the functioning of the algorithms, but most importantly, the regulatory framework enables algorithmic antitrust to be effective whenever algorithmic collusions may arise. On the contrary, algorithmic price discrimination, and more generally of algorithmic-enabled abuse of dominant positions, raise more questions as per the risks of false positives and or false negatives.

Article 102 and Algorithms. Anticompetitive conducts are prohibited under Article 102 TFEU whenever an abuse of a dominant position harming consumers can be evidenced. As an "objective concept," abuses are proven when it can be demonstrated that the dominant firm has implemented business practices that have restricted competition—the intention of the firm to restrict competition being almost irrelevant under Article 102 TFEU.[93] While exploitative abuses have rarely been the primary focus of enforcers under Article 102 TFEU, the ordoliberal influence of this article narrowed down the focus on exclusionary abuses towards rivals. Exclusionary abuses are best assessed in light of the "as-efficient-competitor test" (AEC test).[94] The purpose of this test is precisely to prohibit practices that are not based on the competition on the merits—efficiency-oriented merit.

Economists traditionally differentiate between forms of price discrimination that harm a rival "primary line injury") and those that harm a direct customer of the firm ("secondary line injury"). This section provides an overview of the European treatment of the primary line injury by pricing algorithms. Secondary line injury may generate little if not a harm to consumers as it comes closer to perfect price

[92] Van Cleynenbreugel (2020), p. 436.

[93] C-413/14 P Intel Corp. v. European Commission, September 6, 2017.

[94] Case C-23/14, Post Danmark A/S v. Konkurrencerådet, October 6, 2015.

discrimination.[95] Also, Graef aptly considers that "personalized pricing as such is thus not problematic from a consumer protection law perspective. As long as suppliers do not engage in any misleading or aggressive commercial practices, they are free to customize prices provided they are transparent with consumers about doing so".[96]

How can these potentially new algorithm-enabled abuses of dominance fit into the AEC test and, more generally, into the consumer welfare standard? Two cases of algorithm-enabled exclusionary abuses under Article 102 TFEU will provide insights to answer this question. First, the potential case of Amazon as an algorithmic bias towards private-label products will be discussed in light of the AEC test. Second, the 2017 Google Shopping decision will be scrutinized to assess the relevance of the AEC test in a case of algorithmic leveraging under Article 102 TFEU.

In July 2019, the European Commission opened investigations against Amazon on the suspicion that Amazon might infringe (i) Article 101 TFEU due to anticompetitive use of third-party seller data through standard agreements with marketplace sellers, and (ii) Article 102 TFEU due to the algorithmic distortion of competition evidenced by prominent placement. It is reported that Amazon uses sensitive third-party data and biases its search algorithm to favor private-label products.[97] On Article 102 TFEU potential infringements specifically, it is alleged that products such as the "Amazon Basics" line are systematically promoted on Amazon search results via algorithmic design. Amazon has partially denied such practice in a statement: "The fact is that we have not changed the criteria we use to rank search results to include profitability. We feature the products customers will want, regardless of whether they are our brands or products ordered by our selling partners. As any store would do, we consider the profitability of the products we list and feature on the site, but it is just one metric and not in any way a key driver of what we show customers."[98]

In November 2020, the European Commission sent a statement of objection to the company, thereby paving formal investigations. The general concern is about Amazon's dual role as both a platform and as a retailer—suggesting that this is a new practice whereas every supermarket engages in similar practices:

> We must ensure that dual role platforms with market power, such as Amazon, do not distort competition. Data on third-party sellers' activity should not be used to the benefit of Amazon when it acts as a competitor to these sellers. The conditions of competition on the Amazon platform must also be fair. Its rules should not artificially favor Amazon's own retail offers or advantage the offers of retailers using Amazon's logistics and delivery services. With e-commerce booming, and Amazon being the leading e-commerce platform, a fair and undistorted access to consumers online is important for all sellers."

[95] Botta and Wiedemann (2019), p. 400.

[96] Graef (2018), p. 552.

[97] European Commission (2019).

[98] quoted in Fussel (2019).

Beyond this mere general concern of an alleged "conflict of interests" between Amazon acting as a platform and Amazon acting as a retailer, the specific concern raised by the European Commission relates to Amazon's use of its "Buy Box" and Prime Label. These characteristics allow sellers to gain numerous benefits in the way they reach end-users. The Commission investigates:

> whether the criteria that Amazon sets to select the winner of the "Buy Box" and to enable sellers to offer products to Prime users, under Amazon's Prime loyalty programme, lead to preferential treatment of Amazon's retail business or of the sellers that use Amazon's logistics and delivery services[99]

In other words, does Amazon's algorithm discriminate third sellers to promote some and demote others according to obscure criteria? The Commission wants to investigate how Amazon determines who wins the "Buy Box" since this powerfully shapes the platform's competitive environment. This investigation raises concerns as per the ability and duty of Amazon to disclose its algorithm and the materiality of the competitive harm suffered. The promotion of some sellers may necessarily mean the demotion of other, vice versa. The ranking may well be a zero-sum game for third-party retailers. Also, unfair discrimination among retailers may be counter-productive for Amazon: end-users may end up shopping on alternative platforms such as eBay, Etsy, Shopify, Google Shopping, or any app created by traditional supermarkets. Moreover, it appears that Amazon's algorithm may not discriminate in a way that the European Commission suspects it does. It unavoidably discriminates (after all, it is the raison d'être of algorithms) but from more objective and justifiable criteria.

Indeed, we have scrutinized this aspect earlier.[100] When one looks at the features that impact most in Amazon's algorithm, Amazon's algorithm shows no considerable positive bias by Amazon's algorithm in winning Amazon's Buy Box. In groundbreaking research carried out at Northeastern University, it has been evidenced that, using 4 months of data covering merchants selling 1641 best-seller products, Amazon's algorithm is not designed as to favor its product considerably other criteria are more important.

Where (i) Difference between the seller's price and the current lowest price for the product. (ii) Ratio between the seller's price and the current lowest price of the product. (iii) Positive feedback percentage for the seller. (iv) True when Amazon is the seller of the product. (v) Total feedback count for the seller. (vi) Average customer rating of the seller. (vii) Fulfilled by Amazon (FBA) program concerns third-party sellers who are willing to pay an FBA fee for Amazon to take care of the packaging, the shipping, and the monitoring of delivery of the items sold.

Figure 2 represents the empirical results on an inquiry into Amazon algorithmic design: the higher the weight of a feature (i.e., proxy), the more likely it is to predict who will win Amazon Buy Box (i.e., preferred seller). Therefore, it appears that two price-based features are significantly more important than any other features

[99] Vestager (2019).

[100] Portuese (2020).

Feature	Weight
Price Difference to the Lowest[i]	**36%**
Price Ratio to the Lowest[ii]	**33%**
Positive Feedback[iii]	**10%**
Is Amazon the Seller?[iv]	**10%**
Feedback Count[v]	**6%**
Average Rating[vi]	**3%**
Is the Product Fulfilled by Amazon (FBA)[vii]	**2%**

Fig. 2 Empirical results on an inquiry into Amazon algorithmic design; Source: Compounded figures from Chen et al. (2016)

(respectively 36% and 33%). Positive feedback from consumers (on shipping time, customer service, product quality, etc.) weighs 10% of Amazon's algorithm. However, the very fact that Amazon is the seller as opposed to third-party seller weighs for only 10% in the algorithmic design: the authors thus consider that "although we observe that 'being Amazon' does confer some advantage, we caution that this does not necessarily mean that Amazon has tilted the Buy Box algorithm in their favor".[101] Moreover, a product sold by a third-party seller but for which Amazon handles all logistics (FBA product) only weighs 2% despite Amazon's control of the logistics. The conclusion appears crystal clear: Amazon's algorithm is more tailored towards optimal customer service (price, feedback) rather than biased towards its products. This conclusion is concerned when it is evidenced that, as compared to sellers using algorithmic pricing (meaning, in coherence with the AEC test), Amazon "tends to be ranked lower for products where algorithmic sellers are active."[102] Consequently, while algorithmic profitability derived by self-favoring can be seen as having an influence, such influence plays a considerable minor role compared to the objective customer features playing a much more considerable role in Amazon's algorithmic design.

> Given the breadth of difficulties to examine Amazon's algorithm (or rather because such examination may not generate the coveted results), it may perhaps be this sheer difficulty to assess Amazon's biases in its search algorithm against a hypothetical as an efficient competitor which made necessary, for those who want to take aim at Amazon's algorithm, to target not so much these algorithmic biases but rather the very essence of this bias: the dual role of Amazon as both platform and merchant…[T]he European Commission has focused their efforts in this perceived "conflict of interests." At the same time, Amazon cannot have ownership of the platform and a role in this platform as a seller, the argument goes. In other words, Amazon cannot be the umpire and the player; it cannot pretend to be neutral and be commercially interested. Although attractive and intuitive, this argument lacks legal basis as well as economic soundness: a de facto search neutrality would unduly treat Amazon's platform as an essential facility, and such separation would not be economically rational given the number of similar situations of a dual role both in online platforms

[101] Chen et al. (2016), p. 1344.

[102] Chen et al. (2016), p. 1347.

> and in offline retail. Nevertheless, the simplicity of the rule—a clear (clean?) breakup from the platform with commerce—generates great traction instead of the more complex, yet more evidence-based, scrutiny of the extent to which algorithmic biases are anticompetitive according to the hypothetical AEC test… [I]t appears that the dual of Amazon may not play, as long as the design of its algorithm is concerned, its substantial role in the search results but may, subject to further evidence, be more focused on consumer benefits through price and quality criteria. Obviously, the current investigations and outcome shall shed useful light on both the materiality of this interim conclusion as well as on the remits (and limits) of the algorithmic governance under Article 102 TFEU (Portuese 2020).

Given the difficulty to demonstrate that Amazon unfairly discriminates on its platforms, the European Commission appears stuck in its investigations.[103] Another case was more successful, albeit raising many questions: the Google Shopping decision of 2017.

On 27 June 2017, the European Commission fined Google €2.42 billion for allegedly 'abusing dominance as a search engine by giving an illegal advantage to own comparison-shopping service'.[104] Why did the European Commission impose such a record-breaking fine on Google? According to Competition Commissioner Margarethe Vestager, Google abused its market dominance as a search engine by promoting its comparison-shopping service in its search results and demoting those of competitors' (…) therefore denying 'other companies the chance to compete on the merits and to innovate. And most importantly, it denied European consumers a genuine choice of services and the full benefits of innovation".[105]

The legal arguments of the European Commission are the following: thanks to its complex algorithms, Google has allegedly manipulated the search results of products to promote its platform, Google Shopping, at the expense of competitors. Since the artificial modification of the ranking of search results is equivalent to a price paid by economic actors by manipulating its search results, Google has abused its dominance. It has infringed Article 102 TFEU because it (i) 'has systematically given prominent placement to its comparison-shopping service' and (ii) 'has demoted rival comparison-shopping services in its search results.

In fining Google in 2017 for abusive leveraging of the market dominance held on search engine into the market of comparison-shopping sites with Google Shopping, the European Commission has condemned Google's practice to demote rivals and self-favor its products through discriminatory placements. Beyond numerous legal oddities encapsulated in the decision, the crux of contention, however, pares down to the algorithm design: Panda, the newly introduced algorithm by Google, was explicitly designed to demote competitors' rankings, thereby foreclosing them on the adjacent market (i.e., comparison shopping sites market) to effectively leverage power from its primary market (i.e., search engine). The *Google Shopping* decision[106] concluded that Google's algorithm demoted rivals and promoted Google

[103] Espinoza (2021).

[104] European Commission (2017).

[105] European Commission (2017).

[106] Case COMP/AT.39740.

Shopping comparison shopping results. The European Commission criticized to Google the leveraging of is generic search algorithms (i.e., Google search engine) with specialized search algorithms (say, Google Shopping):

> In response to a user query in Google's general search engine, Google uses generic search algorithms to rank web pages, including those of competing comparison shopping services. These algorithms include the PageRank algorithm...Google also applies a variety of adjustment mechanisms to the results of the PageRank algorithm "to improve the user experience"... Google uses dedicated algorithms to identify and demote automatically websites that do not comply with its Webmaster Guidelines.371 In a minority of cases, Google employees that are part of its "Webspam Team" and "Bad Urls Team" also identify and apply manually demotions to websites that do not comply with the Webmaster Guidelines.[107]

In this decision, the introduction in 2011 of the Panda algorithms by Google seems to be the source of the Commission's concerns:

> Like in the case of [...], set out in recitals (353)-(355), comparison shopping services are prone to being demoted by the Panda algorithm due to the characteristics inherent to those services. This is confirmed by the following Google documents:
>
> (a) A Google blogpost of 21 January 2011 regarding the introduction of the Panda algorithm, which stated that: "we're evaluating multiple changes that should help drive spam levels even lower, including one change that primarily affects sites that copy others' content and sites with low levels of original content.
>
> A blogpost by Matt Cutts of 28 January 2011 regarding the introduction of the Panda algorithm which stated that: "the change was approved at our weekly quality launch meeting last Thursday and launched earlier this week. [...] The net effect is that searchers are more likely to see the sites that wrote the original content rather than a site that scraped or copied the original site's content".[108]

Thus, monitoring of algorithms by Google appears to correspond to some quality control and seldom checks the relevance of the links and websites listed on the search results. Thus, it is dubious to argue that Google should not control the relevance of its search results, although such relevance remains at the core of the search engine's attractiveness.

Be that as it may, the Commission grounds its claim of abusive conduct related to self-favorable positioning and display by Google on the fact that "during the period between 2 August 2010 and 2 December 2016, for the vast majority of the most important comparison shopping services in terms of traffic, their visibility in Google's general search results pages (i) was at its highest at the end of 2010 and beginning of 2011, (ii) was followed by a sudden drop after the launch of the Panda algorithm in the respective EEA country and (iii) no sustainable recovery occurred afterward".[109] Traffic reduction for rivals of Google Shopping appears to coincide with the introduction by Google Search of the Panda algorithm: "That analysis

[107] Google Shopping decision, paras.345–348.

[108] Google Shopping decision, para.358.

[109] Google Shopping decision, paras.361–479.

indicates a lasting decline of the generic search traffic from Google's general search results pages to competing comparison shopping services, notably after the introduction of the Panda algorithm, but also over the longer run. This lasting decline applies to all the competing comparison-shopping services considered in the analysis," the Commission concluded from the web traffic analysis.[110]

This algorithmic-enabled leveraging practice does infer, despite the Commission's denial, that "pure" self-preferencing via algorithmic design becomes prohibited for dominant firms under Article 102 TFEU: self-favoritism becomes Article 102 TFEU violation. It is not the scope of this article to discuss the merits of such finding in terms of the unpredictability and vagueness of the theory of harm. Instead, it is the goal of this section to question the reviewability of such vilipended algorithmic bias. Indeed, how can competition authorities and courts ensure an algorithmic bias towards self-favoring deemed anticompetitive rather than simply a bias grounded on customer experience, service, and consumer welfare? Disregarding that 44% of online shoppers shop directly on Amazon rather than using search engines, the European Commission considered that Google search remains the main gateway for online shoppers. With the misguided definition of the relevant market, the algorithmic antitrust abuse could more easily be found. There is no doubt that the ruling by the CJEU on this case is highly awaited to clarify the ability of firms to constantly improve consumer experience with personalized, algorithmic-enabled search results in an era of fierce competition online and offline.

With the *Google Shopping* decision, European antitrust has entered the age of algorithmic antitrust concerning Article 102 TFEU—and with it, the complex issue of monitoring by antitrust enforcers companies' algorithms. Are algorithms' changes made for quality improvement or anticompetitive purposes–namely, demoting downstream rivals? The question may be more complicated than the Google Shopping decision suggests, and European judges may provide a useful answer to that case and other similar cases.

Algorithmic antitrust in general, and in Europe in particular, deserves particular scrutiny. Without resorting to slogans and catchy answers, this book delves into the complex matter of algorithmic antitrust with a European focus. It provides a wide range of analysis and sheds light on this ever-evolving area of antitrust enforcement that we can now call "algorithmic antitrust."

7 Presentation of the Book

The idea of this book followed a Conference we had the privilege to organize on March 6, 2020, at St Mary's University London. We have brought together a great line of speakers for a conference titled "Algorithmic Antitrust: Enforcing

[110] Google Shopping decision, paras.361–479.

Competition Rules in the Age of Algorithms." A short video clip is available at: https://www.youtube.com/watch?v=p9Z3CFx0NeA.

With the generous support of Linklaters and Concurrences' assistance, the conference proceedings have been published at Concurrences N°3-2020.[111] We are grateful to both Linklaters and Concurrences for having partnered with us on this occasion.

The one-day conference had four sessions. The first session addressed the topic of "Algorithmic Antitrust and Collusive Practices." Prof. Ioannis Kokkoris from Queen Mary's University and Bruce Wardhaugh from the University of Manchester were panelists while I moderated the session. The second session touched upon the issue of "Algorithmic Antitrust and Abuse of Dominance." Moderated by Cento Veljanovski, I was a panelist and Liza Lovdahl Gormsen from the British Institute of International and Comparative Law. The third session scrutinized the issue of "Algorithmic Antitrust and Mergers." Moderated by Philippe Corruble from the Catholic University of Paris, the panelists comprised David Bailey from King's College London, Verity Egerton-Doyle from Linklaters London. Thibault Schrepel moderated the fourth and final session from Utrecht University and Stanford University. Stefan Hunt, the Head of the Digital Markets Unit at the U.K. Competition and Markets Authority, Pierre Kirch from the Catholic University of Paris, and Jonathan Ford from Linklaters London were panelists. The two keynote speakers (morning and evening) were Cento Veljanovski and Stefan Hunt.

The one-day conference provided considerably valuable insights without which the present book would certainly not have been made possible. The increasing worries, fears, and regulatory responses to the impact of algorithms on competition had to be addressed and scrutinized in a more rational, cold-hearted manner. This conference provided such discussion where details were discussed, arguments and not slogans were exchanged, and a middle way between fearful regulatory reactions and complete denial was carved out. Algorithms are considerably efficiency-enhancing, result from ground-breaking technological innovations—antitrust enforcers and academics ought not to overcome that aspect for hasty regulatory prohibitions. However, this does not amount to a *carte blanche* for overtly harmful practices.

Some of the participants at the conference were kind enough to write down their thoughts and analysis as this book's chapters. We are incredibly grateful to them for the time, effort, and thought-provoking ideas they share with us in this book. We hope this book will re-balance the debate regarding the impact of algorithms on competition in a more positive way: over-regulation, the precautionary approach may stifle innovation at the expense of all of us in the name of protecting less efficient, less innovative rivals. This book discusses and raises legitimate concerns relative to algorithms but tries to avoid simplistic and costly answers. We need a serious and rational debate about the impact of technological innovation on the

---

[111] Portuese (2020).

competition. This book may contribute to such debate from a European perspective and concerning algorithms.

In his Chapter, Cento Veljanovski, founder and Managing Partner of Case Associates and fellow in Law and Economics at the Institute of Economic Affairs, explained the economics applied to algorithms and the limited knowledge available to assess their antitrust implications.

Afterwards, Liza Lovdahl Gormsen, Senior Research Fellow and the Director of the Competition Law Forum of the British Institute of International and Comparative Law, argues that Facebook is dominant in the social network market. Its market power stems from its large user base, the data it holds about its users, and barriers to entry. Facebook's dominance in the social network market makes it possible for Facebook to leverage its market power to the detriment of customers and competitors in the online display advertising market. The exploitative conduct in the social network market creates a data advantage for Facebook in the online display advertising market since such data are combined with data obtained from its dominance in the social network market. This generates an unsurmountable competitive advantage in the display advertising market that distorts competition. The strengthening of Facebook's position in the online display advertising market has given it the ability to avail itself of its "must-have" trading partner status and use its advertising services to exclude competitors in market segments into which it wishes to enter. In particular, Facebook has denied advertising services to specific firms, thereby denying them an indispensable outlet to reach customers.

In the next chapter, Verity Egerton-Doyle, Managing Associate in Linklaters' Competition and antitrust practice, and Jonathan Ford, Counsel in Linklaters' Competition, and antitrust practice, examine what theories of harm had been pursued against mergers between algorithm-driven businesses. Theories of harm based on algorithms themselves have been contemplated but have not yet been relied upon to ground intervention. However, mergers between algorithm-driven businesses have come under very close scrutiny. One focus has been on the competitive effect of combining data sets on which algorithm-driven businesses depend. Data-based theories of harm may succeed if it can be shown that the target's data assets are unique and cannot be replicated or that the parties together hold a substantial amount of particular kinds of data. However, given the ubiquity of data generated continuously through online behavior, previous cases show this is a high bar for an authority to meet. Recently, in the context of allegations of historical under-enforcement in digital markets, the charge of "killer acquisition" has been leveled against mergers between algorithm-driven businesses. Authorities are increasingly focused on evidence around valuations and internal documents as critical sources of evidence in determining the appropriate counterfactual in fast-moving dynamic markets.

Chris Pike, Principal for the OECD's working party on competition & regulation, and Gabriele Carovano, Junior Competition Expert at the OECD's Competition Division, describe the benevolent market power of decentralized blockchains. In this optimistic take on the impact of blockchain technology, they argue that blockchains are multisided platforms and that decentralized permission-less blockchains are in effect controlled by markets of gig-working minority shareholders. While they may therefore have a tendency towards concentration and market power based on cross-platform network effects (if the technology takes off), they suggest that these decentralized blockchains will not be able to exercise market power, at least not while they are genuinely decentralized. Their development might therefore be welcomed. They suggest that these blockchains might, in some cases, include matching functions in their protocols that enable them to offer a natural alternative to the big incumbent digital platforms (in which case advertising revenue might instead Now directly to users). Pike and Carovano end by touching upon the proposal that tokenization might also offer a way to internalize the value of the network effects that users bring to a platform. They hence might better enable such blockchains to overcome barriers to entry into platform markets.

Giovanna Massarotto, Academic Fellow at Center for Technology, Innovation, and Competition of the University of Pennsylvania and Research Associate at the Centre for Blockchain Technologies of the University College London, explores blockchain technologies. Permissioned and closed blockchains can, for example, create the perfect conditions for competitors to engage in cartels; smart contracts, on the other hand, can automatize the punishment for any cartel's deviation. Massarotto investigates the relation between competition and blockchain. *Is blockchain the real game-changer for today's centralized digital markets?* She explores whether blockchain can be considered as revolutionary progress also in the context of antitrust.

Pierre Kirch, Adjunct Professor of AI Law at the Catholic University of Paris, and Partner in the Litigation Department at Paul Hastings, spoke about the hiatus between the development of new technology and the grasp of the regulators of the importance of the technology concerning competition rules and regulations and enforcement. As a historical example, the European Commission reviews the current, and now 10-year-old vertical restraints block exemption and the two-block exemptions for horizontal co-operation agreements (on the latter, the consultation period just closed 12 February 2020). Ten years ago, at the time of formulation of its vertical and horizontal guidance, in the form of notices, the Commission barely perceived the importance of the emergence of electronic platforms not only in vertical relationships(distribution) but also in horizontal relationships and even dominance situations (Google, Facebook, etc.). The issue arises of speculation about what the Commission could usefully include, in particular, in both the vertical and horizontal guidelines that will be issued with the future new versions of the vertical and horizontal block exemptions. We know from experience that regulators work in a sort of time vacuum, by which they are consistently way behind the technology.

References

Akman P (2019) Online platforms, agency, and competition law: mind the gap. Fordham Int Law J 43:209

Alexander, J (2020) TikTok reveals some of the secrets, and blind spots, of its recommendation algorithm. The Verge, June 18, 2020
Autorité de la Concurrence and Bundeskartellamt (2019) Algorithms and Competition, November 9, 2019
Baker J (2019) The antitrust paradigm: restoring a competitive economy. Harvard University Press, Cambridge
Botta M, Wiedemann K (2019) To discriminate or not to discriminate? Personalised pricing in online markets as exploitative abuse of dominance. Eur J Law Econ 50:381–404
Bracha O, Pasquale F (2008) Federal Search Commission? Access, fairness and accountability in the law of search. Cornell Law Rev 93(6):1149–1210
Brandeis LD (1934) The curse of bigness. Viking Press, New York
Brayne S, Christin A (2020) Technologies of crime prediction: the reception of algorithms in policing and criminal courts. Soc Probl 2020:1–17
Chen L, Mislove A, Wilson C (2016) An empirical analysis of algorithmic pricing on Amazon marketplace. Proceedings of the 25th International Conference on World Wide Web, April 2016, 1339–1349
Chivot E, Castro D (2019) What the evidence shows about the impact of the GDPR after one year. Center of Data Innovation, June 17, 2019
Citron K, Pasquale F (2014) The scored society: due process for automated predictions. Wash Law Rev 89:1–33
Cleynenbreugel V (2020) Article 101 TFEU's association of undertakings notion and its surprising potential to help distinguish acceptable from unacceptable algorithmic collusion. Anti Bull 65(3):423–444
CMA (2021) Algorithms: How they can reduce competition and harm consumers, January 19, 2021
Cormen TH, Leiserson CE, Rivest RL, Stein C (2009) Introduction to algorithms, 3rd edn. MIT Press, Cambridge
Courtois C, Timmermans E (2018) Cracking the tinder code: an experience sampling approach to the dynamics and impact of platform governing algorithms. J Comput-Mediat Commun 23(1): 1–16
DOJ (2015) Former E-commerce Executive Charged with Price Fixing in Antitrust Division's First Online Marketplace Prosecution, Press release, April 6, 2015
Espinoza J (2021) EU struggles to build antitrust case against Amazon. Financial Times, March 11, 2021
European Commission (2013) Antitrust: Commission fines banks #1.49 billion for participating in cartels in the interest rate derivatives industry, Press Release, December 4, 2013
European Commission (2016) Commission Staff Working Document, Preliminary Report on the E-commerce Sector Inquiry, Brussels, September 15, 2016, SWD (2016) 32 final, Part 1/2, 125
European Commission (2017) Antitrust: Commission fines Google €2.42 billion for abusing dominance as search engine by giving illegal advantage to own comparison-shopping services, Press Release, June 27, 2017
European Commission (2018) Commission fines four consumer electronics manufacturers for fixing online resale prices, Press Release of July 24, 2018
Ezrachi A, Stucke M (2016) Virtual competition: the promise and perils of the algorithm-driven economy. Oxford University Press
European Commission (2019) Antitrust: Commission opens investigations into possible anti-competitive conduct of Amazon, Press Release, July 17, 2019, IP/19/4291
Fussel S (2019) Algorithms are people. The Atlantic, September 18, 2019
Garcia M (2016) Racist in the machine: the disturbing implications of algorithmic Bias. World Policy J 33(4):111–117
Glaubitz A (2020) All Rise: Judicial Algorithms in the Courtroom. The Yale Politic
Graef I (2018) Algorithms and fairness: what role for competition law in targeting price discrimination towards end consumers? Columbia J Eur Law 24(3):540–559
Granka L (2010) The politics of search: a decade retrospective. Inf Soc 26(5):364–374

Hafner K (2006) And if you liked the movie, a Netflix contest may reward you handsomely. New York Times, October 2, 2006
Honore P, Fabre G (2018) European Union – Algorithmic pricing under Article 101 TFEU. Global Competition Review, December 7, 2018
Liptak A (2020) Sent to Prison by a Software Program's Secret Algorithms. The New York Times, May 1, 2017
Mandrescu D (2018) When algorithmic pricing meets concerted practices – the case of Partneo. CoreBlog, June 7, 2018
Nicholas G (2020) Explaining algorithmic decisions. Georgetown Law Technol Rev 4(2):711–730
OECD (2017) Algorithms and Collusion. Competition Policy in the Digital Age, September 14, 2017
Oxera (2018) Algorithmic competition, September 30, 2018
Pasquale F (2015) The black box society: the secret algorithms that control money and information. Harvard University Press, Cambridge
Portuese A (2018) European Algorithmic Antitrust and Resale Price Maintenance: Asus, Denon & Marantz, Philips, and Pioneer Decisions. Competition Policy International, November 2018
Portuese A (2020) Algorithmic Antitrust, Concurrences, Conference Proceedings, N°3-2020
Ray S (2020) Google, Amazon, Microsoft Must Disclose How They Rank Search Results Under New Rules, Forbes, December 7, 2020
Veinott AF (2005) Lectures in Supply-Chain Optimization, Lectures at Stanford University (on file with author)
Vestager M (2017) Algorithms and Competition, Speech at Bundeskartellamt 18th Conference on Competition, March 16, 2017
Vestager M (2019) Commission sends Statement of Objections to Amazon for the use of non-public independent seller data and opens second investigation into its e-commerce business practices, Press Release, November 10, 2020

Algorithmic Antitrust: A Critical Overview

Cento Veljanovski

Abstract This chapter introduces the key issues, economics, and competition concerns surrounding algorithmic antitrust. It provides an overview of recent developments in the economics and legal issues raised by digital platforms and algorithms in the areas of abuse of dominance, algorithmic pricing and collusion, and mergers. The general theme is that while much has been made of the possible anticompetitive effects of the large digital platforms, there is little hard evidence to support many of the core premises underpinning current competitive assessments of large digital platforms and the need for the reform of competition law. This chapter seeks to redress this imbalance.

1 Context

The competition issues raised by algorithms are at the forefront of today's debate on antitrust policy and enforcement. While the word may not be used or even acknowledged, it is at the heart of the internet's operation and the services it provides. The emerging view is that despite the massive innovation and consumers' surplus generated by the large digital platforms, the way they compete is raising concerns. These concerns go beyond isolated breaches of competition law and privacy. They have merged into a clamor for the greater regulation of digital platforms—what some have called '*techlash.*'

The main target of these concerns is a group of companies often referred to as '*Big Tech*'—Alphabet (Google), Facebook, Apple, Amazon, and Microsoft—or by the acronyms GAFAM or FAANG. Other platforms such as Uber, eBay, Airbnb, and comparison websites have attracted attention as part of the platform and '*gig*' economy. Big tech is descriptive—these platforms are undeniably big in terms of market capitalization, users, and coverage, and they are tech companies. Nonetheless there are substantial differences between them. They have different business

C. Veljanovski (✉)
Case Associates, London, UK Institute of Economic Affairs, London, UK
e-mail: cento@casecon.com

A. Portuese (ed.), *Algorithmic Antitrust*, Economic Analysis of Law in European Legal Scholarship 12, https://doi.org/10.1007/978-3-030-85859-9_2

models—Facebook and Google are data-driven advertiser-supported businesses; Apple and Microsoft earn revenues for hardware and software products; Amazon operates a marketplace and is a retailer that takes a share of e-commerce revenues. This means that the business dynamics and drivers, hence competition problems, will differ in type and scale, as will the potential solutions.

The term '*Big Tech*' is also used in the pejorative sense of '*Big is Bad'*, and it seems that the words must be capitalized to emphasize this. To reinforce the point, '*Big Tech'* uses '*Big Data'* and '*Big Analytics'* (read '*Big Algorithms'*) and engages in '*killer acquisitions*.' This journalistic jargon is designed to sensationalize the problems. It juxtaposes big is bad with the looming threat, not of '*Big Regulation'* but '*smart'* regulation. The language is loaded toward the required outcome, and this is unfortunate. This '*big is bad'* view is undergoing a resurgence with calls to return to a more populist approach to antitrust, so-called '*hipster antitrust'*. In the US, this movement harks back to the supposed golden era of antitrust at the turn of the twentieth century when the US Federal government busted the railroad, oil, steel, and tobacco trusts, and where the term antitrust came from. This sees the concentration of private economic power in the economy as inherently bad and that antitrust should protect small businesses and promote a more pluralistic economic structure. To this is added a call that antitrust focus is less on consumers' welfare and more on broader goals such as sustainability, privacy, fairness, tax avoidance, promoting a European digital industry, and so on (Wright and Portuese 2020; Melamed and Petit 2019).

Today big tech is on the back foot. It faces the real and growing prospect of increasing regulation. The EU Competition Commissioner Margarethe Vestager[1] has put Google, Facebook, and Amazon on notice in uncompromising language: "*The biggest threat to competition and innovation comes from platforms that are not just a single business, but the centre of large empires'; 'the expansion of platforms into new markets doesn't undermine competition as it goes, like a bloom of algae that kills off every other form of life as it expands"*.[3] While the calls for more regulation have been resisted by tech leaders, even they now concede albeit reluctantly that the industry should be '*better'* regulated.[2]

These concerns have moved from criticism to official action. The European Commission has undertaken several high-profile investigations of Microsoft, Google, and Amazon, leading to substantial fines and commitments. Many governments have commissioned expert reports into the digital economy—the European Commission's experts' report;[3] the Franco-German competition authorities' report;[4] the Portuguese competition authority's report;[5] a report on digital dominance in the

[1] Vestager (2019, 2020).

[2] Zuckerberg (2020).

[3] Crémer et al. (2019).

[4] ADLC/BKartA (2019).

[5] AdC (2019).

Netherlands,[6] in the UK the Furman Report[7] and the Competition and Market Authority's working paper and interim report on online advertising;[8] and farther afield the Australian Competition and Consumer Commission[9] and Stigler Center report.[10] These are all serious attempts to understand the competition and regulatory concerns raised by the digital sector, assess their validity, and propose possible reforms.

The consensus among most expert reports is for a measured approach to the reform of European antitrust laws. They endorse the consumer welfare approach and the tools available to competition authorities but call for more vigorous enforcement of existing laws with a greater focus on market failures, multisided markets, dynamic considerations, robust theories of harm, and the replacement of market definition with a broader notion of a digital ecosystem.[11]

Others have gone further proposing *ex-ante* sectoral regulation,[12] the reversal of the burden of proof where the platform operators must establish that their proposed merger or actions do not harm competition[13] as opposed to the present legal position, which places the burden of proof to establish an anticompetitive practice on the competition authorities, and more expansive theory of harm. There is also pressure for more protection over the use of personal data. This heightened level of scrutiny has led to changes in the political will to regulate the digital sector. The new and controversial joint responsibilities of the EU Competition Commissioner Vestager for both competition policy and the digital economy indicate the type of afoot change. In the UK, a Digital Taskforce consisting of officials from the Competition and Markets Authority (CMA), Office of Communications (Ofcom), and the Information Commissioner's Office have been formed to advise the UK government on the next steps. Germany proposes to change its laws. The European Commission is consulting on introducing a new competition tool that would allow it to undertake market-wide investigations.[14]

Overlaying all these efforts is the new European Commission's plan to create a European digital sector powered by its vision of '*European technological sovereignty*'—a European society powered by digital solutions rooted in common European values.[15] This reflects the fact that there are no successful European digital platforms and that big tech in Europe is a US-based enterprise. As part of this effort,

[6]van Gorp and de Bijl (2019), MEA&CP (2019).

[7]Furman (2019).

[8]CMA (2018, 2019) and House of Lords (2016).

[9]ACCC (2019).

[10]Stigler Report (2019).

[11]Mateus (2020); Stigler Center (2019); Schweitzer et al. (2018); Furman (2019); Crémer et al. (2019), ADLC/BKartA (2019), Monopolskommission (2015), and ACCC (2019).

[12]Furman Report (2019).

[13]Crémer et al. (2019).

[14]European Commission (2020).

[15]European Commission (2020).

the Commission has launched a public consultation on the Digital Services Act (DSA), which aims to adopt in late 2020, including several inception impact assessments proposing the *ex-ante* regulation of massive online platforms acting gatekeepers that canvasses the possibility of structural remedies.[16]

2 Some First Principles

2.1 What Is an Algorithm?

Algorithms are the workhorse of the digital sector. Whenever you use a computer, you rely on algorithms. Algorithms permit computers to undertake tasks and computations which make them applicable to their users and site operators. At its simplest, an algorithm is a computer code that links inputs to outputs, a bit like a cooking recipe as Rainie and Anderson explain:

> Algorithms are instructions for solving a problem or completing a task. Recipes are algorithms, as are math equations. Computer code is algorithmic. The internet runs on algorithms and all online searching is accomplished through them. Email knows where to go thanks to algorithms. Smartphone apps are nothing but algorithms. Computer and video games are algorithmic storytelling. Online dating and book-recommendation and travel websites would not function without algorithms. GPS mapping systems get people from point A to point B via algorithms. Artificial intelligence (AI) is naught but algorithms. The material people see on social media is brought to them by algorithms. In fact, everything people see and do on the web is a product of algorithms. Every time someone sorts a column in a spreadsheet, algorithms are at play, and most financial transactions today are accomplished by algorithms. Algorithms help gadgets respond to voice commands, recognize faces, sort photos, and build and drive cars. Hacking cyberattacks and cryptographic code-breaking exploit algorithms. Self-learning and self-programming algorithms are now emerging, so it is possible that in the future algorithms will write many if not most algorithms.[17]

Algorithms *per se* do not give rise to antitrust concerns. Maureen Ohlhausen, when the acting chairman of the Federal Trade Commission, noted that *"some of the concerns about algorithms are a bit alarmist . . . An algorithm is a tool, and like any other tool, it can be put to either useful purposes or nefarious ends"*.[18] The quotation above indicates how algorithms run the internet and its many services. As the German and French competition authorities report observes: *"Algorithms provide plethora of beneficial opportunities for the economy and society. For example . . . they can facilitate innovative services, allow for the personalization of products and services, support the optimization of inventories, and/or reduce search costs."*

---

[16] Digital Servies Act package—ex ante regulatory instrument of very large online platforms acting as gatekeeper. https://ec.europa.eu/info/law/better-regulation/have-your-say/initiatives/12418-Digital-Services-Act-package-ex-anteregulatory-instrument-of-very-large-online-platforms-acting-as-gatekeepers.

[17] Rainie and Anderson (2017).

[18] Ohlhausen (2017).

On the other hand, algorithms can facilitate collusive pricing, digital platform self-preferencing, and so on. They give effect to business strategies designed by their corporate entities. But there is a looming concern that one day with the development of artificial intelligence (AI) and self-learning algorithms, algorithms will implement strategies that are not causally linked to human intervention. This would pose challenges for competition authorities and regulators and the customers of and supplier to digital platforms.

2.2 *The Economics*

The starting point of an investigation of the digital sector is to recognize its '*peculiar economics*.' This is set out concisely in the Stigler Center Report:

> The markets where DPs [digital platforms] operate exhibit several economic features that, while not novel per se, appear together for the first time and push these markets towards monopolization by a single company. These features are: (i) strong network effects (the more people use a product, the more appealing this product becomes for other users); (ii) strong economies of scale and scope (the cost of producing more or of expanding in other sectors decreases with company's size); (iii) marginal costs close to zero (the cost of servicing another consumer is close to zero); (iv) high and increasing returns to the use of data (the more data you control, the better your product); and (v) low distribution costs that allow for a global reach. This confluence of features means that these markets are prone to tipping; that is, they reach a point where the market will naturally tend towards a single, very dominant player (also known as "winner takes all markets"). An entrant will most likely be unable to overcome the barriers to entry represented by scale economies and data control, as they are difficult to achieve in a quick, cost-effective manner.[19]

The DG Comp Report similarly states that: *"the presence of strong incumbency advantage – due to network externalities, economies of scale and data access – changes the principles of enforcement of competition policy."*[20] Caution must be exercised when accepting that these factors necessarily imply market failure, insurmountable barriers to entry, and the inevitably of tipping leading to entrenched market power. For example, to treat networks' effects as a barrier to entry is correct only in a highly qualified way. In the presence of network effects, a larger network is more attractive than a smaller network, and hence the smaller network or platform operates at a disadvantage. However, network effects are demand-side economies of scale and scope which measure consumers' benefits. Thus, when it is said that there are significant network effects, one is saying that there are significant gains to consumers from being on one large platform or several interconnected platforms. The presumption is that '*bigness*' is good from a consumer perspective.

---

[19] Zingales and Lancieri (2019, pp. 7–8).

[20] Crémer et al. (2019, p. 54).

Secondly, many of the factors identified in the above quotations—network effects, economies of scale and scope, etc.—are present in other sectors. They have been recognized for at least the last two decades by antitrust authorities. The difference is that they are said to exist in '*extreme*' form in the digital economy such that '*large incumbent digital players are exceedingly difficult to dislodge*'.[21] These factors have been '*turbocharged*' by the growth, power, and increasing bandwidth of the telecommunication networks and devices that underpin the internet. However, it is also the case that there is extraordinarily little evidence supporting the claim that these factors are empirically significant and inevitably lead to abusive anti-competitive outcomes. The network effects may dissipate well below the total user base and be more localized.[22] The fact that the present digital '*ecosystem*,' to use a fashionable term, is dominated by a few large platforms, risks the *ex-post* fallacy of looking at what has materialized to conclude that this validates the '*monopoly view*' digital platforms.

While network and related effects may make markets '*tip,*' they do not obliterate the competition. Tipping is the result of competition '*for the market*' rather than exclusively '*competition in the market*' and based on superior and innovative services. While many commentators view tipping as a once and for all phenomenon—once tipped always tipped—this is not the case. The reality is that it must constantly innovate and provide better and faster services for a platform to maintain its position. The factors that make markets tip can also cause them to unwind in a '*death spiral*' unless there is reason to believe there is an asymmetry in how digital markets respond to growth and decline. The disappearance of Yahoo, Friends United and Google Plus's failure indicates that being the first mover with a relatively large user base and strong financial backing does not guarantee success or sustainable tipping. Moreover, the market tipping hypothesis can result from adopting excessively narrow market definitions that ignore the competition between the larger platforms in adjacent '*markets*' that constrain a digital platform's market power.

It is easy to exaggerate and misapply network effects theories.[23] This was seen during the dot-com boom. Business got carried away with the application of direct network effects, first-mover advantages, and winner-takes-all strategies rushing to convert every brick-and-mortar business into an online platform or portal which would scoop up all the business. As history showed, this was not the case—direct network effects rarely led to tipping; first-movers generally went bankrupt, and winner-takes-all strategies did not work, only burnt up massive amounts of capital.

Competition authorities have in the past been (over) influenced by network effects theories—often pushed forward by lawyers, economists, and consultants working for and against those under antitrust scrutiny—to base their decisions on anticipated network effects. Prime examples are the European Commission's anal-

[21] Crémer et al. (2019, pp. 2–3).

[22] Tucker (2018).

[23] Veljanovski (2001); Spulber (2002); Varian (2018); Tucker (2018).

ysis in the *MCI/WorldCom*[24] and the *Vodafone/Mannesmann*[25] mergers in the late 1990s. The latter argued that the merger would allow the new entity to create a pan-European seamless mobile network offering bundled services to the disadvantage of other operators. As we know, *WorldCom/MCI* never dominated the internet backbone; Vodafone never developed a seamless transnational mobile network.

2.3 Multisided Markets

Digital platforms serve two or more sides of the market, although this is not unique to the digital sector. The platform brings together these two sides and adopts strategies and practices that encourage take-up and resolve the so-called '*chicken-and-egg problem*'.[26] An excellent example of a two-sided market is credit cards, where the value of a credit card depends on its widespread acceptance among both merchants and users—merchants will only accept credit cards if there are many users; consumers will only take-up credit cards if they are widely accepted by merchants (the chicken-and-egg problem). The credit card company brings together those banks and financial institutions that issue credit cards with those banks which act as acquirers who sign up merchants to foster a viable network.

This, in turn, has implications for the way platforms in two-sided markets price their services. In a two-sided market, price serves a balancing function rather than reflecting the costs of supplying one side or the other of the market. One side of the market receives the service at a subsidized rate or for no payment, while the other side pays more than the marginal costs of supplying the services it receives. One side of the market (merchants in the case of credit cards) is the '*money side*' and the other (the card users) the '*subsidy side*.' In more technical jargon, card usage costs are placed on the side with the more inelastic demand. This explains why many digital platforms do not charge their users. Google does not charge its users to search the internet. But there is a *quid pro quo*—Google harvests the personal data of its users and monetizes this by selling the targeted preferences of its users to advertisers. Thus, the paradox of '*free'* services, which some erroneously argue, makes standard economics (and antitrust analysis) redundant and is evidence of predation by platforms such as Google and Amazon. Such glib evaluations are based on the failure to recognize that digital platforms operate in two or more sides of various markets. The multisidedness of digital markets is only now entering the decisional practice of competition authorities. Unfortunately, their analysis still focuses on one side of the market, which is often narrowly defined, as shown by UK merger clearance

[24]Case IV/M.1069 WorldCom/MCI, Commission Decision of 8 July 1998. Case IV/M.1069 WorldCom/MCI, Commission Decision of 8 July 1998.

[25]Case No. COMP/M.1795 Vodafone AirTouch/Mannesmann, Commission Decision of 14 April 2000.

[26]Rochet and Tirole (2003).

decisions,[27] European Commission antitrust decisions[28], and many populist academic discussions.[29]

While the economics of a two-sided market generates many valuable insights, it is difficult to apply and easy to misapply. A fundamental drawback is that there is no agreed operational definition. According to Rochet and Tirole: *"[A] market is two-sided if the platform can affect the volume of transactions by charging more to one side of the market and reducing the price paid by the other in equal amount; in other words, the price structure matters, and platforms must design it to bring both sides on board"*.[30] The OECD states that *"An online platform is a digital service that facilitates interactions between two or more distinct but interdependent sets of users (whether firms or individuals) who interact through the service via the Internet"*.[31] These definitions hardly give clear guidance to lawyers and regulators.[32]

2.4 Big Data

Monetizing user data is crucial to many digital platforms. It '*cross-subsidizes'* search and social networking by Google and Facebook. Nonetheless, the use of personal data has attracted much criticism on privacy grounds and that it acts as a barrier to entry. As the reader should now anticipate, the problems surrounding using data by Google, Facebook, and some other digital platforms are referred to as '*Big Data*'. Again, there is no one adequate definition of big data. Hylton's definition is appealing for present purposes as it relates to algorithms:

> For my purposes, big data refers to digital platforms that enable the discovery and sharing of information by consumers and the harvesting and analysis of data on those consumers by the platform. Because of the enormous quantities of data, the platforms must use algorithms and often machine learning to process the data. Thus, big data includes, in this definition, a reference to the sophisticated processes by which the data are analyzed.[33]

The Furman Report (2019) stated that *"[T]he evidence suggests that large data holdings are at the heart of the potential for some platform markets to be dominated by single players, and for that dominance to be entrenched in a way that lessens the potential for competition"*.[34] While it is true that in some areas of the digital sector, more data is better, there is little evidence that extensive data holdings per se

[27] Lear (2019).

[28] Cases COMP/34.579 MasterCard, COMP/36.518 EuroCommerce, COMP/38.580 Commercial Cards, Commission Decision of 19 December 2007.

[29] Kahn (2017).

[30] Rochet and Tirole (2006, p. 664).

[31] OECD (2019).

[32] Auer and Petit (2015).

[33] Hylton (2019, p. 2).

[34] Furman Report (2019).

entrench digital dominance. Data is not an essential facility, *i.e.,* an asset that is non-replicable and essential for competition. Personal data is extracted by all digital platforms and is replicable at a cost. For example, a study by Chiou and Tucker found that when searches were based on 6 months of data rather than 18 months, the changes in the apparent quality of search results were minimal.[35] This suggests that the possession of historical data confers less of a competitive advantage than is often supposed.

The focus on '*Big Data'* obscures the fact that it is the development and enhancement of intelligent predictive algorithms that are the primary source of the success of search engines, and Google in particular. Google overtook and displaced the then incumbents' Yahoo Search and Alta Vista largely because its PageRank algorithm was superior and its decision to develop its software infrastructure (Google File System) in contrast to Yahoo, which outsourced this and used the more restrictive application-specific solutions of NetApp.[36] As the OECD states, Google's "*PageRank algorithm led to the emergence of a search engine whose quality and convenience were markedly superior to that of incumbents, such as Yahoo! and Altavista. As a result, Internet users soon began flocking to Google*".[37] A good search engine with access to more significant amounts of data has its performance improved, whereas a bad search engine does not. In this sense, the '*barrier*' is a better search engine rather than more data.

On the other hand, proposals to regulate big data can have adverse effects. Proposals for the mandatory sharing of data of larger platforms could reduce the incentives to invest in data collections and analytics, both by incumbents and entrants. The costs of assembling and organizing data can be substantial, including setting lower prices or offering higher quality to attract more users who add to the data. Requiring a large digital platform to share its data with competitors would diminish the incentives to undertake these investments and reduce consumer welfare. Similarly, the incentive for entrants to invest in data collection and analysis will be lower if they are given relatively open access to the data of the large digital platforms.

Nonetheless, moves are afoot for greater access to data while at the same time restricting the use of personal data, which will have conflicting effects on competitive pressures. For example, the UK Open Banking Standards allows fintech competitors to the retail banks to access the latter's customer data with the customer's consent to increase competition from fintech innovators. The European Commission is discussing giving smaller platforms access to large digital platforms to level the playing field. On the other hand, the General Data Protection Regulation EU 2016/679 (GDPR) limits the use of digital data to protect individuals' privacy. At the same time, it limits the ability of smaller digital platforms to expand. Others propose that digital platforms should pay users for the use of personal data. If

---

[35] Chiou and Tucker (2017).

[36] Aron (2016).

[37] OECD (2019, p. 156).

payment were required, the multisided business models of Google, Facebook, and many other digital platforms would be massively affected. Whatever the analysis is underpinning these proposals, one thing is sure—if digital platforms had to pay their users for their data, (a) this would create a barrier to start-ups and smaller platforms, and (b) result in radical changes in the business models of search and social networking sites.

3 Dominance

The five big tech platforms are typically dominant and often vertically integrated. Dominance and vertical integration, especially the latter, raise the specter of exploitative and exclusionary conduct—under Article 102 of the on the Functioning of the European Union (TFEU). Under European competition rules, bigness, more specifically dominance, is not an offense. It is the abuse of '*bigness.*' The more technical vernacular of antitrust '*bigness*' is measured by the share of sales, customers, and revenue of firms in the relevant product and geographical markets. These markets are defined by the price responsiveness test known as the *Small Significant Nontransitory Increase in Price* or *SSNIP* test as set out in the European Commission's (1997) Market Definition Notice (97/C 372/03). The rule of thumb is that a market share of 40% or greater triggers a presumption of dominance, which can be rebutted by analyzing market conditions that point to the constraining effects of competition. A practice that would otherwise be benign and procompetitive will, if undertaken by a dominant firm, carry the presumption of abuse. Under European antitrust, a dominant firm has a '*special responsibility*' not to act abusively.

Consider the treatment of Google by most of the academic literature and expert reports. Google is seen as dominant in the search engine and related markets because it has high market shares. It is also viewed as facing limited competition from much smaller competitors. Since 2017 Yahoo and Ask.com have exited, followed by one significant entrant, Microsoft's Bing, which over the last decade has struggled to gain a 10% market share in EEA and several other search engines such as Kosmos Cuil, DuckDuckGo, and Blekko. Several structural factors of the search and related markets are routinely put forward as barriers to entry. These include the network effects already discussed above together with:

- **Data economies of scale and scope.** Data network and scale effects make their search and social networking algorithms much better than their competitors. The amount and diversity of data sources increase the speed and effectiveness of a search algorithm to predict user preferences and give more relevant results. Google collects data from Chrome, Gmail, YouTube, Google Maps, Google plus, Google analytics, Aggke Apps, and its ad-serving apps Double Click and Ad Mob. It also has a significant presence in other links of the supply of online advertising, including intermediaries such as AdSense.

- **The high fixed cost of developing search engines**. In 2010 Microsoft invested US$4.5 billion to develop its algorithms and physical capacity to operate its search engine Bing. The code used by a search engine can consist of three million lines and cost US$100 million.
- **Absence of multihoming.** While it is relatively easy for users to switch between search engines as they are '*only a click away*', they tend only to use one search engine. To many, this indicates a behavioral barrier among users so that they are somehow '*lock-in*' to the one search engine.

This approach raises several issues concerning dominance. Firstly, most of the above factors simply identify the differences between large and small platforms and do not naturally constitute barriers to entry in the economic sense. They do not explain the high '*market*' share of Google or the small share of its competitors. For example, while Bing has a relatively small market share, it deals with 60 million queries daily, which are sufficient to hone its search algorithms' relevance and predictive ability.

Secondly, digital platforms, even if dominant, are very different beasts from the stereotypical dominant industrial firm. It is trite to observe that digital platforms are innovative and dynamic businesses. Their investment in R&D is vast, at over US$71 billion in 2017. Google's R&D expenditure is significantly greater than its closest rival, Microsoft's annual investment in Bing, which alone would be a reason for the former's success. Many of the critics of the larger digital platforms take a constricted view of dynamic competition in terms of their rivals' claims that they find it difficult to compete with the large platforms. But to translate the disadvantages that competitors face into harm to consumers is not a straightforward exercise. The network effects and other factors that '*disadvantage*' competitors correlate with greater consumers' benefits.

Thirdly, the way antitrust markets are defined, which triggers dominance in the EU antitrust law, is not fit for purpose in a sector where services are free of charge. The search and social networking sides of these platforms have been described as '*attention markets*' where the competition takes place over non-price attributes to attract and maintain users' attention to their platforms and away from other platforms. In exchange, Google and Facebook harvest users' data and monetize it by selling online advertising space. Over 80% of Google's revenues come from advertising and much less for Facebook. The '*attention*' and online advertising '*markets*' are related. Still, the former has no '*price*' while for the other price serves a more complex function and will exceed marginal costs without necessarily being abusive. Increasingly questions are being raised about the use of the price based SSNIP to define antitrust markets. The proposal to merge the attention and advertising '*markets*' into a single antitrust market does not make sense. Perhaps the answer is to use a broader concept such as '*digital ecosystems*'. But this has drawbacks—lack of precision, hard to operationalize, subject to conflicting application, and its inconsistency with Article 102 TFEU's jurisprudence and the European Commission's decisional practice.

Finally, most antitrust investigations follow from complaints from rivals, who are often far from small and financially weak undertakings, and not from consumers. For example, the US Department of Justice's case against Microsoft was essentially lifted from Netscape's '*White Paper*,' it's then-largest rival.[38] Competition agencies' receptiveness to rivals' complaints encourages rivals to use antitrust strategically to game the system and competition authorities to erroneously treat harm to competitors as an indicator of harm to competition and hence to consumers.[39]

The preceding is not to dismiss the possibility that digital platforms can and do engage in abuses designed to inhibit and remove competitive threats. From an antitrust perspective, a dominant vertically integrated digital platform that supplies access to its platform to its downstream competitors can foreclose the downstream and related markets by engaging in a margin squeeze, bundling, predation, refusal to deal, self-preferencing, and degrading, delaying and/or blocking interoperability. A vertically integrated platform operator also collects information on its downstream competitors' users, usage, and services, and its algorithms rank their and its services. It is, therefore, no surprise that the European Commission has investigated, fined, and sought undertakings/commitments from Microsoft, Google, and Amazon.

The European Commission's investigation of the large digital platform started with two lengthy investigations of Microsoft, the first for refusing interoperability to its workgroup operating systems and media player; the second for bundling its web browser Internet Explorer with its PC operating systems.[40] More recently, Google has borne the brunt of the Commission's antitrust scrutiny. In 2017, 2018, and 2019 the European Commission found Google in breach of Article 102TFEU in the comparison shopping,[41] android operating systems,[42] and the brokering of online search advertising markets,[43] respectively (Table 1). Google has appealed all these decisions. These all involved some form of self-preferencing of Google's services resulting from its vertical integration. Google was prosecuted for giving favourable positioning and display to its comparison-shopping service in its search results pages in the Google Shopping decision. The European Commission fined it €2.4 billion. This contrasts with the position taken by other competition agencies.[44] In 2013, the FTC closed its investigation of Google stating that the "*quantitative evidence the Commission examined are largely consistent with the conclusion that Google likely benefited consumers by prominently displaying its vertical content on its search*

[38] Page and Lopatka (2006).

[39] Veljanovski (2010).

[40] Case COMP/39.530 Microsoft (Tying)) Tying of Internet explorer to its PC operating system, Decision of 2009. For in depth discussions of the DoJ's Microsoft case see Page and Lopatka (2006) and McKenzie (2000).

[41] Case AT.39740 Google Search (Shopping), Decision of 27/06/2017.

[42] Case AT.40.099 Google Android, Decision of 18/07/2018.

[43] Case AT.40.411 Google Search (Adsense), Press release 20/03/2019.

[44] Bergqvist and Rubin (2019).

Table 1 European Commission Article 102 TFEU Infringement decisions against digital platform operators

Commission Decision	Abuses	Fine/sanction/ Stage
Microsoft		
Microsoft (interoperability) (2004)	Refusal to supply competitors' work with group server operating system protocols etc. to interoperate with windows; tying windows media player with windows PC operating system.	€860 m/ commitments
Microsoft (Tying) (2009)	Tying internet explorer to Microsoft's PC operating system	€561 m[a]/ commitments
Google		
Google Shopping (2017)	Systematically favouring its own comparison-shopping service over its competitors in its general search results and relegating competitors to the fourth page of search results	€2.40bn
Google Android (2018)	Restrictive practices related to its android operating system including mandatory pre-installation of its proprietary apps on android devices.	€4.30bn
Google AdSense (2019)	Restricting online search advertising market on third party websites using AdSense—exclusive use AdSense for advertising; reserve premium placement for Google search; setting a minimum number of AdSense advertisements	€1.49bn
Amazon		
Amazon Book MFNs & related matters (2017)	Use of '*parity*' or "*most-favoured-nation*" (MFN) clauses between Amazon and publishers to inform Amazon about more favourable or alternative terms offered to Amazon's competitors and/or offer Amazon similar terms and conditions to its competitors for e-books publishers and distributors	Commitments
Amazon Marketplace (2019 in progress)	Investigating conflicts arising from Amazon's dual role as marketplace (platform) and retailer on its platform	
Apple		
Apple—App Store Practices (2019—in progress)	An investigation into whether Apple's rules for app developers on the distribution of apps via the App Store such as the mandatory use of Apple's own proprietary in-app purchase system and restrictions on the ability of developers to inform iPhone and iPad users of alternative cheaper purchasing possibilities outside of apps.	Investigation
Apple- Mobile Payments (2020—in progress)	An investigation into Apple Pay's terms, conditions, and other measures for integrating Apple Pay in merchant apps and websites on iPhones and iPads, Apple's limitation of access to the near field communication (NFC) functionality ("*tap and go*") on iPhones for payments in stores, and alleged refusals of access to Apple Pay.	Investigation

Notes: Many of these decisions have been the subject of lengthy enforcement activity and were or are being appealed at the time of writing

[a]This is the reduced fine after Google's appeal of the Commission's decision

results page."[45] The Google Adsense decision arose out of Google brokering of online search advertisements by Google's AdSense for Search, which provides search results to the owners of '*publisher*' websites. Here Google is acting as an 'advertising broker' at the same time as providing search services. As a broker, Google imposed several terms that restricted its rivals' search activities.

The European Commission has investigated Amazon. First, in 2017 for the use of the most favored nation (MFN) or parity clauses in its dealings with publishers. In July 2019, the European Commission announced that it was investigating Amazon's dual role (i) of providing a marketplace (platform) where independent sellers can sell products directly to consumers; and (ii) as a retailer on its platform. The European Commission's Press Release notes that when providing a marketplace for independent sellers, Amazon continuously collects commercially sensitive data about the activity on its platform and how this is used[46] and selects the winners of the "*Buy Box*". The "*Buy Box*" is displayed prominently on Amazon and allows customers to directly add items from a specific retailer to their shopping carts. Winning a place on "*Buy Box*" seems key for marketplace sellers as a vast majority of transactions are done through it. In 2020, the European Commission launched two investigations into Apple's activities concerning the terms and conditions to access its App Store[47] and those surrounding Apple Pay.[48]

National competition authorities have also been investigating and prosecuting digital undertakings. The European Commission's announced investigation of Amazon in mid-2019 came hard on the heels of the Bundeskartellamt publication of its settlement decision, with Amazon covering similar concerns.[49] In *Streetmap*,[50] the English and Wales High Court looked at Google's entry into the mapping area. It concluded that Google's entry was an innovation that did not constitute an abuse of dominance. In contrast, similar cases heard by Paris Tribunal de Commerce found that Google had sought to foreclose the mapping market in breach of Article 102 TFEU.[51] In 2019, the CMA obtained undertakings to desist from hotel booking sites including Booking.com, Expedia, Trivago, and others for various breaches of consumer protection law, including search results that did not necessarily give the best deal to their customer. All these decisions involve complex, competitive

[45] Fed. Trade Comm'n, File No. 111-0163, Statement Regarding Google's Search Practices, In the Matter of Google Inc. (Jan. 3, 2013) at p. 2. For analysis of this decision see Salinger and Levinson (2015) and Yun (2018).

[46] Case AT.40.462 Amazon Marketplace. Press release '*Antitrust: Commission opens investigation into possible anti-competitive conduct of Amazon*,' European Commission, 17 July 2019.

[47] European Commission, '*Antitrust: Commission opens investigations into Apple's App Store rules*', Press Release, 16 June 2020.

[48] European Commission, '*Antitrust: Commission opens investigation into Apple practices regarding Apple Pay Brussels*,' 16 June 2020.

[49] FCO, Press Release of 17 July 2019, Bundeskartellamt obtains far-reaching improvements in the terms of business for sellers on Amazon's online marketplaces.

[50] STREETMAP.EU LTD V GOOGLE INC [2016] EWHC 253 (CH).

[51] Caccinelli and Toledano (2017).

analysis and novel theories of harm that warrant careful assessment, but beyond the scope of this Chapter.

4 Algorithmic Pricing and Collusion

Pricing algorithms have attracted considerable and, at times, sensational attention from legal scholars and commentators. The impression given by this literature is that pricing algorithms facilitate collusion and pricing practices that gouge consumers and substantially reduce competition across the economy.

4.1 Algorithmic Pricing

Pricing algorithms are widely used to provide consumer-facing online services such as travel and hotel booking sites, comparison sites, and eCommerce. The European Commission's e-commerce report found most retailers track the online prices of competitors *"out of which 67% use automatic software programs for that purpose' with the 78% of those retailers that use software to track prices subsequently adjust their prices to those of their competitors."*[52] These algorithms often improve the pricing of goods and service by enabling surge and dynamic pricing to take account of peaks and troughs in demand and supply, allow personalized and discriminatory pricing, facilitate price comparison websites, and track, monitor, and reacting to competitors' prices.

The competition issues raised by algorithmic pricing are two-fold. The first is the claim that algorithms will increase discriminatory and personalized pricing on e-commerce sites, *i.e.*, charging different prices for the same product or service to different consumers based on their willingness to pay. The competitiveness or otherwise of discriminatory and personalized pricing is a matter of context. To effectively price discriminate requires that the supplier has some market power and can prevent arbitrage by consumers. By engaging in discriminatory pricing, the seller can appropriate a larger amount of consumers' surplus (more money) than would otherwise be the case, increasing their profits. This '*appropriation effect*' raises concerns over fairness and the reduction of demand elsewhere in the economy.

On the other hand, discriminatory pricing has an '*expansion effect*' as it increases the number of transactions/sales. It is output-expanding and therefore alleviates the tendency of the monopolist to restrict output/sales. In theory, a perfectly discriminating monopolist would produce the same output as a competitive market, albeit with a greater transfer of wealth from consumers to producers.

---

[52] European Commission (2017, para. 149).

The second concern is pricing algorithms to facilitate collusion by better monitoring competitors' prices, increasing the speed at which prices are adjusted, and punishing price cutters. Together with developments in artificial intelligence, it is claimed that these factors will increase the incidence of collusive pricing and make autonomous machine-based collusion possible. To date, there have been only a handful of infringement decisions involving pricing algorithms. The US case of *Topkins*[53] concerning the online sale of posters and frames is routinely cited, as is the CMA's similar infringement decision of poster sellers who used automated re-pricing software to monitor and adjust their prices on Amazon's UK website.[54] The European Commission's *Eturas*[55] decision involved travel agents using algorithms to set prices on their online booking platform. There have been two other infringement decisions—*Asus*[56] and *Casio*[57]—where pricing algorithms have been used to enforce resale price maintenance (RPM). All these cases are legally unexceptional in the sense that they fall within the standard antitrust categories of an infringement of Article 101TFEU because the pricing algorithms were used to give effect to price-fixing agreements between human competitors and retailers.

4.2 *Machine-Based Collusion*

Some legal academics and commentators have suggested the more problematic prospect that self-learning algorithms can create and maintain cartels that set prices without human monitoring and inter-firm communications, *e.g.*, Ezrachi and Stucke (2016), OECD (2017). These algorithms are programmed to interact with one another by observing outcomes and to set profit-maximizing prices which may be collusive. This, combined with the '*oligopoly gap*' in current antitrust laws (Article 101TFEU), which requires some form of human agreement or cooperation as the

[53] United States of America v. David Topkins, Plea Agreement, Department of Justice, Antitrust Division, No. CR 15-00201 WHO.

[54] Decision of the Competition and Markets Authority, Online sales posters and frames, Case 50,223, 12 August 2016.

[55] Case C-74/14 Eturas' UAB and Others v Lietuvos Respublikos konkurencijos taryba EU:C: 2016:42, Judgment of the Court, 21 Jan 2016.

[56] European Commission Press Release, Antitrust: Commission fines four consumer electronics manufacturers for fixing online resale prices, Cases AT.40465 (Asus), AT.40469 (Denon & Marantz), AT.40181 (Philips) and AT.40182 (Pioneer), decisions of 24 July 2018.

[57] Decision of the Competition and Markets Authority, Digital piano, and digital keyboard sector: anti-competitive practices 50565-2 (non-confidential), 8 October 2019. Also see OFGEM Infringement by Economy Energy et al., of Chapter I of the Competition Act 1998 with Respect to an Anticompetitive Agreement, July 26, 2019.

basis for illegality, raises the possibility that machine-based collusion will go undetected and unpunished.[58]

The threat of collusion by self-learning pricing algorithms is hotly debated. The pessimistic view is that it poses a significant threat to the competition, which warrants urgent attention. Ezrachi and Stucke, in their book *Virtual Competition,* warn that algorithmic pricing systems will mark the "*end of the competition as we know it*".[59] They suggest that machine-based algorithms increase the extent of collusion—"*pricing algorithms can spread tacit collusion beyond duopolies to markets with five or six large firms.*" Although Ezrachi and Stucke want us to move away from '*slogans*' in this area, they nonetheless contribute their own by describing '*algorithm-enhanced conscious parallelism*' as "*Tacit Collusion on Steroids*".[60] To others, this is an exaggerated hypothesis.[61]

4.3 Why Machine-Based Algorithmic Collusion Is Not a Problem

There are reasons to be skeptical about the prospect of widespread machine-based collusion and the difficulties it poses for law enforcement. This is based on some of the following considerations, among others:[62]

- **No evidence.** There is no evidence, no real-world example, and no antitrust case where self-learning pricing algorithms have colluded, let alone increased the prospect of collusion across the economy after more than half a decade since the publication of *Virtual Competition*, which given the speed that digital services have emerged and grown is equivalent to several lifetimes. Instead, only two unpublished experimental computer simulations by Calvano et al (2019) and Klein (2019) are frequently cited as 'evidence' of the possibility of autonomous machine-based collusion. The idea of machines colluding without human knowledge or intervention is currently viewed as '*science fiction*' to quote the European Commission's Competition Commissioner Margarethe Vestager.[63] This is not to say that self-learning algorithms can collude in the future, as we know yesterday's science fiction is often today's reality.
- **Lack of specifics.** The proponents of machine-based collusion are vague as to which industries are susceptible to machine-based algorithmic collusion. The discussion so far has mainly been abstract based on unsupported generalizations,

[58] Mehra (2016); Ezrachi and Stucke (2016, 2017).

[59] Ezrachi and Stucke (2016, p. 233).

[60] Ezrachi and Stucke (2016, p. 37).

[61] Veljanovski (2020).

[62] Veljanovski (2020).

[63] Vestager (2017).

giving the impression of an impending contagion of pricing bots affecting the whole economy. However, if one looks at the empirical evidence, the predominant type of illegal collusion is the sellers' cartel for intermediate industrial inputs or components. These are business-to-business (B2B) operations between sophisticated direct purchasers. Invariably these cartels have formed in response to structural problems in the industry such as excess capacity and declining prices due to technological advances and entry. On the other hand, pricing algorithms appear to be mainly used for airline, hotel, and events bookings, Uber-like services, and often take the form of dynamic pricing of non-storable products or services; and retail pricing of business-to-consumer (B2C) e-commerce platforms. This would restrict the scope and impact of machine-based collusion should it arise to economy segments.

- **Other conditions must exist for algorithmic collusion.** Effective, sustainable collusion requires specific structural and behavioral conditions conducive to cartelization in the affected markets. While machine-based pricing algorithms may be able to dispense with human and machine communications between rivals, they nonetheless will be confined to industries that are concentrated with significant barriers to entry, transparent pricing, and the other factors typically listed as required for collusion by competition authorities (such as the next point), rather than the technical possibility of machine-based pricing algorithms. This further limits the sectors at risk and whether they often substitute for human ways of colluding.
- **Inconsistent with discriminatory and personalized pricing**. In a rush to list the potential transgressions of digital platforms, Ezrachi and Stucke say that Google, Amazon, and others will engage in price and non-price discrimination.[64] However, as they are aware discriminatory and personalized pricing and competition based on non-price terms and quality are in practice hostile to successful collusion. Simple economic logic tells us that collusion is more likely where the good is homogeneous and sold at a single transparent price. This is because monitoring price divergences for a standardized product is easier and cheaper. Where prices differ among customers for the same product or the product has different quality attributes and prices, it is hard for pricing algorithms to locate a stable collusive set of prices.
- **Executives are unlikely to be able to hide behind machines.** The claim that there is a severe gap in cartel laws rests on the premise that management and shareholders can wash their hands of collusion by claiming that they were unaware of how the pricing algorithm worked and that it would collusively set artificially high prices. The law is sufficiently elastic to blow this defense apart. These are the same executives who commissioned the computer scientists to develop and maintain the pricing algorithm software and authorized its use to set prices.

[64] Ezrachi and Stucke (2016, Part III).

- **Debate US-centric.** The focus of many articles is the legal position under US antitrust. EU law, specifically Article 101TFEU, is potentially more flexible and can be widened to incorporate machine-based collusion under the rubric of '*concerted practice*'. In recent years, the scope of Article 101TFEU has been progressively widened from '*classic sellers*' cartels where executives meet in '*smoked filled rooms*' to include information exchange, third-party facilitators, unilateral price signaling, and even being present in the same room as members of the cartel while refusing any involvement and taking no collusive actions. The concept of concerted practice, which is cooperation that falls short of an agreement, in EU law seems sufficiently broad to capture unilateral actions among pricing algorithms that have the effect of generating artificially high prices.
- **Over-reliance on whistleblowers/leniency.** There is an enforcement gap from competition authorities' over-reliance on whistleblowers, leniency programs, and prosecutions based on the '*object*' provision of Article 101(1) TFEU, which has failed to adopt a proactive effects-based enforcement strategy. The failure to invest in expertise and technology to detect cartels generally invites firms to use more difficult-to-detect forms of collusion. This is changing. Competition authorities are now beginning to invest in and draw on digital technologies and proactive enforcement based on screening techniques. The CMA's recent formation of a data unit "*to better understand the impact that data, machine learning, and other algorithms have on markets and people*"[65] is an example of how competition authorities are responding.

5 Mergers

Mergers and acquisitions by digital platforms have led to two related concerns. The first and most graphic is the claim that digital platforms have made '*killer acquisitions*' of potential competitors; and the second is that conglomerate mergers enhance the market power of the acquiring platform by exploiting network effects and data and product economies of scope. As observed by the Chief Executive of the CMA:[66]

> Over the last decade, Amazon, Apple, Facebook, Google, and Microsoft combined—the so-called GAFAM quintet—have made over 400 acquisitions globally, with more than half of these—close to 250—just in the most recent five years. Some of these acquisitions have had exceptionally high valuations. However only a handful of these mergers have been scrutinized by competition authorities, and none have been blocked. As an economist, these statistics naturally lead me to question whether we as competition authorities have got the

[65] CMA appoints Stefan Hunt to top digital role,' Press Release, 18 May 2018. https://www.gov.uk/government/news/cma-appoints-stefan-hunt-to-top-digital-role.

[66] Coscelli (2019).

> balance right. Is it right that across all 400 of these acquisitions, there has not been a single prohibition? On this basis, is it possible to argue that we have correctly balanced the risks of under- and over-enforcement?[67]

The Lear Report (1999), using available public information, found that in 2008 to 2018, Google acquired 168 companies, Facebook acquired 71 companies, and Amazon acquired 60 companies, i.e., around an average of 15, 6, and 5 annual acquisitions, respectively. Mergers that some commentators regard as potentially anti-competitive such as between Apple/Shazam (2018), Microsoft/LinkedIn (2016), Facebook/WhatsApp (2014), and Google/Doubleclick (2008), were all approved by the European Commission; and the mergers between Facebook/Instagram (2012) and Google/Waze (2013) by the (then) UK Office of Fair Trading.

5.1 Killer Acquisitions

A '*killer acquisition*' can be defined as the acquisition of innovative targets to preempt future competition.[68] The term comes from a study of acquisitions in the pharmaceuticals sector. Some evidence was found that '*Big Pharma*' had acquired a potential competitor in a small number of cases (6% of the sample).[69] Many believe that the same thing is happening in the digital sector. Several commentators have cautioned against using evidence from the pharmaceutical sector to extrapolate to the digital platforms and whether there has been many genuine pharma '*killer acquisitions*'.[70] Nonetheless, the meager empirical evidence has not prevented the claim from being repeated and applied to the digital sector. For example, the Furman report states: "*[Q]uantitative evidence on the effects of mergers in the digital economy is limited*".[71] Yet it then refers to the pharma study to audaciously claim that "*[T]his research, in combination with wide-ranging evidence gathered through extensive consultation with experts, supports the Panel's expectation that at least some of the acquisitions that large digital companies have made will have been problematic*".[72] This is no basis for concluding that there is a problem, let alone grounds for policy and legal reforms.

While there have been criticisms of the clearance of some mergers such as *Facebook/WhatsApp,*[73] *Google/DoubleClick*[74], and *Facebook/Instagram*, these have not amounted to a general case of the '*failure*' of the EU merger clearance to

[67] Lear Report (2019).

[68] OECD (2020b).

[69] Cunningham et al. (2019).

[70] Grise et al. (2020).

[71] Furman Report (2019, para. 1.154).

[72] Furman Report (2019, para. 1.155).

[73] Case M.8228 Facebook/WhatsApp, Decision of 17 May 2017.

[74] COMP/M.4731 Google/DoubleClick, Decision of 11 March 2008.

block '*killer acquisitions.*' More systematic studies of the M&A activity in the digital sector find no evidence of a killer acquisition problem. Gautier & Lamesch study of 175 mergers and acquisitions during 2015–2017 failed to find evidence of killer acquisitions.[75] The authors of the study define merger or acquisition targets to be in the killer zone if they are *"(1) in the core segment of the acquirer, (2) continued under the original brand name after the acquisition, and (3) have a substantial user base".*[76] Based on these criteria, only one acquisition potentially qualified as a '*killer application'*—Facebook's acquisition in 2016 of Masquerade a young startup that had developed a photo filter app that became rapidly popular. The large digital platforms used M&A activity primarily to strengthen their core market segments and rarely expanded into new activities. The study concluded that *"tech giants ... acquisition appears to be a substitute for in-house R&D".*[77] Most of the acquired products were shut down post-acquisition, which suggests that GAFAM mainly acquires a firm's assets (functionality, technology, talent, or intellectual property) to integrate them into their ecosystem rather than the products and users themselves. Latham et al. confirm these results.[78] They examined the 409 acquisitions made between 2009 and 2020 to identify transactions where the target firm could have plausibly threatened the acquirer's '*core*' business, and the valuation was large enough to mask a market power premium plausibly. They conclude that '*killer acquisitions'* were rare and found that had the acquisition not taken place, the purchaser would have entered the same space as the target, thus *"flipping the traditional "killer" acquisition narrative on its head."*[79]

5.2 Conglomerate Mergers

A conglomerate merger is where an undertaking acquires an entity operating in an adjacent market. Thus, the merger does not increase concentration in the relevant product market and does not give rise to the prospect of significantly lessening competition by removing an independent rival. For these reasons, conglomerate mergers generally escape competition law scrutiny. This is being reconsidered given the dynamics of digital platforms where complementary products can be bundled, and data leveraged across markets, to give the acquirer advantages interpreted as barriers to entry.[80] Predictably lawyers and economists have developed more complex theories of harm, suggesting the need for greater scrutiny of conglomerate mergers. One of these is the '*envelopment theory'* that recasts the leverage theory of

[75] Gautier and Lamesch (2020).

[76] Id.

[77] Id.

[78] Latham et al. (2020).

[79] Id.

[80] Bourreau and de Streel (2019); OECD (2020a).

monopoly where a dominant platform operator in one market enters another market by bundling or tying together the two platform products: so-called '*privacy policy tying*'.[81] Provided there is a significant overlap of users those in the second market offering a narrower range of products find they are unable to compete. This can also occur from the acquirer's access to more data and its ability to cross-subsidize services in the second market.

There are other theories of harm. A merger between two networks offering different products to the same user groups can restrict competition even if the products offered to capture consumer attention are different. Yet others have hypothesized that digital platforms use conglomerate mergers to create a branded '*ecosystem*' and a '*one-stop shopping experience*', making it difficult for smaller platforms with more limited offerings to compete. Or a horizontal merger enables the dominant platform to coordinate parallel exclusionary conduct, such as resale price maintenance or most favored nation (MFN) or parity clauses, across multiple markets.

These leverage theories of harm have been around for some time, although not focusing on the greater accumulation of user data. In the telecoms sector, there have been endless analyses of the disadvantages that single product access-seekers have in competition with larger operators who provide platform access benefiting from economies of scale and scope when offering double and triple play bundles (telephony, broadband, mobile, etc.).

Despite the above theories, there is little evidence to support that conglomerate mergers have harmed competition and consumers. While the Chief Executive of the CMA has questioned whether competition authorities have been too permissive (see above), his speculations are not borne out by the Lear Report, commissioned by the CMA, which concluded:

> While we have identified some gaps in the way that the Authorities analysed these cases, it is not always clear whether competitive harm has arisen as a result of such gaps. The decisions taken in Facebook/Instagram and Google/Waze may have represented missed opportunities for the emergence of challengers to the market incumbents but have also likely resulted in efficiencies. The decisions taken in Priceline/Kayak and Amazon/The Book Depository appear less controversial, as the level of competition in the markets concerned does not seem to have been substantially affected by the mergers.[82]

Others see the current merger clearance as adequate and point to numerous examples of large communications conglomerates who appeared to be making critical acquisitions at the time, but which failed, such as the *AOL/TimeWarner* and *MySpace/News Corp* mergers, and Yahoo's acquisitions.

---

[81] Condorelli and Padilla (2020).

[82] Lear Report (2019, para. II.268).

5.3 Merger Reforms

Despite the lack of evidence that competition authorities have waved through anti-competitive acquisitions, governments are pressing ahead with reforms. So far, these have focused on plugging to perceived '*gaps*' in the law which have allegedly allowed anti-competitive M&As to slip under the 'antitrust radar' due to (1) relatively high merger thresholds which have allowed smaller strategic acquisitions; and (2) the benign treatment of conglomerate mergers. These *gaps* in the law have led to several proposed reforms, including:

- Some countries such as Austria and Germany have moved fast to introduce new lower merger notification thresholds.
- The European Commission's expert report[83] recommended that the Commission "*should put less emphasis on the analysis of market definition, and more emphasis on theories of harm and identification of anti-competitive strategies.*" The experts recommend that mergers be assessed in the broader '*digital ecosystem'* and treat conglomerate mergers as horizontal mergers in the same '*technological and users*' space.
- The Furman Report proposes pre-notification and a "*balance of harm approach to killer acquisition, which considers the scale and likelihood of harm in merger cases involving potential competition and harm to innovation*".[84] It also proposed that dominant platforms be designated as having Strategic Market Status (SMS), which would attract greater scrutiny, reverse the burden of proof and be subject to *ex-ante* regulatory obligations.
- The Lear Report calls for a more forward-looking merger clearance process that takes better account of technological developments. It recommends that the CMA name the digital companies with a strategic market status required to give advanced notice of intended acquisitions.[85]

6 Concluding Observations

The '*monopoly view*' of the large digital platforms is gaining traction, as is the need for greater regulation. For the most part, this is based on theory, market shares, and competitor complaints and not a detailed empirical examination of the effects of large digital platforms on consumer welfare and competition. To say that network effects are rife in the digital sector and that algorithms can be used as anti-competitive devices does not tell whether they are responsible for anticompetitive practices and their significance.

---

[83] Crémer et al. (2019, pp. 3–4).

[84] Furman Report (2019).

[85] Lear Report (2019).

One is reluctant to ask for further analysis of the sector given the large and growing number of reports that have so far been published. What is needed is a more balanced perspective and to move away from selective generalities to a deeper empirical understanding of the digital sector and its interplay with competition, regulation, and economic welfare. In particular, the empirical significance of data and users' direct and indirect network effects is urgently needed. Despite the limited and indeed contrary evidence that killer acquisitions are a major problem, the debate must move to a factual analysis of M&A activity in the digital sector. Considering the findings of several independent reports, merger regulation has not been permissive.[86] It is accepted that repeated and lengthy antitrust investigations of Article 102 TFEU infringements may not be the most effective way to regulate the sector. But it is also the case that the theories of harm underpinning these investigations are often *ad hoc* and not well worked out. The emerging situation is a wall of regulation falling on the large digital platforms based on a *'big is bad'* thesis and theoretical propositions that have yet to be fully explored or tested. This is not to diminish the claim and evidence that the large digital platforms are asserting market power or the need to evolve regulation of the sector that is fit for purpose in some areas.

References

ACCC (2019) Digital Platforms Inquiry - Final Report. Australian Competition, and Consumer Commission

AdC (2019) Digital ecosystems, Big Data and Algorithms - Issues Paper. Autoridade da Concorrência. July

ADLC/BKartA (2019) Algorithms and Competition. Joint Report of the Autorité de la Concurrence and Bundeskartellamt

Aron M (2016) Why Google Beat Yahoo in the War for the Internet. Techcrunch, May 22

Auer D, Petit N (2015) Two-sided markets and the challenge of turning economic theory into antitrust policy. Anti Bull 60:426–461

Bergqvist C, Rubin J (2019) Google and the Trans-Atlantic Antitrust. Univ. of Copenhagen Faculty of Law Research Paper No. 2019-73, 2019, https://papers.ssrn.com/sol3/papers.cfm?abstract_id=3354766

Bourreau M, de Streel A (2019) Digital Conglomerates and EU Competition Policy. ETNO. http://www.crid.be/pdf/public/8377.pdf

Caccinelli C, Toledano J (2017) 'Assessing Anticompetitive Practices in Two-Sided Markets: A Comparative Analysis of four Antitrust Proceedings against Booking.com' presented at 28th European Regional Conference of the International Telecommunications Society (ITS): Competition and Regulation in the Information Age, Passau, Germany, 30 July – 02 August 2017

Calvano E, Calzolari G, Denicolò V, Pastorello S (2019) Artificial Intelligence, Algorithmic Pricing and Collusion. CEPR Discussion Paper 13405. Available at SSRN: https://ssrn.com/abstract=3304991

Chiou L, Tucker CE (2017) Search Engines and Data Retention: Implications for Privacy and Antitrust. NBER Working Paper No. w23815

[86] Lear Report (2019).

CMA (2018) Pricing Algorithms - Economic working paper on the use of algorithms to facilitate collusion and personalised pricing. Competition & Market Authority, CMA94

CMA (2019) Online Platforms and Digital Advertising - Market Study Interim Report. Competition & Market Authority

Condorelli D, Padilla J (2020) Harnessing Platform Envelopment in a Digital World. https://papers.ssrn.com/sol3/papers.cfm?abstract_id=3504025

Coscelli A (2019) 'Competition in the Digital Age: Reflecting on digital merger investigations', speech to the *OECD/*G7 Conference on Competition and the Digital Economy. https://www.gov.uk/government/speeches/competition-in-the-digital-age-reflecting-on-digital-merger-investigations

Crémer J, de Montjoye Y-A, Schweitzer H (2019) Competition Policy for the Digital Era: Final Report. European Commission

Cunningham C, Ederer F, Ma S (2019) 'Killer Acquisitions', March 22

European Commission (1997) Commission Notice on the definition of relevant market for the purposes of Community competition law (97/C 372 /03) OJ C 372, 9.12.1997, pp 5–13

European Commission (2017) Final Report on the E-commerce Sector Inquiry, European Commission Staff Working Document, COM (2017) 229 final, 10 May

European Commission (2020) Communication: Shaping Europe's Digital Future, 19 February

Ezrachi A, Stucke ME (2016) Virtual competition: the promise and perils of the Algorithm-driven economy. Harvard University Press

Ezrachi A, Stucke ME (2017) Artificial intelligence and collusion: when computers inhibit competition. Univ Ill Law Rev, pp 1776–1810

Furman J (2019) Unlocking Digital Competition, Report of the Digital Competition Expert Panel, HM Treasury

Gautier A, Lamesch J (2020) Mergers in the Digital Economy. CESifo Working Paper 8056, January

Grise J, Burns D, Giordano E (2020) The no kill zone: the other side of pharma acquisitions. Online at Competition Policy International.com

House of Lords (2016) Online Platforms and the Digital Single Market. Select Committee on European Union 10th Report of Session 2015–16

Hylton KN (2019) Digital platforms and antitrust law. Neb Law Rev 98:272–296

Kahn L (2017) Amazon's antitrust paradox. Yale Law J 126:710–805

Klein T (2019) Autonomous Algorithmic Collusion: Q-Learning Under Sequential Pricing. Tinbergen Institute Discussion Paper - TI 2018-056/VII

Latham O, Tecu I, Bagaria N (2020) Beyond killer acquisitions: are there more common potential competition issues in tech deals and how can these be assessed? Anti Chronicle 2(2):26–37

Lear (2019) Ex post Assessment of Merger Control Decisions in Digital Markets - Report to the Competition Market Authority

Mateus AM (2020) Is there a Consensus on Antitrust for Big Tech?. SSRN Electronic Journal

McKenzie RB (2000) Trust on trial – how the microsoft case is reframing the rules of competition. Perseus Publishing

MEA&CP (2019) Factsheet – Dutch position on competition policy in relation to digital platforms. The Netherlands Ministry of Economic Affairs and Climate Change

Mehra SK (2016) Antitrust and the Robo-seller: competition in the time of algorithms. Minnesota Law Rev 100:1323–1335

Melamed AD, Petit N (2019) The misguided assault on the consumer welfare standard in the age of platform markets. Rev Ind Organ 54:41–774

Monopolskommission (2015) Competition Policy: The Challenge of Digital Markets. Special Report 68

OECD (2017) Algorithms and Collusion - Note from the European Union. AF/COMP/WD (2017) 12

OECD (2019) An Introduction to Online Platforms and Their Role in the Digital Transformation. https://doi.org/10.1787/53e5f593-en

OECD (2020a) Roundtable on Conglomerate Effects of Mergers - Background Note by the Secretariat, DAF/COMP (2020)2, 30 April

OECD (2020b) Start-ups, killer acquisitions and merger control: Background note by the Secretariat. http://www.oecd.org/daf/competition/start-ups-killer-acquisitions-and-mergercontrol.htm

Ohlhausen M (2017) Should We Fear the Things That Go Beep in the Night? Some Initial Thoughts on the Intersection of Antitrust Law and Algorithmic Pricing. Remarks from the Concurrences Antitrust in the Financial Sector Conference, New York, May 23. https://www.ftc.gov/public-statements/2017/05/should-we-fear-things-go-beep-night-some-initial-thoughts-intersection

Page WH, Lopatka JE (2006) The microsoft case – antitrust, high technology, and consumer welfare. University of Chicago Press

Rainie L, Anderson J (2017) Code-Dependent: Pros and Cons of the Algorithm Age. Pew Research Center, 8 February, https://www.pewresearch.org/internet/2017/02/08/code-dependent-pros-and-cons-of-the-algorithm-age/

Report S (2019) Stigler committee on digital platforms - main report. George Stigler Center, Univ Chicago

Rochet J-C, Tirole J (2003) Platform competition in two-sided markets. J Eur Econ Assoc, 990–1029

Rochet J-C, Tirole J (2006) Two-sided markets - a progress report. Rand J Econ 37:645–667

Salinger MA, Levinson RJ (2015) Economics and the FTC's Google investigation. Rev Ind Organ 46:25–57

Schweitzer H et al (2018) Modernizing the Law on Abuse of Market Power. Report for the Federal Ministry of Economic Affairs and Energy

Spulber DF (2002) Famous fables of economics – myths of market failures. Blackwells

Stigler Report (2019) Stigler committee on digital platforms – main report. George Stigler Center, Univ Chicago

Tucker C (2018) What have we learned in the last decade? Network effects and market power. Antitrust 32:72–79

van Gorp N, de Bijl P (2019) Digital Gatekeepers - Assessing Exclusionary Conduct, Report commission by the Netherland ministry of Economic Affairs, 7 October

Varian H (2018) Use and abuse of network effects. In: Guzman M (ed) Towards a just society: Joseph Stiglitz and twenty-first century economics. Columbia University Press

Veljanovski C (2001) EC antitrust in the new economy – is the European Commission's view of the network economy, right? Eur Compet Law Rev 22:115–121

Veljanovski C (2010) Strategic Use of Regulation. In: Baldwin R, Cave M, Lodge M (eds) The Oxford handbook of regulation. Oxford University Press

Veljanovski C (2020) Pricing Algorithms as Collusive Devices. draft

Vestager M (2017) Speech at the Bunderskartellampt, 18th Conference on Competition, Berlin, 16 March

Vestager M (2019) Competition in the Digital Economy. IECD/G7 Conference, Paris, 3 June

Vestager M (2020) Shaping a Digital Future for Europe. Symposium on Digitalisation, The Hague, 3 February. https://ec.europa.eu/commission/commissioners/2019-2024/vestager/announcements/shaping-digital-future-europe_en

Wright J, Portuese A (2020) Antitrust populism: towards a taxonomy. Stanford J Law Bus Financ 25:131–181

Yun JM (2018) Understanding Google's search platform and the implications for antitrust analyses. J Compet Law Econ 14:311–329

Zingales L, Rolnik G, Lancieri FM (2019) Stigler Committee on Digital Platforms: Policy Brief. September 2019

Zuckerberg M (2020) We Need More Regulation of Big Tech. Financial Times, 17 February

Algorithmic Antitrust and Consumer Choice

Liza Lovdahl Gormsen

Abstract This chapter considers how algorithms affect competition and what their implications are for competition policy. With the economy going digital, a huge number of great innovations have materialized. Consumers have greatly benefitted from these innovations. However, several antitrust issues have emerged. This chapter looks at both the consumer benefits as well as the antitrust issues. It examines contemporary reports to determine whether algorithmic innovations have produced competition law concerns such as tacit collusion or price personalization. Other more sophisticated issues include the increase in nudging strategies from digital platforms.

1 Introduction

Algorithm's feed of data and data is—or ought to be—an essential issue for antitrust enforcers. The ability of a firm to collect extremely large amounts of data and process them through sophisticated algorithms to reveal patterns, trends, and associations (collectively known as '*big data*') adds a new dimension to market power. Possessing data can lead to significant innovations, but it can also create considerable concentrations in specific markets. Data can affect entry conditions by making it more or less difficult for a firm to enter or compete, particularly for firms needing data as an input to compete in a specific market. There is a belief that simple algorithms with lots of data outperform sophisticated algorithms with little data partly because of the opportunity for algorithms to learn through trial and error.[1] According to Peter Norvig, Google's director of research, Google "*. . .don't have*

This chapter develops the arguments set out in an article 'Algorithms & Competition Law' published in Competition Policy International (2020). I am grateful to Enrique Bravo, who has provided great research assistance on this chapter.

[1] Ezrachi and Stucke (2016b, p. 16).

L. L. Gormsen (✉)
British Institute of International and Comparative Law, London, UK
e-mail: l.lovdahlgormsen@biicl.org

A. Portuese (ed.), *Algorithmic Antitrust*, Economic Analysis of Law in European Legal Scholarship 12, https://doi.org/10.1007/978-3-030-85859-9_3

better algorithms than everyone else; we [Google] just have more data."[2] While big data raises many legal, moral and ethical issues, such as cybersecurity and the undertakings' accountability for the actions of their algorithms,[3] this article focuses on the implications of data and algorithms for competition policy. It also analyses algorithms from a fresh perspective, meaning the increased exploitation of consumer bias and prediction of preferences following the nudge theory as developed by Richard Thaler and Cass Sunstein.

2 Competition Law in Digital Markets

2.1 Algorithm Input

An algorithm is only as good as the data input. The volume of data is of particular significance concerning the operation of algorithms. With data input, algorithms can predict trends and behaviors or assess the likelihood for certain events to occur from the deduction or inference from new information.[4] Deep learning (the design and development of innovative, self-learning algorithms) software and algorithms crunch large datasets, thereby 'learning' to recognize patterns in digital representations of sounds, images, and other data.[5] Deep learning allows algorithms to carry out a myriad of functions relating to pricing decisions, matchmaking, planning, logistics, online communications, and e-commerce. As a result of deep learning, algorithms can understand and translate languages, identify images, write news articles, and analyze medical data for example. Advancements in data science have led to the ability to learn fast and deep from big data with the aid of algorithms that access and analyze vast amounts of information quickly. The analysis of data, performed through algorithms and advanced data processing techniques (*i.e.,* big analytics), becomes more valuable to the extent that it allows for specific patterns to be found and new correlations to be made between several datasets coming from a combination of different data sources.[6]

2.2 Consumer Benefits

Algorithmic developments have been a great driver for the growth of the digital economy, which has brought essential consumer benefits. Firstly, the collection and

[2]O'Reilly (2010).

[3]Stucke and Grunes (2016, p. 1).

[4]De Filippi (2014).

[5]Hof (2014).

[6]De Filippi (2014).

processing of data have conferred upon digital firms the ability to identify new trends and develop new products and services of particular relevance for users.[7] Secondly, detailed knowledge of consumers' preferences and behaviours can be derived from data mining. This knowledge allows digital firms to target ads and products better, supply personalized services, and increase consumer retention and loyalty. Targeted advertising, in turn, can increase sales and revenues for marketers and merchants.[8] Algorithmic personalized advertising can potentially reduce advertisement investment that is wasted when addressed to consumers uninterested in the advertised product[9] and reduce consumer annoyance (at least as compared with non-targeted advertising, since consumers can perceive targeted advertising as less vexatious or even as informative[10]). Thirdly, based on observed behavior, big data enables the redesign and improvement of services, business processes, strategies, and efficiency in general (for example, big data can be used to speed up transactions and reduce the likelihood of product returns).[11] Lastly, big data has contributed significantly to the emergence of business models under which digital services and content are offered to consumers at zero prices. Under this business model, firms ('*platforms*') offer consumers a free product or service on one side (the '*user side*') and earn their income on the other side (the '*paying side*') from selling advertisers the ability to access these consumers with targeted behavioral ads. The latter will be discussed in more detail later in the chapter.

2.3 *Antitrust Issues*

2.3.1 Leverage and Nudging Strategies

The OECD describes the development of artificial intelligence ('AI') in the following way: '(...) *AI became more effective tool after the development of algorithms that teach machines to learn, an idea that evolved from the study of pattern recognition and learning theory, and which would establish the new branch of machine learning.*[12] A key element of AI is its ability to simulate or reproduce thinking patterns that have naturally been exclusive to human beings. As with almost any kind of technological development, its effects could be either positive or negative depending on how AI is deployed. An algorithm could be useful to improve, for example, decision-making processes such as comparing prices for goods and services at a large scale. However, the downside is that algorithms

[7] Monopolkommission (2015, p. 30).

[8] CMA (2015, p. 50).

[9] Blattberg and Deighton (1991, pp. 8–11).

[10] Monopolkommission (2015, p. 31).

[11] CMA (2015, p. 93).

[12] OECD (2017).

could have been designed for less benign purposes, such as maximizing profits as opposed to help consumers find the best prices. This section is divided into two parts. Part one looks at data and how its quantity is relevant for the improvement and effectiveness of AI. Part two discusses how nudging strategies can be designed utilizing using AI as a way to achieving leveraging.

2.3.1.1 AI and Data

For example, user data collected in one market in the search engine market or social network market can improve quality in another market, in the online display advertising market. Where the same data can be used in two or more markets, an incumbent can benefit from a 'domino effect': it can leverage its dominant position in market A, which is derived from its data advantage, to cause a connected market B to tip, even where traditional incumbent firms already serve market B.[13] There are numerous examples of this trend. For instance, due to its dominance in the market for online search Google was able to identify data that was useful for the digital maps market. Google Maps soon became the market leader after Google expanded onto this segment, quickly displacing the theretofore-market leader MapQuest.[14] Google repeated this move in many 'vertical' segments, such as travel, local, and shopping, recently fined by the European Commission (the 'Commission') for abusing its dominant position with its comparison-shopping service.[15]

Additionally, data-linkage has enabled Google to extend its dominance in online search onto numerous related online segments, such as mobile operating system (Android), web browser (Chrome), email service (Gmail), video streaming site (YouTube), mapping service (Google Maps), website analytics tool (Google Analytics), cloud platform service (Google Apps), display advertising technology (DoubleClick and AdMob). A one firm scenario dominating numerous online markets is inconsistent with a competition policy that seeks to keep markets open and ensure entry and exit dynamism. Worse still, data collected online can be used as an input to gain dominance in other 'offline' markets. For instance, mapping data is of the essence for the development of autonomous cars.[16] Google already has mapping technology (Google Maps), in addition to the crowd-sourcing app Waze, which provides real-time traffic, accident, and police information. As a result of increased use of these services, Google can improve its mapping technology, thereby gaining the upper hand in the race for the development of self-driving cars. Indeed, this may be one of the reasons why Google's self-driving technology division

---

[13] Prüfer and Schottmüller (2017).

[14] Consumer Watchdog (2010).

[15] European Commission (2017).

[16] NTTDATA (2015).

(Waymo) *"is widely considered to be the front-runner among companies developing autonomous technology."*[17]

As a consequence of the 'domino effect,' insurmountable barriers to entry are likely to arise. Any entrant that wishes to compete in an online platform market (for example, in a search engine, social network, or App store market) must build a platform capable of providing services with the ability to compete with the incumbent. Setting up a platform demands high investments in R&D. For example, the Federal Trade Commission found that search and search advertising platforms "require enormous investments in the technology and infrastructure required to crawl and categorize the entire Internet", noting that Microsoft invested in 2010 more than USD 4.5 billion to develop its algorithms and building the physical capacity necessary to operate Bing.[18] In addition, the collection, storage, processing, and analysis of user data involves substantial fixed costs and low or negligible marginal costs,[19] which means that established firms have cost advantages over entrants in this regard. But setting up the platform is not enough. To launch a practical challenge (and therefore to have access to the data necessary to compete), competitors must attract a sufficiently large user base. To this effect, they must develop an infrastructure capable of matching that of the incumbent. For example, any company intending to launch a serious challenge against Google in the search market cannot rely on search query data. Instead, it must find a way to gather data from other sources, especially browsing and locational data, to give rise to economies of scope and thereby enhance the quality of its search results. Not even Microsoft, with its deep pockets, has been able to achieve that.

Something remarkably similar has occurred in the e-commerce segment. By embarking upon a strategy of sustaining losses and investing aggressively at the expense of profits and integrating across multiple business lines aided by the data, it can collect and process. Amazon created an infrastructure that cemented its leading position. In addition to being a retailer, Amazon is an advertiser, delivery and logistics network, a payment service, a credit lender, an auction house, a book publisher, a producer of TV shows and films, a hardware manufacturer, and a vendor and a leading provider of cloud services. Substantial synergies, derived from data-driven economies of scale and scope, enable Amazon to optimize its operations in all business segments above, synergies, which competitors in individual segments cannot necessarily match. To compete effectively against Amazon, taken as a whole, any entrant would have to invest heavily in each of such segments. In addition, Amazon avails itself of data to make strategic business decisions.

For example, Amazon has used sales data gathered from Amazon Marketplace to sell products that have proved successful and popular. It has been reported that Amazon has begun selling 25% of the top items first sold by Marketplace vendors in

---

[17] Palmer (2017).

[18] FTC (2013).

[19] CMA (2015, p. 75).

the women's clothing retail segment.[20] In this way, Amazon avoids the initial costs and uncertainties surrounding introducing new products and sells products, which are a proven success, to the direct detriment of those vendors who assumed the initial risk. Accordingly, Amazon uses the advantages arising from vertical integration, in particular, the very fact that some of its customers are also its competitors. It has been reported that Amazon has had recourse to insights derived from its cloud computing service to make investment decisions.[21] Amazon can tell which cloud customers need more server capacity, thereby obtaining clues about the business and technologies that are gaining tractions, clues that venture capital firms do not have.[22] Aided by data, Amazon can safely and successfully expand onto many segments, thereby consolidating its position and financial strength.

Data is not only the most relevant aspect brought by the digital economy but also the most contentious.[23] While some key traits are still disputed, such as whether a dataset is fungible or not, two essential definitions are helpful to understand the role of data in digital markets. First, data is a necessary input, processed by platforms to improve algorithms. Second, data reflects the price paid by consumers for accessing certain services offered by platforms, specifically those that operate in two-sided markets where one of the markets is the digital advertisement market. Concerning the former, data is extracted by platforms in consumer-facing markets. Consumers must provide basic information details to sign up, for example, to a social media (*i.e.*, name, age, education, and workplace).

While using social media, they also provide further information reflecting hobbies, interests, and generally data about their commercial preferences (*i.e.*, following specific brands such as retailers, supermarkets, or newspapers). This raw material in the form of data is then processed by the platform and used in another segment, the digital advertisement market, to sell advertisement slots. As the platform extracts more data, the effectiveness of its advertisement service is expected to increase accordingly. Advertisers (*i.e.*, businesses buying advertising slots) are aware that consumers spend time in digital platforms, which is a privileged opportunity to publicize products and services. Considering the rich datasets held by digital platforms, those datasets can target advertisements for a specific group of consumers. This has enabled platforms to leverage from consumer-facing markets into the digital advertisement. This is, however, a necessary consequence of the sophistication of the algorithms developed by platforms, as this enables them to target consumers effectively. The greater the data extracted in consumer-facing markets, the better the platform becomes at selling advertisement by, for example, improving algorithms that are used in search advertisement (*i.e.*, search engines) or advertise (*i.e.*, social media). This strategy works as a vicious circle as one market

[20] Soper (2016).

[21] Reuters (2011).

[22] Id.

[23] Gormsen (2020).

complements the other. Thus, the digital advertisement sector is more likely to be fully controlled by traditional market players operating in consumer-facing markers.

2.3.1.2 Nudge and AI

Nudging strategies can be used to influence people's decision-making processes. It is a relevant feature that ought to be considered by competition policymakers when they review potential harmful effects arising from the use of algorithms, as it can be a valuable tool for leveraging. Before analyzing the competition issues associated with it, a brief overview of nudge will be discussed.

Nudge reveals an uncomfortable truth as it suggests that human beings are prone to making decisions that affect their well-being. Thaler and Sunstein suggest that human beings are, in reality, less intelligent than they think they are. This challenge the benchmark set by neo-classical economics. Nudge tells a different story as it argues that *homo economicus* ('*econs*') exists only in the realm of economists' sci-fi literature. Decision-making is influenced (*i.e.,* nudged) by cognitive or emotional limitations that are natural to human thinking. The way choices are introduced influences decision-making. Thaler and Sunstein use the example of a students' cafeteria manager who could increase or decrease the consumption of specific products by 25% simply by altering the way food is displayed.[24] While this example corresponds to a brick-and-mortar shop, the same logic applies to an online shop, as will be explained below. The way the website is designed can influence consumer's behavior.

Nudge also highlights individuals' preferences for the *status quo*, where they tend to stick to preordain standards or default options. At this point, Thaler and Sunstein are particularly persuasive as they use the example of how phone manufacturers could shape consumers' decisions, as they will most likely stick to default settings.[25] The *status quo* preference is explained concerning type 1, also known as an automatic system, and type 2, reflective system. Type 1 thinking is pretty many decisions made quickly, without hesitation reflecting ordinary situations such as going to work, having breakfast in the morning, and checking your email once in a while. Thaler explains that type 1 reflects instinctive decisions.

On the other hand, type 2 thinking is more cautious, not quick, and requires analysis. Therefore, it is expected that as type 2 is costlier in terms of time and effort, typically, most of the decisions only require faster and simpler type 1 thinking. Thaler and Sunstein explain the interaction between the two thinking systems in the following way: '(...) *Econs never make an important decision without checking with their Reflective Systems (if they have time). But humans sometimes go with the answer the lizard inside is giving without pausing to think* (...).'[26] A link between

[24] Thaler and Sunstein (2012).

[25] Id.

[26] Id.

nudge and AI is how they have a complementary role. The former explains the individuals' decision-making process failures, while the latter can be used as a tool to guide or influence this same decision-making process.

A nudge is a tool capable of being used for either improving or worsening decision-making. This is important for two reasons. First, anyone can be a choice architect. Not just policymakers but also merchants and intermediaries such as online platforms. The example used by Thaler and Sunstein regarding a students' cafeteria is practical, as the same idea applies to online shops where the way they are designed can nudge consumers into acquiring sponsored products—those from merchants that have paid for the advertisement to the online platform—as opposed to decisions based on best price and the best quality. For example, this could be the case of Amazon when it lists products with the label '*Amazon's choice.*' This label is highly controversial as some consumers may think that Amazon has tested or endorsed the product. It may be just a marketing strategy as algorithms assign this label based on questionable evidence.[27] There are good reasons to be skeptical about this practice. Again, it is unlikely that consumers will apply type 2 thinking when browsing Amazon. It is simpler, faster, and easier to click a couple of links and buy whatever they are looking for, guided by the recommendation provided by Amazon's algorithms.

Second, Thaler has proposed a new name for nudging strategies that operate in reverse. This means that if nudge effectively means facilitating choice in a specific direction, 'sludge'—as Thaler calls it—makes it harder to exercise such choice: '*So, sludge can take two forms. It can discourage behavior in a person's best interest, such as claiming a rebate or tax credit. It can encourage self-defeating behavior, such as investing in a deal that is too good to be true.*'[28] An example of the latter is where consumers sign-up for a free 30-day trial of an online service with automatic enrolment to the paid service without previous notification before the trial expires. Sludge was described in the report entitled "*The behavioral science of online harm and manipulation, and what to do about it*" from the Behavioural Insights Team (the 'BIT report') as a tool used to make consumers worse off. Elisabeth Costa and David Halpern write in the BIT Report that '*the conscientious nudger seeks to design systems and processes to help people make better choices for themselves. They use defaults to make it easier to save, rank deals based on best value, and tell us what others like us do. Thaler has coined the term 'sludge' to describe the deliberate use of these tactics to thwart us from acting in our best interests. (...) There is plenty of sludge offline, notably in administrative paperwork burdens (...), but online environments (and their jarring interaction with offline processes) allow sludge to thrive'*.[29] As explained in the BIT report, AI can be designed to take advantage of cognitive limitations or emotional responses from individuals, this is manifested in

[27] McKinley (2019).

[28] Thaler (2018).

[29] BIT Report (2019).

two categories. First, consumer bias and, second, the prediction of preferences. Both issues are explained below.

Consumer bias consists of the exploitation of cognitive limitations or psychological weakness from consumers.[30] For example, the acquisition of the Amazon Prime membership could give the impression that such membership entails a unique benefit expressed in free shipping of certain items. However, it is a marketing strategy to nudge consumers into buying more products listed on Amazon.[31] In the same vein, hotel booking sites that provide information to consumers are sometimes highlighted in bold letters such as '*5 people viewing*' or '*last room available*. This was one of the findings from the CMA in its market study on hotel booking sites in 2019, also known as pressure selling.[32] These messages try to nudge consumers into acquiring the product or the service without making them think (too much). Another issue is that there is no way for consumers to verify these 'advisory' messages powered by an algorithm.[33] As troubling as it may already seem, these examples are not the most concerning aspect of algorithms. As social networks such as Facebook gather more and more data from consumers, they seek to develop new services as a consequence of their dataset increasing over time. For example, in Australia, it was reported that Facebook's algorithms could deduce when a teenager is in a vulnerable state, and therefore this could be an opportunity for targeted advertisement.[34]

The prediction of preferences is another potential area of concern involving AI and algorithms.[35] This is not exclusive to online markets as behavioral economics show that it is possible to nudge consumers into buying a product, for example, in a brick-and-mortar store simply by the way products are displayed. Another situation involving the prediction of preferences is the use of defaults. For example, consumers may tend to stick with default preferences in smartphones or a different technological gadget. There is a perception that factory settings are equivalent to best settings or an enhancement of functionality of some sort. This is a consequence of type 1 thinking, rapid and effortless thinking that usually leads to bad outcomes in specific situations. However, on reflection, a consumer may realize those default settings may have nothing to do with performance or best quality but rather a choice made by the manufacturer based on other considerations such as a payment from a provider to pre-install its products were the case in *Google Android*.[36] Because of the massive flow of data, AI can predict preferences in a much more effective way. This is not surprising as it is expected that creative content will be widespread on online platforms shortly. Innovative content is considered the next generation of personalised advertisement consisting of algorithms to personalize users' experience

[30] Id, 13–14.

[31] Id 13.

[32] CMA (2019).

[33] BIT report (2019, p. 13).

[34] Id; Levin (2017).

[35] BIT report (2019, pp. 22–23).

[36] Case AT.40099, Google Android (Google Android).

on the website.[37] For example, the way the news is presented to each consumer to meet histheirrsonal preferences. This is nothing new, as websites such as YouTube recommend content such as news based on user's preferences (i.e., the previous history using the website).

Another example is Netflix, as it customizes images for each user to attract its attention and maintain engagement with the platform.[38] It is not surprising that Netflix has valued its recommendation system at US$ 1 billion.[39] The main advantage of this recommendation system is capturing user's attention and the reduction of cancellation rates. A report on online targeting published by the Centre for Data Ethics and Innovation in February 2020 highlights this feature: '*Online targeting systems' effectiveness lies in their ability to predict people's preferences and behaviors. [...] They collect and analyze an unprecedented amount of personal data, tracking people as they spend time online [...] This enables them to predict how users will react when shown different items of content. Their predictions are used to decide what content to show people to optimize the system's desired outcome. People's responses to this content are then collected and fed back into the system in an iterative cycle.*'[40] As will be explained below, nudging strategies are not merely a theoretical possibility but more a reality, as the *Google Shopping* case shows.

2.3.2 Consumer Choice

The presence of the same tech giants across many industries has harmful effects on consumer choice. Take the example of Android. As Google SVP & General Counsel noted: '*...while Android is free for manufacturers to use, it's costly to develop, improve, keep secure, and defend against patent suits. We provide Android for free and offset our costs through the revenue we generate on our Google apps and services we distribute via Android.*'[41] Through a zero-priced and cross-subsidized strategy, Google has effectively used Android to protect its dominance in the online search market[42] and foreclose the market for licensable mobile OS. Android's competitors such as Symbian, Windows, Blackberry, and others could not endure Google's data-driven, zero-price-based style of competition[43] since they did not have the required infrastructure, access to data, and financial strength to compete on these terms. In turn, Android secured Google's access to a permanent and valuable stream of data from Android users, strengthening its dominance in the online search

[37] Koponen (2019).

[38] Ha (2019).

[39] Centre for Data Ethics and Innovation Report (2020, p. 26).

[40] Id. 14.

[41] Walker (2016).

[42] European Commission (2018).

[43] Dunn (2016).

market. As a consequence, there are no credible alternatives to Google search. If consumers do not want to use Android (for example, given its data protection policy), they are only left with Apple's iOS.

Consumer choice has also been impaired through other routes. Consumers are increasingly worried about the protection of their data and want more privacy-friendly options. However, privacy protection is the kryptonite of online advertising-funded business models. Mergers and acquisitions have proved highly successful in quashing this threat. Think of WhatsApp's 1-dollar-a-user subscription fee business model that sought to protect users' privacy. When acquired by Facebook in 2014, WhatsApp had a business model that was not designed for fast revenue growth, only user growth. Its business model consisted of providing a free service for a year and then charging an annual 1-dollar subscription fee after that. WhatsApp had an aversion to adopting an advertising model for a social messenger service because WhatsApp founders were primarily committed to protecting user privacy given the 2013 mass surveillance revelations in the Edward Snowden affair. After WhatsApp's acquisition by Facebook, the latter amended WhatsApp's privacy policy to allow data to be shared with Facebook,[44] to the detriment of those consumers who prefer higher levels of privacy protection.

Another example of reduced consumer choice can be seen from Amazon's expansion efforts. As explained, Amazon is both a book publisher and marketer. Consequently, it can produce and promote its content on Amazon Marketplace, to the detriment of publishers that offer their content on that platform. This advantage has put pressure on booksellers and publishers, thereby spurring consolidation amongst them in the US.[45] This trend has had deleterious effects on both authors and readers, *"leaving writers with fewer paths to market and readers with a less diverse marketplace".*[46] Additionally, given book publishers' dependence on Amazon Marketplace, Amazon can impose higher fees on them, thereby affecting publishers' business model to impairs consumer choice even further, as publishers are less able to invest in a range of books. Publishers have reportedly responded to Amazon's fees by both publishings fewer titles and focusing mainly on books by celebrities and bestselling authors, as a result of which readers are *'presented with fewer books that espouse unusual, quirky, offbeat, or political risky ideas, as well as books from new and unproven authors.'*[47]

2.3.3 Price Algorithms

As more companies and industries switch to computer algorithms to improve their pricing models, customize services, and predict market trends, big data and big

---

[44] Bindi (2017).

[45] Khan (2016, p. 766).

[46] Id.

[47] Authors United (2015).

analytics can provide novel ways to achieve and sustain collusion, even without a formal agreement or human interaction. In a traditional cartel case, executives of competitors secretly reach an agreement to fix prices, allocate markets, or restrict output. However, under current technology, computer algorithms can be used as the messenger that the cartel members program to implement the agreement and monitor and punish any deviation from it. For example, in 2015, the US Justice Department charged the members of a price-fixing cartel agreement, the purpose of which was to fix, increase, maintain and stabilize the prices of some posters sold in the US on Amazon Marketplace. To implement the agreement, David Topkins, and his co-conspirators *'agreed to adopt specific pricing algorithms for the sale of the agreed-upon posters to coordinate changes to their respective prices.'*[48] Here the algorithm was just an extension of the humans' cartel agreement, and therefore this case is an example of express collusion.

The effects of price discrimination on welfare are ambiguous. However, an argument can be made in the sense that, given the effectiveness of pricing algorithms in extracting consumers' wealth, 'almost perfect' price discrimination may justify intervention. Indeed, price discrimination is likely to enable a dominant firm or a group of firms to exploit consumers and increase barriers to entry or expansion.[49] In this connection, the UK Competition and Markets Authority found that *'where a firm users consumer data to separate different groups of customers and offers a different price to each group, [small competitors or entrants] would not have a substantial fixed base of existing customers, and so may be unable to compete as successfully to target customers through offering them lower prices.'*[50]

2.3.4 Tacit Collusion and Personalized Pricing

Computer algorithms can be used to facilitate the conditions necessary for stable tacit collusion.[51] Traditionally, many competitors make it harder to designate a hub for coordination, monitor deviations, and implement effective punishments for cheating members. However, algorithms can allow for coordination, monitoring, and punishment to take place in less concentrated markets, as their ability and speed in collecting and analysing data makes the number of firms monitor and agree with less relevant.[52] In addition, algorithms have the inherent ability to increase market transparency and frequency of interaction amongst competitors,[53] features that make industries more prone to collusion.[54] Indeed, the French and German competition

[48] United States v Topkins, CR 15-00201 WHO Plea Agreement 4 (ND Cal 2015).

[49] Ezrachi and Stucke (2016a, pp. 118–119).

[50] CMA Report (2015, 3.48).

[51] Brooke Group, v Brown & Williamson Tobacco Corp, 509 US 209, 227 (1993).

[52] OECD Report (2017).

[53] OECD Report (2017, p. 22).

[54] Id. 21.

authorities have noted that *'[e]ven though market transparency as a facilitating factor for collusion has been debated for several decades now, it gains new relevance due to technical developments such as sophisticated computer algorithms. For example, by processing all available information and thus monitoring and analyzing or anticipating their competitors' responses to current and future prices, competitors may easier be able to find a sustainable supra-competitive price equilibrium which they can agree on.'*[55]

In their book *Virtual Competition*, Ezrachi and Stucke explore a number of scenarios where algorithmic technology enhances the risk of collusive outcomes. In one of those scenarios, which they call '*the Predictable Agent,*' each competitor programs its algorithm to monitor price changes and swiftly react to any competitor's price reduction. In addition, they also program their algorithms to follow price increases when sustainable. That is to say, where others timely follow price rises so that no competitor benefits from keeping prices lower.[56] Since these algorithms can assess and adjust prices within milliseconds, they can readily match a rival's discount, thereby eliminating the incentive to discount in the first place. Accordingly, in a scenario dominated by similar pricing algorithms that enable interdependence, there is a real risk of higher prices.[57]

Additionally, pricing algorithms may allow for more effective price discrimination. In economics, perfect price discrimination (also known as first-degree price discrimination) amounts to a scenario where a seller charges each customer the maximum price, they are willing to pay (*i.e.,* their reservation price). In a perfect price discrimination scenario, the seller captures the entirety of consumers' surplus (the difference between the price a consumer pays for a given product or service and his reservation price).

While this scenario has been hitherto more theoretical than real, pricing algorithms, fed by a constant stream of up-to-date data on consumer preferences and revealed interests, may categorize consumers in narrow groups and charge each of such groups different prices determined based on their estimated reservation price.[58] The effects of learning-by-doing are the critical enablers of this development. Pricing algorithms can observe and assess the reaction of users and predict how a user will likely react under certain circumstances. Based on predictive capabilities, users are categorized into subgroups of like-minded, like-price-sensitive individuals that share common biases, interests, and preferences. This subgrouping also enables the algorithm to approximate the user's reservation price, observe behavior and adjust more accurately. Accordingly, *'the more times the algorithm can observe what you and others within your grouping do under various circumstances, the more experiments it can run, the more it can learn through trial and error what your*

[55] Autorité de la Concurrence and Bundeskartellamt (2016, pp. 14–15).

[56] Ezrachi and Stucke (2016a, p. 61).

[57] Id, (2016, p. 62).

[58] Newman (2014).

group's reservation price is under different situations, and the more it can recalibrate and refine.'[59]

The report '*Unlocking digital competition*' (the '*Furman report*') focused on the two classic themes: algorithmic collusion and personalized pricing. Collusion between competitors, as explained, is typically known as a situation where different undertakings agree on the fixing of a minimum price. The effect of this agreement is the suppression of competition, as prices will remain unchanged. Algorithmic collusion could deliver this same outcome but absent an explicit agreement between the parties, effectively resembling tacit collusion.[60] In personalized pricing, the algorithm will set prices according to the personal data it has from each consumer.[61] For example, if the algorithm infers that a consumer is unlikely to purchase alcohol, the price displayed will be lower than a consumer with an opposite interest. Price discrimination of this kind could prove to be efficient as goods and services are allocated by a market-based mechanism (*i.e.,* prices). However, this practice is susceptible to be questioned on the grounds of fairness. There are three critical conclusions and recommendations from the Furman report on this subject. First, the Furman report concludes that there is little evidence regarding pricing practices.[62] Second, it suggests that companies should be held accountable for the algorithms they use by explaining their functionalities and how they have mitigated potential anti-competitive effects.[63] Third, it advised a close relationship between the Competition Markets Authority (the 'CMA') and the 'CDEI' as the latter has been formed to provide recommendations on using data and AI.

In 2018, the CMA published a paper entitled*: 'Pricing algorithms – Economic working paper on algorithms to facilitate collusion and personalized pricing.*[64] This paper distinguished between two potential competition issues on pricing algorithms: (i) the use of algorithms to monitor pre-existing collusion agreements;[65] and (ii) algorithmic collusion involving tacit collusion.[66] The CMA's working paper considered the first scenario as nothing particularly new. According to the CMA, this could be analyzed using the tools applicable to similar agreements outside the digital world. There are already cases dealing with this same subject.[67] In 2016, the CMA fined Trod Ltd. £163,371 for concerting prices with another competitor. The CMA found evidence of the agreement (i.e., previous communications between the parties), and then the illegal behavior was implemented by using re-pricing

[59] Ezrachi and Stucke (2016b).

[60] Furman Report (2019).

[61] Id, para.3.164.

[62] Id, paras.3.163, 3.166.

[63] Id, para.3.171.

[64] CMA (2018).

[65] Id. para5.2.

[66] Id.

[67] Id.

software.[68] In the second situation, the analysis depends on the type of algorithm being analyzed. The more complex the algorithm—and, therefore, the more self-sufficient—the greater the danger for competition. The CMA raised three issues in this regard. First, a potential scenario where the danger is much subtler occurs when an entire industry uses pricing algorithms developed by the same provider to achieve similar outcomes.[69] Second, markets posing greater risk are those already susceptible to tacit coordination, such as highly concentrated markets or those offering homogenous products where the introduction of algorithms is an additional element contributing to tacit collusion.[70] Third, algorithmic collusion is unlikely to happen in highly competitive markets, with differentiated products and low barriers to entry and expansion.[71] A more general conclusion from the CMA's working paper is the finding that algorithms are constantly evolving. The development of much more self-sufficient algorithms is at the moment uncertain.[72]

A report prepared for the European Commission in 2017 on online market segmentation ('*Online market segmentation report*')[73] analyzed different personalized practices, including targeted advertising and personalized pricing. The report included a mystery shopping exercise consisting of eight European countries (Czech Republic, France, Germany, Poland, Romania, Spain, Sweden, and the UK) in four different markets: televisions, shoes, hotels, and airline tickets ('*mystery shopping exercise*'). The exercise included four scenarios, search engine review, price comparison websites, browser research (i.e., browsers provided by different providers), and mobile devices. On personalized pricing, the online market segmentation report concluded that there is no consistent evidence of price personalization in the four markets is analyzed.

While there was some price personalization between personalization and non-personalization scenario (*i.e.,* the personalized scenario applied only if the platform holds data from the consumer), it detected a price difference of 6% in identical products.[74] However, the price difference detected was less than 1.6%.[75] These numbers show that there is little evidence of this practice in consumer-facing platforms. This does not mean, of course, that this practice may not be implemented in the future. For this purpose, periodical monitoring is necessary. If, however, this issue is viewed from consumers' perspective, there are, in principle, low information costs for them to detect these practices. For example, a group of friends booking a holiday trip. It would be relatively easy for them to compare prices for flight tickets and hotels and realize that they have been charged different amounts for the same

---

68 Case 50223 (12 August 2016) Online sales of posters and frames. CMA.

69 CMA, (2018, para.5.35).

70 Id, para.5.37.

71 Id.

72 Id, pp. 4–5.

73 Ipsos et al. (2018).

74 Id, p. 190.

75 Id.

services. It may generate reputational damage for the providers involved as a consequence of the massive backlash. The mystery shopping exercise also found that potentially vulnerable consumers to online personalization are: (i) the elderly, (ii) people with low educational attainment, (iii) those who have difficulty making ends meet (iv) those inexperienced with online shopping.[76] Those with less knowledge are likely to be the most affected by personalization driven by algorithms.

The same report also detailed the three main benefits of online personalization as perceived by consumers. First, targeted adverts facilitate access to exciting products (42%), the reduction of irrelevant ads (23%), and the funding of free content (20%). Second, personalized ranking and offers enable finding interesting products (34%), save time when browsing (23%), and allows a selection of products that match consumers' needs (23%). Third, personalized pricing allows websites to offer special promotions (22%), getting the best prices (21%), and increasing the choice of products (15%).[77] As can be seen, consumers also experience tangible benefits as a consequence of algorithms. However, as will be explained below, these benefits contrast with the competition issues detected in digital markets.

The debate on algorithms focused on pricing practices provides an interesting discussion from an academic perspective. It involves questioning if competition rules, such as whether Article 101 TFEU, remains fit for purpose as discussed by the German Bundeskartellamt and the French competition authority.[78] This report concluded that there is at the moment no evidence of pricing algorithms: *'It should be kept in mind, however, that algorithms, like digital markets as a whole, are rapidly evolving. Hence, the emergence of algorithmic collusion cannot be ruled out. [...] To this end, authorities should continue expanding their expertise on algorithms in an exchange with each other and interacting with businesses, academics, and other regulatory bodies. Such an effort is in line with the more general tendency of authorities to devote more resources to the challenges posed by the ongoing digitalization.'*[79] The absence of evidence is, of course, not a guarantee that this problem may not arise in the future. There has two critical implications for both competition enforcers and commentators in this regard. Firstly, as mentioned previously, competition authorities must remain vigilant and periodically conduct tests to find evidence of this practice.

According to the Furman report, businesses using algorithms must exercise particular care: *'The Panel considers as a general principle that businesses who use algorithms should take all reasonable steps to understand, and be prepared to explain, how their algorithms work, how they interact with other firms' algorithms, and how they have mitigated against any potential biases or anti-competitive consequences'.*[80] Second, the absence of evidence on pricing practices involving

[76] Id, p. 167.

[77] Id, p. 168.

[78] Autorité de la Concurrence and Bundeskartellamt (2019).

[79] Id, p. 77.

[80] Furman Report (2019, para.3.171).

algorithms does not mean that the debate is settled. The debate on algorithms should be further explored from different angles as AI provides several challenges for competition policy. A large part of the debate on digital platforms is focused on regulating or limiting prices expressed in the amount of data provided by consumers. This does not mean that algorithmic collusion or personalized pricing could never occur, as it may happen in oligopolistic markets where competitors use algorithms to set monetary prices, as explained by the CMA in a report on this matter.[81] It could also happen in vertically integrated platforms, such as Amazon. However, the problems are that the relevance of the use of algorithms goes far beyond pricing practices, and as will be explained below, there is little evidence of this practice. The growing obsession from both competition enforcers and commentators with this same issue does not help, as the debate is still price centric.[82]

3 The Google Shopping Case: Leverage, AI, and Nudge

The use of AI had already played a significant role in competition enforcement when used as a tool for leveraging, mainly through nudging strategies. In the Google Shopping case, the Commission fined Google €2.42 billion for displaying its comparison-shopping website on Google's search engine platform in a much more prominent way.[83] The Commission considered that Google was leveraging its market power from general search engines into price comparison websites, a different market segment.[84] The decision itself cuts across different areas and has a myriad of relevant topics for discussion. However, the analysis below focuses on the theory of harm developed by the Commission and how it reflects possible future competition enforcement patterns in digital platforms. Google's objective with this practice seemed to be exploiting inertia in consumers by using its search engine (*i.e.*, platform) to nudge consumers into using another service provided by Google. In this specific case, artificial intelligence—an algorithm—was demoting rivals' websites. This is one of the Commission's findings: *'Comparison shopping services are prone to be demoted by the [. . .] algorithm due to the characteristics of those services.'*[85] This same behavior was in line with the exploitation of inertia in consumers. They tend to select search results based on their location (*i.e.*, first search results) as these are more prominently displayed. The Commission held:

> '597. . . . the Conduct is likely to reduce the ability of consumers to access the most relevant comparison-shopping services. This is for two reasons.

[81] CMA (2018, para.5.37).

[82] Schrepel (2020).

[83] Case AT.39740—Google Shopping.

[84] Id.

[85] Id. para.352.

> 598. In the first place, . . . users tend to consider that search results that are ranked highly in generic search results on Google's general search results pages are the most relevant for their queries and click on them irrespective of whether other results would be more relevant for their queries. . . .
>
> 599. In the second place, Google did not inform users that the Product Universal was positioned and displayed in its general search results pages using different underlying mechanisms than those used to rank generic search results. ... while the "Sponsored" label may suggest that different positioning and display mechanisms are used, that information is likely to be understandable only by the most knowledgeable users.[86]

The *Google Shopping* decision has far-reaching consequences. It should not only be seen as just another competition infringement, as it also has a prescriptive element. This decision could also be understood as establishing a precedent on how to design or program algorithms in the future. This can be analyzed from two different perspectives. First, one of the fundamental reasons that triggered competition enforcement, in this case, was the existence of Google's dominant position and the consequences deriving from it. Google was accused of leveraging its market power from general search engines into comparison-shopping websites. The notion of leveraging as applied by the Commission is closely related to ordoliberalism. According to ordoliberals, the market structure should be protected from dominant undertakings as this affects the right to compete in the market. The CJEU, for example, has been sympathetic towards this school of thought. In *Michelin I,* it held: *'A finding that an undertaking has a dominant position is not in itself a recrimination but simply means that, irrespective of the reasons for which it has such a dominant position, the undertaking concerned has a special responsibility not to allow its conduct to impair genuine undistorted competition on the common market.'*[87]

The approach taken by the CJEU seems to resemble a broad approach to the notion of abuse of dominance. A broad approach is not necessarily negative, as it could be helpful to quickly adapt competition enforcement in new markets such as digital platforms. According to Van den Bergh, the Ordoliberal approach has clear implications on enforcement patterns: *'The competitive system has already been harmed by the simple presence of a dominant firm and should not be further weakened. For example, a refusal to supply can be prohibited as an abuse of a dominant position, irrespective of whether such conduct is perfectly lawful when practiced by its non-dominant competitors.'*[88] Viewed from a more comprehensive perspective, it could be argued that competition policy for the digital era with a highly intrusive character is nothing new. Previous decisions, such as the *Microsoft Windows Media Player* case, were at that time regarded as an example of the ordoliberal approach, which is intrinsic to EU competition policy.[89]

---

[86] Id. paras.597–599.

[87] Case 322/81 (1983) NV Nederlandsche Banden Industrie Michelin v Commission of the European Communities. ECLI:EU:C: 1983:313. Para.57.

[88] Van den Bergh (2017, p. 109).

[89] Alhborn and Evans (2009).

Second, the consequences of this decision are far-reaching as Google's future developments over its platform will need to consider its own profitable interest and the development of a competitive digital market. This includes designing an algorithm that does not restrict a rival's access to its platform. This position allows a reflection from two different perspectives (i) potential clashes with innovation as online platforms will have to develop new products (i.e., design algorithms) in line with competition policy goals. (ii) whether competition policy should be enforced with a view of promoting competition in the digital market and its implications.

Hefty fines were also imposed in *Google Android* (€4.34 billion) involving the tying of different Google products in mobile phone systems and the granting of commercial incentives to mobile phone operators to pre-install Google products, the restriction on the development of apps without Google's previous approval.[90] In 2019, Google was fined again (€1.49 billion) for restricting rivals' from offering advertisements in Google's search engine results. The Commission decision, however, remains unpublished.[91] A common element in the Google saga and—perhaps the root of the problem—seems to be Google's dominant position in general search engines. As explained before, perhaps this specific market segment has become so relevant in the digital economy that there is little doubt about its public utility character. This could be analyzed in the same way as telecoms and energy because there are economic reasons to regulate the platform (*i.e.,* controlling market power) and social considerations (*i.e.,* relevance for consumers). With or without sector-specific regulation in the EU, the Commission seems to have already decided what its role will be in the digital economy.

As can be seen, AI is also a valuable tool for leveraging and reinforcing the never-ending circle of improving advertisement systems based on data extracted from consumers. The debate on AI and competition is far from being limited to tacit collusion or price personalization. Both practices could prove incompatible as either price are fixed by an algorithm or personalized for each consumer. The danger posed by intelligent content and the endless personalization cycle supported by massive extraction of data from consumers should be added to the list of competition concerns brought by AI.

4 Conclusion

Data is, maybe by far, the most salient feature for algorithmic technology. Under a consumer welfare approach to competition policy, it could be argued that the consumer benefits flowing from the use of algorithms in the digital economy are amplified as a result of data-driven efficiencies. However, many antitrust issues

[90] Google Android.

[91] Case AT.40411—Google Search (Ad Sense).

associated with algorithmic technology and how to deal with these remains a challenge for competition policymakers in the years to come.

As the digital world keeps evolving at an unprecedented pace, it will be ever harder for competition authorities to keep the pace and scrutinize the development of algorithms. The issue remains how to tackle this issue with effective but proportionate measures. As outlined in the Furman report, one possible approach is to require developers and beneficiaries of algorithmic-driven businesses to explain how these tools have been programmed and how they operate so to better assess whether they are likely to produce anticompetitive effects in the market. While this measure may seem onerous at first glance, in reality, it places the burden of providing information on the party that is better placed to submit it. This is the developer or beneficiary of the algorithm. Anyhow, the alternative—leaving the market as it is now—could prove to be more harmful to competition and consumers in the long term.

References

Alhborn C, Evans DS (2009) The microsoft judgment and its implications for competition policy towards dominant firms in Europe. Antitrust Law J 75(3):887–932

Authors United (2015) Letter to the Assistant Attorney General Baer, *Authorsunited.net,* August 14, 2015. Available at http://www.authorsunited.net/july/

Autorité de la Concurrence, Bundeskartellamt (2016) Competition Law and Data, May 10, 2016. Available at https://www.bundeskartellamt.de/SharedDocs/Publikation/DE/Berichte/Big%20Data%20Papier.pdf?__blob=publicationFile&v=2

Bindi T (2017) WhatsApp, Facebook to face EU data protection taskforce. Zdnet, October 27, 2017. Available at https://www.zdnet.com/article/whatsapp-facebook-to-face-eu-dataprotection-taskforce/

BIT Report (2019) The behavioural science of online harm and manipulation, and what to do about it. An explanatory paper to spark ideas and debate by Elisabeth Costa and David Halpern. The Behavioural Insight Team. Available at https://www.bi.team/wp-content/uploads/2019/04/BIT_The-behavioural-science-of-online-harm-and-manipulation-and-what-to-do-aboutit_Single.pdf

Blattberg RC, Deighton J (1991) Interactive marketing: exploiting the age of addressability. Sloan Manage Rev 33(1):5–15

Centre for Data Ethics and Innovation (2020) Review of online targeting: Final Report and recommendations, Centre for Data Ethics and Innovation, February 2020. Available at https://assets.publishing.service.gov.uk/government/uploads/system/uploads/attachment_data/file/864167/CDEJ7836-Review-of-Online-Targeting-05022020.pdf

CMA (2015) The commercial use of consumer data. Report on the CMA's call for information. Available at https://assets.publishing.service.gov.uk/government/uploads/system/uploads/attachment_data/file/435817/The_commercial_use_of_consumer_data.pdf

CMA (2018) Pricing algorithms. Economic working paper on the use of algorithms to facilitate collusion and personalised pricing, October 8, 2018. Available at https://assets.publishing.service.gov.uk/government/uploads/system/uploads/attachment_data/file/746353/Algorithms_econ_report.pdf

CMA (2019) Hotel booking sites to make major changes after CMA probe. Press Release, February 9, 2019. Available at https://www.gov.uk/government/news/hotel-booking-sites-to-makemajor-changes-after-cma-probe

Consumer Watchdog (2010) Traffic Report: How Google is Squeezing Out Competitors and Muscling into New Markets, A Study by Inside Google, June 2, 2010. Available at https://www.consumerwatchdog.org/resources/TrafficStudy-Google.pdf

De Filippi P (2014) Big data, big responsibilities. Internet Policy Rev 3(1). Available at https://policyreview.info/articles/analysis/big-data-big-responsibilities

Dunn J (2016) There's no hope of anyone catching up to Android and iOS. Business Insider, August 23, 2016. Available at https://www.businessinsider.com.au/smartphone-market-shareandroid-ios-windows-blackberry-2016-8#:~:text=As%20noted%20by%20a%20new,%25%20and%200.1%25%2C%20respectively

European Commission (2017) Antitrust: Commission fines Google €2.42 billion for abusing dominance as search engine by giving illegal advantage to own comparison shopping service. Press Release, June 27, 2017. Available at https://ec.europa.eu/commission/presscorner/detail/en/MEMO_17_1785

European Commission (2018) Antitrust: Commission fines Google €4.34 billion for illegal practices regarding Android mobile devices to strengthen dominance of Google's search engine. Press Release, July 18, 2018. Available at https://ec.europa.eu/commission/presscorner/detail/en/IP_18_4581

Ezrachi A, Stucke M (2016a) Virtual competition: the promise and perils of the algorithm-driven economy. Harvard University Press, Cambridge

Ezrachi A, Stucke M (2016b) Online platforms and the EU digital single market, Written evidence (OPL0043), in submission of *the House of Lords, 10 Report of Session 2015-16, Online Platforms and the Digital Single Markets,* April 20, 2016. Available at http://data.parliament.uk/writtenevidence/committeeevidence.svc/evidencedocument/eu-internal-marketsubcommittee/online-platforms-and-the-eu-digital-single-market/written/23223.html

FTC (2013) Statement of the Federal Trade Commission Regarding Google's Search Practices, In the Matter of Google Inc. FTC File Number 111-0163, January 3, 2013. Available at https://www.ftc.gov/system/files/documents/public_statements/295971/130103googlesearchstmtofcomm.pdf

Furman Report (2019) Unlocking Digital Competition, Report of the Digital Competition Expert Panel, March 2019. Available at https://assets.publishing.service.gov.uk/government/uploads/system/uploads/attachment_data/file/785547/unlocking_digital_competition_furman_review_web.pdf

Gormsen LL (2020) The Importance of Antitrust in the Digital Economy. Digital Freedom Fund, March, 2, 2020. Available at https://digitalfreedomfund.org/the-importance-of-antitrust-inthe-digital-economy/

Ha A (2019) Netflix is experimenting with different episode orders for 'Love, Death & Robots'. Techcrunch, March 19, 2019

Hof RD (2014) Is artificial intelligence finally coming into its own? MIT Technol Rev March 29, 2016

Ipsos, London Economics, Deloitte (2018) Consumer market study on online market segmentation through personalised pricing/offers in the European Union. *Request for Specific Services 2016 85 02 for the implementation of Framework Contract EAHC/2013/CP/04, Final Report.* Available at https://ec.europa.eu/info/sites/info/files/aid_development_cooperation_fundamental_rights/aid_and_development_by_topic/documents/synthesis_report_online_personalisation_study_final_0.pdf

Khan L (2016) Amazon's antitrust paradox. Yale Law J 126:746–747

Koponen J (2019) Get ready for a new era of personalized entertainment. Techcrunch, April 14, 2019

Levin S (2017) Facebook told advertisers it can identify teens feeling 'insecure' and 'worthless'. The Guardian, May 1, 2017

McKinley J (2019) What does 'Amazon's Choice' Actually Mean? Reader's Digest, August 21, 2019. Available at https://www.rd.com/article/what-does-amazons-choice-mean/

Monopolkommission (2015) Competition Policy: The Challenge of Digital Markets. Special Report No 68. Available at https://www.monopolkommission.de/images/PDF/SG/s68_fulltext_eng.pdf

Newman N (2014) The costs of lost privacy: consumer harm and rising economic inequality in the age of Google. William Mitchell Law Rev 40(2):849–889

NTTDATA (2015) Automative 4.0, Sensing the road ahead for tier 1 suppliers. NTT DATA Deutschland, München. Available at https://de.nttdata.com/-/media/NTTDataGermany/Files/2019-EN-WP-Automotive-40.pdf

O'Reilly T (2010) 'Whole Web' is the OS of the future. CNET, March 18, 2010. Available at https://www.cnet.com/news/tim-oreilly-whole-web-is-the-os-of-the-future/

OECD (2017) Algorithms and Collusion – Competition policy in the digital age. Available at http://www.oecd.org/daf/competition/Algorithms-and-colllusion-competition-policy-in-thedigital-age.pdf

Palmer A (2017) Looks Like Apple Just Killed the iCar. The Street, August 23, 2017

Prüfer J, Schottmüller C (2017) Competing with Big Data. Tilburg Law School, Research Paper, No 06/2017

Reuters (2011) Amazon finds startup investments in the 'cloud'. Reuters, November 9, 2011

Schrepel T (2020) The fundamental unimportance of algorithmic collusion for antitrust law. Harv J Law Technol, February 7, 2020. Available at http://jolt.law.harvard.edu/digest/thefundamental-unimportance-of-algorithmic-collusion-for-antitrust-law

Soper S (2016) Got a hot seller on Amazon? Prepare for e-tailer to make one too. The Star, April 30, 2016

Stucke M, Grunes A (2016) Big data and competition policy. Oxford University Press, Oxford

Thaler R (2018) Nudge, not sludge. Science 361(6401):431

Thaler R, Sunstein C (2012) Nudge: improving decisions about health, wealth, happiness. Penguin Books, New York

Van den Bergh R (2017) Comparative competition law and economics. Edward Elgar Publishing, Cheltenham

Walker K (2016) Android's Model of Open Innovation. Google Europe Blog, April 20, 2016. https://blog.google/topics/google-europe/androids-model-of-open-innovation/

Algorithms, Big Data, and Merger Control

Verity Egerton-Doyle and Jonathan Ford

Abstract The ubiquity of algorithms has profound implications for the way businesses compete, perhaps most critically, through their use to harness and extract value from big data. Data has been variously described as "*the new oil*" and "*the new currency*", amongst other metaphors. Both these descriptions help to conceptualise data as a valuable, fungible asset, which can be leveraged to the competitive advantage of the firm holding it. But if data is the new oil, it is the crude oil and algorithms make up the rest of the supply chain necessary to obtain value from it. It would therefore seem obvious that the data held, and algorithms used by, merging parties would come under scrutiny in merger reviews of what we describe in this chapter as "*algorithm-driven businesses*". The purpose of this chapter is to catalogue the various ways in which analysis of algorithms (and big data) have featured in merger control decisions thus far, in the hope it may shed light on how practice may evolve going forwards.

1 Introduction

Recent years have seen digital competition become a (if not *the*) key focus of competition policy. There is an apparent consensus, at least among authorities, that there has been underenforcement in the digital sector, especially in merger control. Competition authorities have been heavily criticised for failing to identify potential competitive harms in mergers between algorithm-driven businesses, in acquisitions made by "*dominant*" tech platforms like Google, Amazon, Facebook, and Apple (the "*GAFAs*"). A key theme of the plethora of policy papers and retrospective analyses performed by authorities, governments, and independent experts, is that competition authorities have lacked sufficient technical knowledge and expertise to fully evaluate the competitive effects, and identify potential competitive harms, of mergers between algorithm-driven businesses. In recognition of

V. Egerton-Doyle · J. Ford (✉)
Linklaters LLP, London, UK
e-mail: verity.egerton-doyle@linklaters.com; Jonathan.ford@linklaters.com

A. Portuese (ed.), *Algorithmic Antitrust*, Economic Analysis of Law in European Legal Scholarship 12, https://doi.org/10.1007/978-3-030-85859-9_4

the importance of better understanding digital markets, and critically data and algorithms, competition authorities around the world have spent the past few years "*tooling up*", employing data scientists and conducting studies of digital markets to enable them to evaluate the impact of big data and algorithms on competition. To date, algorithms themselves have rarely been critical to the competitive assessment of mergers, with only one case at EU level where an authority "*intervened*" (*i.e.*, required remedies or prohibited a merger) either because of, or in relation to, algorithms or data (*Microsoft/LinkedIn* (EC 2016a) where an interoperability remedy was accepted). It is clear however that analysis of algorithms and data will come under increasing scrutiny in merger control in the digital sector going forwards. While authorities now have new tools and expertise to draw on, analysis will inevitably be shaped by previous decisional practice.

The purpose of this chapter is to catalogue the various ways in which analysis of algorithms (and big data) have featured in merger control decisions thus far, in the hope it may shed light on how practice may evolve going forwards. The "*catalogue*" in this chapter is organised by reference to the kinds of theories of harm pursued by authorities. The first part considers the horizontal unilateral effects theories of harm considered in mergers between business offering or using algorithms, as well as online platforms that use algorithms to execute their competitive strategy. The second part considers cases in which non-horizontal foreclosure theories of harm have been considered in mergers of algorithm-driven businesses, exploring the potential for a merged entity to use their algorithms to hinder interoperability between programmes, or access to key datasets to the disadvantage of competitors and consumers. Parts 1 and 2 demonstrate that intervention in mergers between algorithm-driven businesses has been rare: on a static view of horizontal competition, merging parties have generally not been considered particularly close competitors, and vertical theories of harm have generally not been made out because authorities have concluded merging parties have no incentive to foreclose competitors, often due to the knock-on effects foreclosure strategies would have on the "*other side*" of multi-sided markets.

It is a virtual certainty that this "*hands off*" approach to mergers of algorithm-driven businesses will not continue, but higher levels of intervention may require authorities to free themselves from traditional horizontal and vertical analysis on a static basis when considering mergers of algorithm-driven businesses. Assessment of dynamic competition has already become an important focus of merger control. Dynamic theories of harm, including those focusing on "*killer acquisitions*" and platform envelopment strategies straddle traditional horizontal and non-horizontal theories of harm, but seem to offer the richest ground for more intervention going forward. However, they also pose complex questions around evaluating alternative counterfactuals in the face of inherent uncertainty around how technology will develop. Part three covers dynamic theories of harm and concludes that as authorities focus more on dynamic theories of harm in digital markets (and beyond), algorithms (and algorithmic innovation) will become a critical aspect of merger review going forwards.

We focus on the decisional practice of the European Commission and the UK's Competition and Markets Authority ("*CMA*"). The CMA is given particular focus not only because the authors are London-based, but because of its unique position in the digital mergers debate. Thanks to its elastic jurisdictional rules and in particular its ability to review mergers even where the target has limited (or no) turnover, the CMA has been one of few authorities, or in some cases the only authority, to review some of the most significant digital mergers that have shaped the modern landscape. In recent years therefore, the CMA has arguably been the leading authority globally in willingness to shape novel theories of harm to facilitate intervention in mergers between algorithm-driven businesses.

2 Horizonal Unilateral Effects

2.1 Mergers Between Algorithm/Analytics Software Providers

All software relies on algorithms to some extent, but it is informative for present purposes to consider how authorities have typically approached mergers between parties where the *purpose* of the software is to run an algorithm—*i.e.,* analytics software, as opposed to software offered for content creation (*e.g.*, the Microsoft Office suite), or consumption (*e.g.,* gaming). Analytics softwares have been defined as "*software that supports the major business functions needed by commercial organisations to manage their business effectively*".[1] In line with its general approach to software markets, within a broad market for enterprise applications software, the Commission has identified a market for business analytics which it described as "*tools that allow data mining, ad hoc query capabilities, reporting functions, scorecards, and modelling*" (*SAP/Business Objects* (EC 2007, para. 11)). Within this market, the Commission has considered:

- *Functionality*: The Commission has considered distinguishing between "*query, reporting and analysis*" tools and "*advanced analytics*" tools, which carry out data mining and statistics.[2] The Commission has also considered whether to segment analytics software which is used for customers' promotional and sales activities (*IMS/Cegedim* (EC 2004a)).
- *Industry*: Given specificities of algorithmic software requirements, the European Commission has also considered segmentation by the industry at which the software is targeted—*e.g.,* retail, insurance, etc.—although the EC has typically left this open. For instance, *Sanofi/Google/DMI/JV*[3] involved the development of an integrated digital e-medicine platform by Google for the delivery and

[1] Oracle/Sun Microsystems (2010a, para. 24); Oracle/PeopleSoft (2004b, para. 17)).
[2] SAP/Business Objects (EC 2007, para. 15); IMS/Cegedim (EC 2004a, para. 103–105).
[3] EC (2016a).

monitoring of insulin/glucose for diabetics. The notifying parties argued that it was not necessary to distinguish a separate market for healthcare data analytics on the basis that, while different rules apply for safety and privacy reasons, this need not apply to the actual analytics itself and the algorithms used to carry out the analysis (para. 45). The Commission left the precise definition open, noting that competitor respondents took different views on the issue, with some considering algorithms to be "*data agnostic, and not industry-specific*" and others noting that "*healthcare data analytics is much more diverse and complex and therefore would require more sophisticated algorithms [...] than those used for other types of data*" (para. 46).

These data analytics mergers are useful background to understand the competitive impact of algorithms. However, theories of harm pursued by the European Commission in these cases have followed well-trodden ground and cases have typically been cleared unconditionally at Phase I,[4] noting that the relevant software markets themselves are typically fragmented with low barriers to entry/expansion within a broad geographic market definition (typically EEA-wide and potentially global in scope).[5]

The practice of the CMA is similar. For example, in the CMA's recent decision in *Google/Looker Data* (2020b), the CMA considered a horizontal overlap in the "*frame of reference*" for business intelligence tools, which it describes as "*types of application software designed to analyse, visualise and interpret business data in support of corporate decision-making processes*" (p. 1). In dismissing horizontal concerns, the CMA considered the functionality of Google and Looker's business intelligence products and concluded Google's tool was narrowly focused on advertising performance and therefore not suitable as a general tool for many enterprise customers, which was corroborated in internal documents and market testing. The horizontal assessment consumes only five of the 66 pages of the CMA's decision, which is primarily focused on vertical links relating to web analytics and online advertising services, discussed further below. These cases therefore provide some insight into how authorities have viewed competition in markets for algorithms themselves. As authorities improve their own technical understanding of these markets and even involve data scientists in competitive assessment, it will be interesting to see whether the way product markets are defined, and competition is analysed, evolves.

[4]BNP Paribas Fortis / Belgacom / Belgian Mobile Wallet (EC 2013); Publicis / Omnicom (EC 2014a); Sanofi / Google / DMI / JV (EC 2016b); Verizon / Yahoo (EC 2016c).

[5]IMS / Cegedim (EC 2004a, para. 110).

2.2 *Platform Mergers/Acquisitions*

The major global tech platforms operate using a range of business models,[6] but the common trait they share is that they operate in markets that are at least two- if not multi-sided. Another feature common to many but not all digital platforms is that on at least one side of the market, no monetary price is paid for the service offered/ provided. To take the most cited examples, Google and Facebook offer their search and social media services (respectively) at no monetary price to their users. Rather, users "*pay*" for the services by giving Facebook and Google their data, which Google and Facebook monetise through the sale of targeted advertising. Digital platforms use algorithms to mediate the two (or more) sides of the market and so algorithms and data constitute an essential aspect of these platforms' business models, either as their core functionality (*e.g.,* Google's search) and/or creating the dataset from which they generate their advertising revenues (*e.g.,* both Facebook and Google).

Acquisitions by platforms can offer the opportunity to generate efficiencies by improving their algorithms' functionality and related to this, accumulate data. Mergers between such businesses may therefore affect competition on both (or all) sides of the market, and failure to fully analyse all sides of multi-sided markets has been a key criticism of historical practice. For example, the Lear Report, which the CMA commissioned to review its (and its predecessors') prior decisional practice in digital mergers, concludes that "*current business models and monetization avenues should represent an unavoidable step for the development of a ToH because, quite simply, market power is not exerted for its own sake, but has the ultimate objective of increasing profits*"[7] and that such investigation could uncover additional potentially anti-competitive effects of a merger. Again, challenges require close assessment of how algorithms and data are used—can arise where only one side of the market pays a monetary "*price*" for the service. This section reviews how authorities have grappled with these issues in the (notoriously few) cases that have come before them, looking at paying and non-paying sides of the market in turn.

2.2.1 Analysing a Merger's Impact on the "Paying" Side of a Market

The main assessment of most platform merger reviews has typically been on the "*paying*" side of the market (though with some notable exceptions). For example, in *Google/Waze*[8] the CMA's predecessor authority, the Office of Fair Trading ("*OFT*") focussed solely on the effect that the merger could have had on the user side of the market, and notes that as such apps are provided for free and "*monetized elsewhere.*" The OFT's failure to give any detailed consideration to monetization channels and

---

[6] Caffarra (2019).

[7] Lear (2019, para. II.264).

[8] OFT (2013).

evaluated the potential adverse effect of the merger in the markets where the monetization occurs was criticised in the Lear Report.[9] Given how these businesses generate their revenues, cases that have come before the authorities have typically focussed on the impact of a merger in the online advertising market. When Facebook acquired Instagram in 2012, the OFT considered the impact of the merger in the supply of online display advertising. At the time, Instagram was a free mobile photo app for sharing on Instagram itself or on other social networks and did not offer online display advertising; the authorities' assessment therefore focussed on the potential for the platforms to compete and concluded that the merging parties were not close competitors. A few years later, the European Commission assessed the impact of Facebook's acquisition of WhatsApp on online advertising services, even though WhatsApp was not at the time offering online advertising services. The Commission concluded that even if WhatsApp were to enter online advertising, a sufficient number of competitors would remain (*Facebook/WhatsApp*[10]).

In assessing the impact of these mergers on the advertising side of the market, there was no in-depth analysis of the impacts of the algorithms used by the parties on competition. However, these two cases have been held up as the "*poster children*" of perceived underenforcement against mergers in the digital sector. Andrea Coscelli, chief executive of the CMA, has addressed this issue directly in a 2019 speech in which he notes that *"the so called GAFAM quintet – have made over 400 acquisitions globally, with more than half of these – close to 250 – just in the most recent 5 years" … [h]owever only a handful of these mergers have been scrutinised and none have been blocked"*.[11] The Lear Report notes that "*the advertising revenue per hour spent on Facebook and Instagram is significantly larger than that of their rivals, suggesting that the merged entity is able to command higher prices.*".[12] The Lear Report goes on to identify limitations in the way the OFT assessed closeness of competition, which include the OFT's focus on the number of downloads rather than engagement with the platform (which would have required analysis of the data/ algorithms used by the parties) (pp. 70–71).

2.2.2 Analysing a Merger's Impact on the "Free" Side of the Market

Assessing the impact on the "*free*" side of the market can raise more significant challenges for authorities. While economic theory has no difficulty in describing the provision of data as a "*price*" for use of the service,[13] it is a price that is more difficult to measure (and therefore more difficult to evaluate the effects of a merger upon) than one paid in cash. Similarly, given customers are not actively paying for the

[9] Lear (2019, pp. 117–118).

[10] EC (2014b, para. 179).

[11] Gov.uk. (2019).

[12] Lear (2019, p. iv).

[13] Arrieta Ibarra et al. (2017); Carrascal et al. (2013).

service they provide, it can be difficult for market participants to give views on the impact of a merger in a way useful to authorities, making market testing challenging. Perhaps the most obvious conceptual theory of harm in the context of a "*free*" product would be that the accretion of market power would allow providers of "*free*" platforms to begin charging for their use.

However, this is not a theory that has gained significant traction in cases involving platforms thus far given the nature of these companies' business models. In *Facebook/WhatsApp*[14] for example, the Commission appears to accept that users of consumer communications apps expect the app to be provided for free, noting this to be "*standard practice*" (para. 90) and highlighting that a customer survey confirmed customers are highly price sensitive. In fact, the Commission refers to concerns raised by market participants that WhatsApp would increase its fees not to generate higher revenues, but to encourage users to switch to Facebook Messenger (which in turn would allow Facebook to generate higher advertising revenues through accumulation of data), though these concerns were dismissed.

For example, in other cases, the OFT's decision in Priceline/Kayak—the fact customers are not charged for use of the platform is taken as a given, and the possibility of price increases is not considered (paras 63–66). Excluding the possibility of starting to charge for a previously "free" service, analysing the impact of the merger on the non-paying side of the market requires an analysis of non-price effects. A range of theories of harm have been mooted in both policy literature and decisional practice, including increasing the data "*price*" by degrading the privacy protections for users, degrading the quality of the algorithm (*e.g.,* worsening the functionality of the platform), and using data to exploit customers—*e.g.,* through price discrimination, and reducing innovation. These three theories of harm are discussed in turn below.

2.2.2.1 Privacy as a Parameter of Competition?

A key question which has arisen in algorithm-driven markets is whether privacy could be considered a parameter of competition, and whether businesses with market power may have the ability to "*deteriorate*" privacy (or put another way, to increase the data "*price*" for using their service). This is of course part of a broader debate around the ability of dominant platforms in particular to "*leverage*" privacy, which has been the subject of dominance enforcement. The most relevant case being the Bundeskartellamt's decision against Facebook and the subsequent appeals, which are ongoing. There are no UK or EU merger control decisions at the time of writing where a privacy-based theory of harm has grounded intervention in the merger. The typical approach of competition authorities has been that "*any privacy related concerns flowing from the increased concentration of data*. . .*do not fall within the*

[14] EC (2014b).

scope of the EU competition law rules but EU data protection" (*Facebook/WhatsApp*[15]).

Privacy considerations have nonetheless featured in the Commission's decisions. In *Facebook/WhatsApp*,[16] the Commission relied in part on the privacy policies of the merging firms and lack of incentive to merge such data (bolstered by examination of the parties' internal documents) to clear the merger. However, Facebook was later fined for misleading the European Commission over its ability to consolidate customer data. The Commission expressed the view that customers value privacy and would switch if WhatsApp's privacy standards degraded, noting that a high number of German users switched from WhatsApp to Threema in 24 h following announcement of the transaction, apparently due to privacy concerns (para. 174). Similarly, in *Microsoft/LinkedIn*[17] the Commission considered the possibility of reducing consumer choice regarding privacy protection (para. 50) and noted that (consistent with *Facebook/WhatsApp*[18]) its market investigation revealed that privacy is an important parameter of competition and driver of customer choice.

Calls for scrutiny of privacy issues in a merger control context have been growing louder. In the context of the ongoing review of Google's planned acquisition of fitness tracker maker Fitbit, the European Consumer Organisation published a position paper expressing competition concerns including in relation to the potential for Google to "*degrade Fitbit's current relatively better privacy rights and security protections, leading to reduced consumer choice in privacy options*".[19] The European Data Protection Board has required that Google conduct a privacy impact assessment of the acquisition of Fitbit prior to notifying to the European Commission for approval and said expressly that it "*stands ready to contribute its advice on the proposed merger to the Commission if so requested*".[20]

In the face of this pressure, Commissioner Margrethe Vestager has stressed that privacy-related issues be reviewed by data-protection authorities rather than competition authorities. Other enforcers, including the President of the French competition authority, Isabelle da Silva, have argued that the situation is ripe for change: "*The issue of mergers' effects on privacy has come to the fore as tech giants increasingly seek to boost their troves of data to enter new markets, offer innovative services and attract more advertising spending.*"[21] Outside of a merger context, forthcoming reforms to German Competition Law will give the Bundeskartellamt greater power to intervene—without the need for establishing a competition infringement—in the conduct of large platforms, including in relation to privacy.[22]

[15] EC (2014b, para. 164).

[16] EC (2014b).

[17] EC (2016c).

[18] EC (2014b).

[19] BEUC (2020, p. 11).

[20] Newman (2020a).

[21] Newman (2020b).

[22] Chazan and Espinoza (2020).

Enforcement in a behavioural context will force authorities to consider more explicitly and in-depth the extent to which privacy can truly be leveraged as a competitive parameter. Assuming the conclusion is that it can, these learnings will no doubt eventually start to influence merger control going forwards.

2.2.2.2 Degrading the Quality of the Algorithm

Several cases have also considered the possibility that a merger could allow the merged entity to deteriorate their offer to customers or reduce investment in improving its offer to the non-paying side of the market. Given platforms generate their revenue through monetisation of both data and users' attention in targeted advertising, authorities have generally found that even where the merged entity would have the ability to deteriorate its offer, it would not have the incentive to do so due to the risk of loss of advertising revenues (*i.e.*, impacts on the other side of the market). For example, in *Facebook/WhatsApp*[23] the European Commission accepts the Parties' submission that "*should the merged entity introduce or raise its prices or stop innovating, customers could easily switch to competing services which are available free of charge and which will provide new features and better-quality services*" (para. 91). Concerns have also been raised about the impact of mergers on innovation in product areas adjacent to the merging parties' core products, discussed further below under dynamic theories of harm.

2.2.2.3 Use of Data to Exploit Customers

The possibility of algorithms and data to allow for targeted price discrimination has been flagged in many policy reports. For example, the UK Furman Report (commissioned by the government to assess whether the UK competition regime is fit for the digital age) notes the possibility of "*each customer being offered an individual price based on what the business infers they are willing to pay*", though found that there is little evidence of this happening in practice.[24] The U.S. Counsel of Economic Advisers reached the same conclusion that "*examples of personalised pricing remain fairly limited*" and "*many of them can be addressed by enforcing existing antidiscrimination, privacy and consumer protection laws*".[25]

In its Phase I decision in *Amazon/Deliveroo*,[26] the CMA outlined a "*behavioural discrimination*" theory of harm, in which the CMA examined whether "*inframarginal customers*"—*customers who would not switch away if prices rose or quality worsened—would be discriminated against on price or quality as a result*

[23] EC (2014b).

[24] Digital Competition Expert Panel (2019, paras. 3.164 to 3.165).

[25] US Counsel of Economic Advisers (2015, p. 2).

[26] CMA (2019).

of the merger" (para. 375). One example the CMA gave was if Deliveroo used data from Amazon to adjust their algorithm such that the set of restaurants visible to inframarginal customers would include only more expensive restaurants (from which Deliveroo would receive higher commission revenue). The parties submitted that they would not have the ability to share customer data, in part because of their data protection obligations. While the CMA did not seem to agree (for reasons that are unclear due to the level of redaction in the decision), it found that neither Amazon nor Deliveroo had an incentive to share customer data. The CMA referred to *"risk to [Amazon's] reputation and consumer trust (in particular its commitment to a global policy of not selling customer data to third parties)"* (para. 372).

It is far from clear as a matter of economics that price discrimination is always welfare depletive, and many economists would argue it can generate efficiencies and in fact be pro-competitive. Consideration of price discrimination in a merger control context therefore raises complex economic questions. The CMA did not need to wrestle with these because it was able to dismiss the "*behavioural discrimination*" theory of harm, on the basis that Amazon would not be able to internalise the full benefits arising out of Deliveroo's increased profitability due to its limited (~16%) equity stake. This will clearly not be a factor in all mergers, and it will be interesting to see if this theory of harm arises again in future cases, and if so, how pro- and anti-competitive effects of price discrimination are weighed. While the *Amazon/ Deliveroo* case was referred for an in-depth investigation, the CMA's Phase II inquiry did not pursue behavioural discrimination as a theory of harm.

3 Non-Horizontal Foreclosure

Given the inter-related nature of many digital businesses, there can be significant efficiencies drawn from vertical integration, particularly in relation to data. However, vertical integration can also raise the risk of exploiting data or assets to the disadvantage of competitors and consumers. There are two broad categories of vertical theory of harm which can be seen in mergers of algorithm-driven businesses: those in which foreclosure could be carried out through erecting barriers to interoperability, or on the other hand refusing access to data itself. We address each in turn.

3.1 Interoperability

One key focus of competition authorities in assessing the competitive impact of algorithms has been the possibility that a merged entity may amend its application programming interfaces ("*APIs*") in a manner that would foreclose competitors, by blocking (or making more difficult) interaction between competitors' platform or programmes and those of the merging parties. As the name suggests, an API is a programming interface determining the interaction between multiple pieces of software. The availability of APIs is critical in the context of important platforms like operating systems, hardware, and powerful social media platforms. For example, the availability of the APIs for the iPhone allows app developers to "*build in*" a camera function without the need to write their own camera interface which would interpret the input from the iPhone's hardware.

In a number of mergers, particularly involving platforms, competition authorities have explored whether the merging parties may be able to develop their algorithms in a manner that forecloses competitors by blocking or reducing interoperability between their platform or software and competing products. As far back as *Microsoft's* acquisition of *Skype* in 2011, the Commission explored whether Microsoft would integrate Skype and Windows/Office software and be likely to degrade Skype's interoperability with competing operating systems and platforms. Ultimately, the Commission was not convinced that Microsoft would have any incentive to degrade interoperability since Skype's product value is mainly based on its large active user base.[27] However, later, in *Microsoft/LinkedIn*,[28] after finding that LinkedIn's features could be integrated into Office (a stated rationale for the deal), the Commission concluded that the transaction could lead to foreclosure of LinkedIn's competitors, by refusing access to Microsoft's APIs (required to interoperate with Microsoft's products and to access user data stored in the Microsoft cloud). The Commission also considered broader concerns around tying and bundling of Office with a LinkedIn application but concluded that these were not well founded based on the parties' strategic plans and user preferences. The Commission noted that Microsoft was "*well aware of the benefits that those practices would create in terms of increased user base and activity of LinkedIn and, as a result, of increased monetisation opportunities*" (paras. 331–332). Microsoft ultimately offered commitments to maintain current levels of interoperability for other social networks with Microsoft Office's suite of products through the so-called Office add-in program and Office APIs; and granting competing social networks access to 'Microsoft Graph,' a gateway for software developers to access data stored in the Microsoft cloud.

Competition authorities have often explored interoperability as a theory of harm in transactions involving online platforms. For instance, in *Facebook/Instagram*,[29] the OFT considered whether Facebook would prevent Instagram users uploading photos to other social networks or deteriorate the quality of the Instagram's API connection with rival social networks (para. 31) and in *Google/Looker Data*,[30] the CMA assessed interoperability issues relating to products outside the Google ecosystem (*e.g.*, competing data warehouses) and competing business intelligence tools. However, crucially in these mergers, competition authorities have generally (*Apple/Shazam* being the exception, where the Commission concluded that even if the

[27] EC (2011, paras. 145–150).

[28] EC (2016a).

[29] OFT (2012).

[30] CMA (2020b).

ability and incentive existed, such conduct would not result in foreclosure of Apple's digital music streaming competitors[31]) concluded that the platform would not have the incentive to engage in such a foreclosure strategy, either because it would diminish the value of the platform (*Facebook/Instagram*[32]) and/or such a strategy would not be profitable (albeit that this has not been uncontroversial). For instance, the Lear Report suggested that the OFT in *Facebook/WhatsApp* ought to have considered the dynamic impact of incentives if for instance Instagram became a must-have product.[33]

There are at least two critical differences between *Microsoft/LinkedIn* and the *Facebook* and *Google* cases. First, switching operating system is not as easy as switching in social media; in the latter, switching is "*free*" and multi-homing is common. Second, Microsoft's revenues come directly from software sales rather than being dependent on numbers of software users to generate revenues on the "*other side*" of the market. Given these differences, establishing an incentive to foreclose will always prove more difficult in relation to multi-sided platforms. Given the ability of companies to readily change and amend algorithms and the interaction between different layers of digital markets, we continue to expect scrutiny of such interoperability theories going forward.

Two cases ongoing at the time of writing promise to shed further light on the interoperability issue. First, in the European Commission's referral of *Google/FitBit* to a Phase 2 review, the Commission said that it would examine the merger's impact on Google and Fitbit's offerings in digital healthcare, and whether Google might have the incentive to degrade interoperability with rival wearables. It is also understood that the DOJ is considering interoperability between Fitbit and non-Android (Google) devices in its ongoing review of that transaction. Second, the CMA is currently reviewing *Facebook's* acquisition of *Giphy*. Although the theories of harm to be explored are not yet clear, on announcement, the social media provider confirmed that, while it intended to integrate the GIF provider into its Instagram ecosystem, it promised that Giphy's partners will continue to have the same access to Giphy's APIs.[34] Both cases should shed further interesting light on this complex area.

3.2 Accumulation of Data

The accumulation and consolidation of data have been the driving rationale behind many mergers in recent years. The mere consolidation of data does not *prima facie* lead to an ability to increase price or degrade quality or range of service to customers,

[31] Paragraph 286.

[32] OFT (2012, para. 37).

[33] Lear (2019, section II.81).

[34] Facebook (2020).

but a key focus in reviews of data-driven mergers has instead been the potential for vertical foreclosure of competitors. To evaluate a data foreclosure-based theory of harm, it is instructive first to consider some of the economic characteristics of data. Data has a unique set of economic characteristics, but each dataset's value will depend on a range of factors. Quality, accuracy, and completeness are self-evidently critical to the value of any data set. Data is non-rivalrous (*i.e.,* use by one party does not negate its use by another) and non-depletable (*i.e.,* it does not run out) and depreciates over time and at different rates for different information. Different kinds of data also have different costs of acquisition. The cost of acquisition and the duration of time for which data retains its currency are the two critical factors that influence data's value.[35] Critically in the context of mergers, certain datasets when combined can be more valuable than the sum of their parts, and this has been a key focus in some merger reviews. The ability to extract value from data is also increasingly dependent upon having tools to collate and analyse it—*i.e.*, using algorithms.

For instance, in *Telefónica/Vodafone/Everything Everywhere/JV*[36] the Commission examined concerns that the mobile networks JV would use basic customer data such as age, residential status and profession, and location and social behaviour data to foreclose providers of data analytics or advertising services from a unique customer database. Third parties argued that the uniqueness of this database lay in the ability to couple other forms of data (which were relatively ubiquitous) with location data, meaning that the JV would be "*uniquely placed*" to reach the consumer at a certain "*right moment*".[37] However, the Commission concluded that none of the components of the JV's database were unique—mobile apps (Apple and Google) had access to location data, competing payment service providers (PayPal) had access to campaign response data, and social networks (Facebook and LinkedIn) had access to behaviour data. Concerns about the accumulation and control of data was also a focus in *Microsoft/LinkedIn*, although these were not deemed credible not least given that "*LinkedIn's business model, and the value of the data it collects, are based on its users' willingness to update their profiles and engage with LinkedIn services,*" noting that this would be undermined should users become aware that their data will be shared.[38]

Given the scale and breadth of data controlled by them, accumulation of data has been a focus of attention in mergers involving online platforms. For instance, the Commission examined whether Facebook would use WhatsApp's user data to improve the targeting of Facebook's advertising activities, eventually dismissing this theory on the basis that it would necessitate a change to WhatsApp's privacy policy and a matching exercise between individuals' Facebook and WhatsApp profiles (though Facebook was later fined for providing misleading information in

---

[35] Oxera (2018).

[36] EC (2012).

[37] EC (2012, para. 544).

[38] EC (2016a, para. 247).

this respect). Similarly, in *Google/Looker*,[39] the CMA concluded that Google would not be likely to foreclose rival BI tool providers from accessing Google-generated data sources post-merger as it was unlikely to be profitable. Similar issues were considered in *Apple/Shazam*, in which the Commission also considered the potential for the transaction to give Apple commercially sensitive information on its competitors, in particular Spotify, and whether it could lead to any anticompetitive effects. The Commission was persuaded that Apple would not have the incentive to do so—in part in reflection of its "industry leading-positions on privacy",[40] but concluded more generally that there would be no anticompetitive effect.

While the data held by merging parties has come under scrutiny in mergers between algorithm-driven businesses (and there is clear overlap with interoperability concerns as demonstrated by *Google/Looker*[41]), stand-alone data concerns are yet to ground intervention. The sheer volume of data available, from multiple sources, means competition authorities have been reluctant to conclude that any target's data assets are unique and cannot be replicated.[42] Many commentators have nonetheless argued that even if data is ubiquitous, the combination of particularly rich sets of consumer data and the ability to extract value from them through sophisticated algorithms, is only available to a small pool of companies.

Such concerns may be particularly acute in mergers where the parties together hold a substantial number of particular kinds of data which is harder to replicate—for example health data (and announcements from the Australian regulator's review of Google*/Fitbit*[43] suggest it will be a particular focus in that case). The European Commission referred the merger to a Phase 2 investigation in August 2020, and its final decision is due between writing and publication, in January 2021. The Commission's press release on referral to Phase 2 cited concerns that the acquisition of "key insights about the life and health situation" of Fitbit users could give Google a (further) advantage in online advertising services, with a dataset that rivals could not match. Google had offered a commitment not to use Fitbit's data for advertising, saying the deal is about "devices not data", but the behavioural remedy offer was insufficient to resolve the Commission's concerns.

We predict the accumulation of data will receive greater scrutiny in future "*GAFA*" cases and it remains to be seen whether we might reach a "*tipping*" point where authorities seek to restrict the volume and diversity of data held by a limited number of online platforms. Outside of a merger control context, the CMA's Digital Advertising Market Study has focused on this very issue and recommended possible reforms to remedy perceived competitive harms. At the time of writing the CMA is finalising its Digital Taskforce Report, which is expected to build upon the work of the Digital Advertising Market Study and include a recommendation the UK

[39] CMA (2020b).

[40] Paragraph 245.

[41] Id.

[42] See for example, Apple / Shazam, paragraph 328.

[43] Id.

government establish a special regulatory regime for acquisitions by platforms with "Strategic Market Status", which would subject all acquisitions them to mandatory CMA review and potentially lower the standard of proof the CMA needs to meet to intervene in a merger.

4 Looking Forward: Dynamic Theories of Harm

Scrutiny of—and intervention in—mergers between algorithm-driven businesses has increased dramatically over recent years. As noted at the outset, there is an emerging consensus among authorities and policymakers globally that there has been an undesirable accumulation of market power in the hands of large tech companies, *inter alia*, through the practice of large tech platforms buying up nascent businesses. A traditional consideration of "*static*" metrics of existing competition would typically not find such mergers to be problematic, as they result in no—or very low—increments to market share, meaning that authorities have focussed increasingly on "*dynamic*" or potential competition.

The concept that the acquisition of nascent business could raise competition concerns has its genesis in the influential empirical study from the pharmaceutical sector from 2018. The study showed that pipeline drugs of acquired companies were less likely to be developed where the acquirer's portfolio included overlapping drugs—i.e., the development was "*killed*". The study estimates that 5.3–7.4% of acquisitions reviewed were "*killer*" acquisitions.[44] The killer acquisitions concept has since been applied to the tech sector and beyond. In the UK, the Furman Report[45] says that in the absence of similar empirical data for tech acquisitions, the pharma study can be considered informative, and notes concerns that "*in some instances, large digital companies have acquired smaller innovative companies in spaces adjacent or overlapping with their main activity, as a so-called killer acquisition strategy, designed to eliminate potential future rivals.*" (para. 3.51). The Report recommends explicitly that "*The CMA should take more frequent and firmer action to challenge mergers that could be detrimental to consumer welfare through reducing future levels of innovation and competition, supported by changes to legislation where necessary.*" (para. 3.54).

Heeding this call even prior to any legislative reform, the CMA has pursued theories of harm based on dynamic competition in a number of cases in involving algorithm-driven businesses since the publication of the Furman Report in 2019, including *Amazon/Deliveroo* (CMA 2020a) (already covered above), *Sabre/Fare Logix*[46] (airline booking software merger, blocked by the CMA after the DOJ in the

[44] Cunningham et al. (2020).

[45] Digital Competition Expert Panel (2019).

[46] CMA (2020c).

US had lost its attempt to block the merger in court), *Experian/Clearscore*[47] (free credit scores merger, abandoned after being provisionally blocked) and *PayPal/iZettle*[48] (mobile offline and online payments, cleared in Phase II). The CMA is expected to release revised merger assessment guidelines outlining its approach to dynamic theories of harm between writing and publication.

The European Commission's Report on *Competition in the Digital Age*,[49] citing the same study from the pharma sector, takes a slightly different perspective. It finds that the shuttering of a target's pipeline of innovation is not the typical scenario in the digital realm, but more common is a scenario where the nascent business' offering is integrated into the "*ecosystem*" of the acquirer, where the acquisition allows the acquirer to build on its (frequently data-based) economies of scope. The report suggests that a useful framework for reviewing these mergers is a conglomerate theory of harm, focusing on the effects of the merger on the market position of the (conglomerate) ecosystem and the barriers to entry protecting it. The authors suggest that acquisitions may be problematic in combining parties' positive network effects, reinforcing barriers to entry to the "ecosystem" and simultaneously eliminating the risk that the target attracts the acquirers' users. The report cautions that "*theories of harm should be limited to cases of highly entrenched dominance when the possibility of entry is limited,*" and that these would succeed where in the counterfactual, the target could have succeeded on a stand-alone basis, or been acquired by an alternative (presumably less or non-dominant) competitor (and where efficiencies cannot be proven to offset the anticompetitive effect) (p. 121).

The focus on the potential for tech acquisitions to be "*killers*" has been very much international. In February 2020, the FTC announced a study into acquisitions made by Google, Facebook, Apple, Amazon and Microsoft over the past decade that had not at the time been notified to US antitrust enforcers, which could lead to enforcement action against historical transactions.[50] Separately, FTC commissioner Rohit Chopra has advocated for the FTC to use this power more often, noting that some deals—including those motivated by the acquisition of consumer data—"*fly below the radar*".[51] Similarly, in Australia the ACCC's digital platforms inquiry report recommended a change to the merger law to be able to consider the "*nature and significance of assets, including data and technology, being acquired*" as part of its merger review.[52] This recommendation was made to address the importance of data in digital markets, and the competitive advantage presented by data. The ACCC specifically named Google's acquisition of Waze as a situation in which data-based theories of harm may have justified an intervention.

[47] Id.

[48] CMA (2019).

[49] Crémer et al. (2019).

[50] Parts (2020).

[51] Id.

[52] ACCC (2019).

The debate over "*killer*" acquisitions raises the more fundamental question of whether dominant tech platforms should be forced to "*build*" rather than "*buy*" new products and services. There have been calls for legislative reform to have a presumption against acquisitions by dominant tech platforms, including the former Chief Economist of the European Commission,[53] and Margarethe Vestager has mooted the idea of shifting the burden of proof in certain tech mergers to the parties to show the deal is *not anticompetitive*.[54] Such proposals are premised on the belief—held by many authorities—that because of digital markets' propensity to "*tip*", the costs of failing to intervene are particularly high. Such reform would remove from competition authorities the burden of establishing an appropriate counterfactual, which has typically been one of the key hurdles to intervention in such cases, as demonstrated by retrospective reviews. The Lear Report highlights the difficulty of constructing the counterfactual in cases where the target is a young firm at an early stage of its development. Among other examples, it highlights that in *Google/Waze*[55] the OFT considered a theory of harm based on Waze's potential as a disruptive force in the market going forward. This was dismissed in large part due to the uncertainty of Waze's future growth projections because of Waze's relatively small presence in the UK, which did not afford it sufficiently significant network effects to accelerate its growth and uncertainty with respect to partnerships that Waze was finalising (as well as the presence of competitors).[56] It is also clear that authorities could predict a *more competitive* future than eventuates in practice. For example, *Microsoft/Yahoo Search*[57] noted that the cost of developing and updating the algorithm was a high barrier to entry (para. 111), and also that "[*t*]*he is starting point for this assessment is the fact that the transaction will remove one provider of an algorithmic search engine from the market*" (para. 202), but that the new platform could compete more effectively with Google.[58]

While the "*killer*" or "*reverse killer*" acquisition theory of harm does not necessarily require or involve close analysis of merging parties' algorithms (though it may), in many respects it could be considered the natural evolution of the theories discussed above in a dynamic context. When concerns are framed in this manner, they present a theory of harm which, if proven, is difficult if not impossible to remedy appropriately. Such "*prohibition risks*" are therefore clearly an important consideration for any merger between algorithm-driven businesses.

[53] Caffarra et al. (2020).

[54] Espinoza and Fleming (2019).

[55] OFT (2013).

[56] Lear (2019, para. II.267).

[57] EC (2010b).

[58] Chirita (2018, p. 21).

5 Conclusion

Thousands of pages have been written by authorities, policymakers and the broader antitrust community about how authorities "should" be thinking about mergers between algorithm-driven businesses. Whether or not criticism of previous (lack of) enforcement is considered legitimate, we are now in a new era in which competition authorities will scrutinise such mergers more closely and intervene more often.

The decisional practice reviewed in this chapter shows that authorities have generally struggled to find grounds for intervention based on "*traditional*" and static assessment of horizontal and vertical theories of harm. However, it seems likely that the increased focus on dynamic competition may allow the complex interrelationships between market participants—especially for multi-sided markets—to be more fully evaluated and translated into theories of harm. Clearly, an important aspect of this will be a full understanding and analysis of the way that merging parties' algorithms and datasets affect competition in their own—and adjacent—markets.

At the same time, new challenges lie in wait. Ongoing cases in other areas of competition law (*e.g.,* dominance enforcement against Google, Amazon and Apple, and the UK's Digital Advertising Market study) are likely to indirectly influence and inform merger control practice going forward. Historically, theories of harm pursued in *Microsoft/Skype* and *Microsoft/LinkedIn* were no doubt influenced by previous antitrust enforcement (*Microsoft (bundling)*[59] and *Microsoft (tying)*[60]). In the present day, it is understood that third parties complained in the *Google/Fitbit* case that Google would have the ability and incentive to favour Fitbit devices in its search results[61]—a theory of harm derived from dominance enforcement. Further advances in technology will inevitably raise new challenges. With the growth of artificial intelligence, machine learning and self-learning algorithms (with little to no human oversight), it may be even more difficult for competition authorities to accurately assess how competition will evolve and the impact of these algorithms in rapidly evolving markets.

While some reform in the EU and UK is on the horizon, it is not yet known whether calls for legislative changes to make intervention in algorithm-driven mergers easier for authorities will be heeded by governments, and if so, what form these will take. In the meantime, authorities will need to work with existing tools to put the learnings of authorities' policy work into practice. There are cases under review at the time of writing—in *Google/Fitbit* and *Facebook/GIPHY*—which will need to address head-on the issues covered by this chapter.

[59] EC (2004c).

[60] EC (2009).

[61] Sisco and Ebersole (2020).

References

ACCC (2019) Digital platforms inquiry – final report. Retrieved from https://www.accc.gov.au/publications/digital-platforms-inquiry-final-report

Arrieta Ibarra I, Goff L, Jiménez Hernández D, Lanier J, Weyl EG (2017) Should we treat data as labor? Moving beyond 'free'. Am Econ Assoc Pap Proc 1(1)

BEUC (2020) Google-Fitbit Merger: Competition concerns and harms to consumers. Retrieved June 19, 2020 from https://www.beuc.eu/publications/beuc-x-2020-035_google-fitbit_merger_competition_concerns_and_harms_to_consumers.pdf

Bhageshpur K (2019) Data is the new oil - and that's a good thing. Forbes. Retrieved June 18, 2020 from https://www.forbes.com/sites/forbestechcouncil/2019/11/15/data-is-the-new-oil-and-thats-a-good-thing/#1519fbf57304

Caffarra C (2019) "Follow the Money" – Mapping issues with digital platforms into actionable theories of harm. Concurrences e-Competitions e-Bulletin. No91579. Retrieved from https://ecp.crai.com/wp-content/uploads/2019/09/e-Competitions-Special-Issue-Cristina-Caffarra.pdf

Caffarra C, Crawford G, Valletti T (2020, May 11) 'How tech rolls': Potential competition and 'reverse' killer acquisitions. VOX. Retrieved on June 19, 2020 from https://voxeu.org/content/how-tech-rolls-potential-competition-and-reverse-killer-acquisitions

Carrascal JP, Riederer C, Erramilli V, Cherubini M, de Oliveira R (2013) Your browsing behaviour for a Big Mac: economics of personal information online. Proceedings of the 22nd International Conference on World Wide Web. May 2013. pp 189–200

Chazan G, Espinoza J (2020, February 4) Tech companies face clampdown in Germany over competition fears. Financial Times. Retrieved from https://www.ft.com/content/39559796-4698-11ea-aee2-9ddbdc86190d

Chirita AD (2018) Data-driven mergers under EU competition law. In: Linarelli J, Akseli O (eds) The future of commercial law: ways forward for harmonisation. Hart, Oxford

Competition & Markets Authority (2019) *PayPal/iZettle*

Competition & Markets Authority (2020a) Amazon/Deliveroo

Competition & Markets Authority (2020b) *Google/Looker Data*

Competition & Markets Authority (2020c) *Sabre/Farelogix*

Competition & Markets Authority (2020d) *Experian/Clearscore*

Competition & Markets Authority (2020e) *Facebook/Giphy*

Crémer J, de Montjoye Y-A, Schweitzer H (2019) Competition Policy for the digital era: Final Report at page 121. https://doi.org/10.2763/407537

Cunningham C, Ederer F, Ma S (2020) Killer Acquisitions. https://doi.org/10.2139/ssrn.3241707

Department of Justice (2020) *Google/Fitbit*

Digital Competition Expert Panel (2019) Unlocking digital competition, Report of the Digital Competition Expert Panel. Gov.uk. Retrieved from https://assets.publishing.service.gov.uk/government/uploads/system/uploads/attachment_data/file/785547/unlocking_digital_competition_furman_review_web.pdf

Espinoza J, Fleming S (2019, October 30) Margrethe Vestager eyes toughening 'burden of proof' for Big Tech. Financial Times. Retrieved on June 19, 2020 from https://www.ft.com/content/24635a5c-fa4f-11e9-a354-36acbbb0d9b6

European Commission. (2004a) *Case M.7337 – IMS / Cegedim*

European Commission. (2004b) *Case M.3216, Oracle / PeopleSoft*

European Commission. (2004c) *Case No COMP/C-3/37.792 Microsoft (bundling)*

European Commission. (2007) *Case M.4944 - SAP / Business Objects*

European Commission. (2009) *Case No COMP/C-3/39.530 Microsoft (tying)*

European Commission. (2010a) *Case M.5529 - Oracle / Sun Microsystems*

European Commission. (2010b) *Case M.5727 – Microsoft / Yahoo! Search Business*

European Commission. (2012) *Case M.6314 – Telefónica UK / Vodafone UK / Everything Everywhere / JV*

European Commission. (2013) *Case M.6967 – BNP Paribas Fortis / Belgacom / Belgian Mobile Wallet*

European Commission. (2014a) *Case M.7023 – Publicis / Omnicom*

European Commission (2014b) *Case No COMP/M.7217 – Facebook / WhatsApp*

European Commission (2014c) *Case No COMP/M.6281 – Microsoft / Skype*

European Commission (2016a) *Case No COMP/M.8124 – Microsoft / LinkedIn*

European Commission (2016b) *Case M.7813 – Sanofi / Google / DMI / JV*

European Commission (2016c) *Case M.8180 – Verizon / Yahoo*

European Commission (2017, March 16) Bundeskartellamt 18th Conference on Competition, Berlin, 16 March 2017 – Speech: Algorithms and competition. Retrieved on June 19, 2020 from https://wayback.archive-it.org/12090/20191129221651/https://ec.europa.eu/commission/commissioners/2014-2019/vestager/announcements/bundeskartellamt-18th-conference-competition-berlin-16-march-2017_en

Facebook (2020) Facebook Welcomes GIPHY as Part of Instagram Team. Retrieved June 18, 2020 from https://about.fb.com/news/2020/05/welcome-giphy/

Gov.uk (2019) Competition in the digital age: reflecting on digital merger investigations. Retrieved June 3, 2019 from https://www.gov.uk/government/speeches/competition-in-the-digital-age-reflecting-on-digital-merger-investigations

Lear (2019) Ex-post Assessment of Merger Control Decisions in Digital Markets. Retrieved June 18, 2020 from https://assets.publishing.service.gov.uk/government/uploads/system/uploads/attachment_data/file/803576/CMA_past_digital_mergers_GOV.UK_version.pdf

Newman M (2020a, May 18) Big Tech's personal data hoard raises EU antitrust, privacy concerns. Mlex. Retrieved from https://www.mlex.com/GlobalAntitrust/DetailView.aspx?cid=1166873&siteid=190&rdir=1

Newman M (2020b, February 19) Google asked by EU data-protection regulators to review privacy impact of Fitbit deal. Mlex. Retrieved from https://mlexmarketinsight.com/insights-center/editors-picks/area-of-expertise/data-privacy-and-security/google-asked-by-eu-data-protection-regulators-to-review-privacy-impact-of-fitbit-deal

Office of Fair Trading (2012) *ME/5525/12 Facebook / Instagram*

Office of Fair Trading (2013) *ME/6167/13 Google / Waze*

Oxera (2018) Consumer Data in Online Markets. Retrieved June 18, 2020 from https://www.oxera.com/wp-content/uploads/2018/07/Oxera-Consumer-data-in-online-markets.pdf.pdf

Parts S (2020, February 12) FTC will move fast on study of big tech deals. Glob Compet Rev. Retrieved on June 18, 2020 from https://globalcompetitionreview.com/article/usa/1214428/ftc-will-move-fast-on-study-of-big-tech-deals

Sisco J, Ebersole J (2020, May 21) Google-Fitbit review by US DOJ examines data, interoperability. Mlex. Retrieved from https://www.mlex.com/GlobalAntitrust/DetailView.aspx?cid=1191281&siteid=191&rdir=1

The Economist (2017) The world's most valuable resource is no longer oil, but data. Retrieved June 18, 2020 from https://www.economist.com/leaders/2017/05/06/the-worlds-most-valuable-resource-is-no-longer-oil-but-data

U.S. Counsel of Economic Advisers (2015) Big Data and Differential Pricing. Retrieved from https://obamawhitehouse.archives.gov/sites/default/files/whitehouse_files/docs/Big_Data_Report_Nonembargo_v2.pdf

Reasons to be Cheerful: The Benevolent Market Power of Decentralised Blockchains

Chris Pike and Gabriele Carovano

Abstract We remain uncertain as to the prospects of a Blockchain revolution, nevertheless, in this chapter, we focus on the reasons for optimism, and in particular, why we think that decentralised permission-less blockchains might offer the prospect of radical pro-competitive and inclusive efficiencies, and hence might contribute to a pro-competitive industrial policy. Given these possibilities we therefore expect that blockchain will continue to capture the attention of policymakers that are keen to deliver shared prosperity in a post-COVID world. We suggest that competition agencies might explore whether actions by incumbents and regulators might create barriers to the emergence of a particular type of Blockchain, specifically decentralised permission-less blockchains with platform functionality.

1 Introduction

Blockchain technology has in recent years captured attention and funding based on its promise to build trust among multiple parties without the need for a trusted intermediary. Blockchain technology is born out of government-funded research on game-theoretic Byzantine consensus.[1] Blockchain technology offers the prospect of a more efficient way to build trust in transactions; trust in a product's provenance or trust in a contract's execution. In competition policy, the focus of work on

The authors can be contacted at: chris.pike@fideres.com; Gabriele.carovano@kcl.ac.uk. We thank Antonio Capobianco, Pedro Caro de Sousa, Pedro Gonzaga, Konstantinos Stylianou, and Thibault Schrepel for their helpful comments and discussion.

[1] Shrier (2020, p. 20).

C. Pike (✉)
Fideres LLP, London, UK
e-mail: chris.pike@fideres.com

G. Carovano
King's College, London, UK
e-mail: Gabriele.carovano@kcl.ac.uk

A. Portuese (ed.), *Algorithmic Antitrust*, Economic Analysis of Law in European Legal Scholarship 12, https://doi.org/10.1007/978-3-030-85859-9_5

blockchains has, since the OECD's thought-leading work on the topic began in 2018, been on the possible anti-competitive risks posed by the technology, and the question of whether there is anything new about these risks. There have also been predictions that blockchains will prove the death of antitrust law, or that vigilant enforcement of antitrust law threatens blockchain development. However, while there might conceivably be a conflict between contract law and blockchains (we are not equipped to comment on this possibility), we do not see a conflict between competition law and blockchain, any more than there is a conflict between competition law and email or electricity.

While we remain uncertain as to the prospects of a Blockchain revolution, in this chapter, we therefore focus instead on the reasons for optimism, and in particular, why we think that decentralised permission-less blockchains offer the prospect of radical pro-competitive and inclusive efficiencies, and hence might contribute to a pro-competitive industrial policy. We therefore expect that blockchain will continue to capture the attention of policymakers that are keen to deliver shared prosperity in a post-COVID world. We suggest that competition agencies might explore whether actions taken by incumbents and regulators might create barriers to the emergence of a particular type of Blockchain, specifically decentralised permission-less blockchains with platform functionality.

2 Clarifying Terminology

First, however, some clarifications. Contrary to some accounts, blockchain does not eliminate the need for intermediaries, as it still requires third-party intermediaries, although they do not need to be 'trusted.' Instead, where intermediaries are decentralised and appropriately incentivised by the rules or protocols of a Blockchain, they can be relied upon to operate truthfully whilst remaining self-interested. This means potentially untrustworthy intermediaries can nevertheless be trusted to act as the user would wish them to.

The strength of the Blockchain brand also obscures important distinctions between (i) blockchain and distributed ledger technologies (DLTs); between (ii) public and private blockchains, and between (iii) permission-less and permissioned blockchains.

The terms blockchain and DLT are often used interchangeably, but while all blockchains are DLTs, not all DLTs are blockchains.[2] For example, since the issuing of Satoshi Nakamoto's Bitcoin white paper,[3] alternative 'non-blockchain' distributed ledger systems have emerged, such as directly acyclic graphs (DAG-DLTs). These do not require creating a chain of blocks and instead use alternative crypto-economic mechanisms to reach consensus. Directed Acyclic Graphs (DAGs) consensus mechanisms, instead of bundling data together into blocks that are then confirmed one after another, require newly added data to reference and validate

[2]Shrier (2020, p. 22).

[3]Nakamoto (2008).

past data. Usually, each new transaction would have to reference and validate two transactions that came before. In doing so, the network comes to form a graph of converging and confirmed transactions. If a node incorrectly validates a past transaction, that node's transaction would fail to be confirmed by other participants. Similarly, 'Public' and 'permissionless' are not synonyms, and nor are 'private' and 'permissioned.'[4] The public/private nature of a blockchain refers to whether access to use a given blockchain is subject to a previous authorization or not. In contrast, a blockchain's permissioning refers to the powers that a user can exercise on a blockchain. For example, the Libra (now Diem) blockchain developed by Facebook is a permissioned but public blockchain (originally it planned to become permissionless, though these plans have now been abandoned).[5]

In 'permission-less' blockchains, anyone with the necessary equipment can become a validator and so the number of validators can be numerous. Validators are usually compensated with a mixture of transaction fees and new tokens that are created and used as the platform's currency (the total number of which are determined by the protocols of the blockchains). Meanwhile, users' identity can be either pseudonymized or (in some cases, see Monero) totally anonymized so that anybody can observe the actions that have taken place on the blockchain between active parties, but with the security that it is extremely difficult to identify users. This eradicates the need to hire a trusted third party (e.g., a notary, bank, etc.) to verify an action or transaction, and allows these to be collectively verified by a crowd of validators, who do not know the participants, and who are individually unable to verify. Verification is then the result of a degree of consensus across the crowd of validators. Consequently, to sabotage the verification process requires coordination amongst large numbers of pseudonymized validators.

Instead, in 'permissioned' blockchains, validators are selected by a controlling firm or consortia of firms. This reintroduces the need for a higher degree of trust in the third party, and so the premium that can be charged by those that are trustworthy potentially increases costs, relative to permission-less blockchains. The need for consensus across validators can also be loosened, potentially leading to a single-validator verification process. Unlike the permission-less variation, where access to a blockchain's history is normally public, in a permissioned blockchain, this may be private, and hence restricted to well-defined users, or remain public. Finally, it should be noted that in both public and private variations, the detailed contents of the transactions, that is, not the meta-data, might be encrypted to provide greater privacy (enabling validators to undertake so-called 'zero-knowledge proofs' in which they verify a block of transactions without knowing the contents of the transactions). However, seen from a competition policy perspective, permissioned blockchains are not special, and are in many ways little more than an industry consortia or joint venture. The risks of these are well known, and to the extent that there are peculiarities, these have been set out.[6] We therefore do not consider these

[4] Jayachandran (2017).

[5] Libra (2020).

[6] Pike and Capobianco (2019); OECD (2018); Pike and Capobianco (2020).

further. Rather we focus on the truly radical innovative aspect of blockchain—the decentralised permission-less variant.

3 The Nature of a Permission-Less Blockchain's Role Within a Market

3.1 A Platform

Blockchains are platforms that strive to attract both users and validators. Additional hardware developers, software developers, application developers, exchanges, oracles, etc. may also strengthen the platform. As a result, cross-platform network externalities are likely to arise since the more users a platform obtains, the higher the value of its tokens and the rewards to validators. Similarly, the higher the number of validators, the better the security, speed, and costs of the verification process for users (provided there is sufficient competition between validators). It follows that blockchains need to set incentives to get both sides on-board.

As with other multi-sided platforms (e.g., advertising-based media services), each blockchain platform may compete with other blockchain platforms with the same application, or with non-blockchain (non-platform) alternative technologies that have the same application (e.g., subscription-based media services). It therefore does not follow that there is a specific blockchain market. Nor that a blockchain will comprise its own separate market. What matters when identifying a particular blockchain's competitors is therefore its users' and validators' view of the substitutability between these different technologies.

3.2 Pricing

The pool of validators in permission-less blockchains is potentially countless. These validators are paid by both the platform (via newly minted tokens) and by the users in exchange for their services (via a transaction fee). Blockchain protocols, at the beginning of their lifecycle, may use newly minted tokens to attract validators by funding their recruitment without discouraging users with high transaction fees. However, as the production of newly minted tokens gets reduced until it ends (so-called halving), the balance of validators' income shifts towards transaction fees.

As a platform, the balance of pricing between users and validators is particularly important to a blockchain's success. For example, on Bitcoin, users post a transaction price that they are willing to pay to validate their transactions. They can observe transaction prices that other users have posted in order to make sure their posted price is sufficiently attractive to be validated within a timeframe that meets their needs. For instance, urgent transactions can be posted with higher fees to ensure they are validated quickly. Transaction fees are set through an auction mechanism. When validating capacity is constrained compared to demand, transaction fees will therefore increase, while low-margin operations may get postponed, and after a period, might even be dropped entirely. To increase price, validators will therefore need to either change the price-setting process by modifying the blockchain protocols, or to collectively refuse to validate low priced transactions. However, the number and pseudonymity of validators, combined with the fact that they hold tokens earned through their validation work that give them a stake in the Blockchain being broadly adopted, makes coordination to raise prices through either mechanism extremely difficult and often undesirable for validators.

3.3 Control

Permission-less blockchains are decentralised organisations. They have no governing body. Rather they are governed by the collective decision-making of their validators on the protocols that define the working-mechanism of the blockchain. When the consensus of validators is against adopting certain changes to protocols that developers may have proposed, they may therefore reject them, equally if they are against maintaining an existing protocol, even one created by the founder of the Blockchain, they can modify it. The minority of validators may react by 'forking' the Blockchain to create a new variant.

Consequently, decentralised permission-less blockchains are better seen as a huge employer-owned mutual (e.g., John Lewis), that votes on the firm's decision-making, while being unable to delegate decision-making to a board, nor even to recognize one another. Like an oversized board, the validators may try to agree on the price that should be set. However, as noted, the prospects of countless pseudonymous validators successfully agreeing either to boycott validation of low-margin blocks, or adopt new 'price-raising' protocols, appears far-fetched. In a sense, they might be seen as a gig-working co-operative who collectively determine the blockchain's offer to users (like Partners in a law firm), while individually having to follow the collectively determined protocols (like drivers on a ride-sharing platform). To the extent that they follow strict protocols in the gig-work they do for the blockchain, these validators would appear unlikely to be considered to be independent contractors (as, for example, is claimed in the case of ride-sharing platforms). If they are workers or employees, they would not face the risk of being accused of colluding with one another (this is being tested in the *United American Corp. v. Bitmain, Inc.* complaint).[7] However, whether they are employees or independent contractors, trying to control price-setting will, as noted above, be extremely challenging.

[7] Stylianou (2019).

4 Reasons to be Cheerful

During the tech-lash, techno-optimism or techno-utopian perspectives have become desperately unfashionable. This is perhaps unsurprising as the memory of ‘do no evil’ fades, and ‘extract the rewards that innovation deserves,’ or ‘rationally exploit market power’ prove both less snappy and somewhat underwhelming. In start contrast to the height of our previously towering ambition for the tech sector, the hope is now simply that they will refrain from abusive behaviours. Therefore, what follows is most likely ill-advised, hopelessly naïve, and may date extremely badly. However, where is the fun in reticence?

Let us begin by saying that like many innovative technologies before it, blockchain creates an opportunity to reduce prices, improve quality, and disrupt the market power of incumbent firms. It is a general-purpose technology that has multiple uses and can potentially impact a wide range of markets. While the most popular applications of blockchain have thus far been in the financial sector, the technology may substantially affect numerous other sectors, including legal services, notaries, data storage, energy, and transport. Indeed, it is already being used to improve global supply chains, and pilots are underway on its ability to authenticate the ownership of intellectual property rights, land rights, identity data, health records, online votes, pollution certificates, search query data, stock, pensions, insurance schemes and many other assets.

4.1 *Reducing Transaction Costs and Expanding Output*

Underlying this broad range of potential uses is the way in which a blockchain platform can create an efficient ‘marketplace’ of validators that cost a fraction of the price that trusted intermediaries are currently able to charge for their services. It is true that the issue of the energy required to power permission-less blockchains still needs to be solved (one existing blockchain currently absorbs the average daily power usage of Austria).[8] However, if a solution is possible, then the magnitude of the reductions in transaction costs will challenge both existing payment systems and existing intermediaries, creating opportunities for new entrants to thrive. In addition, this reduction in transaction costs in downstream markets may facilitate the adoption of new business models. For example, by allowing smaller firms and specialists to set themselves up as viable businesses to whom larger firms outsource work or functions, rather than keeping it in-house.

[8] Vincent (2019).

4.2 *Clashing with the Tech Titans*

One possibility that some have predicted is that blockchain will disrupt and replace the leading digital platforms. The two most interesting articulations of this theory are driven in the first case by the tokenisation process that many blockchains adopt, and secondly, by the potential that blockchains offer for practical steps that improve users' control of their data. We explore each of these below.

4.2.1 Tokenisation

The first version of this theory is that the offering of free tokens offers a costless way for new entrants to reimburse users for the value of the network effects they bring to the platform.[9] Indeed ideally, blockchains might seek to design protocols that target additional token-drops at influential users as they grow, for instance to target the points on the 'S-curve' of network adoption where a platform can take off or run out of steam. However, to do so early adopters would need to be willing to take a long-term view and water down the value of their own tokens in exchange for the uncertain prospect of the blockchain's growth.

This is an interesting addition to the entry strategies of a new entrant facing a dominant platform. In a sense this recognises that the tokens are investment securities that are being awarded with a view to the future value of the blockchain. However, it is also possible that a token simply offers a user a share of the added value that they are bringing to the network, and hence is not a speculative investment instrument any more than a discount for referring your friends and family would be. Nevertheless, given the move towards regulating ICOs as securities like stocks, bonds, and derivatives, we might in any case expect that the issuing of tokens by start-up blockchain platforms will quickly cease to be the straightforward process that it has been.

4.2.2 Creating a Decentralised Alternative to Digital Platforms

A second theory is that decentralised blockchains may offer an alternative to centralised digital platforms. It is certainly possible, for example, that the trust generated by a blockchain might mean that alternative trust building mechanisms such as rate-and-review systems may become obsolete. For example, where validation by a blockchain provides confidence in the authenticity of a product or automates the pay-out of an insurance claim in certain circumstances, the need for a crowd-sourced review of the reliability of a seller might not be necessary. However, blockchain technology does not itself offer matching or searching algorithms that

[9] Catalini and Tucker (2018).

drive many of the important cross-platform network effects that power these platforms.

For example, the matching function in general search is the algorithm that matches users' search queries with a webpage, the matching function in hotel-booking is the algorithm that matches users' search queries to hotels, and the matching function in professional, social, and telephone networks is the look-up that connects users to their peers, friends, and families. Without these matching functions, the user reviews offered by platforms are of little value. Therefore, to really challenge the digital platforms will therefore require that applications offering this functionality are built on the blockchain. If matching or searching applications that work on a blockchain are built by firms, this will risk simply reproducing the same bottleneck of access to the user that the existing platforms enjoy. Therefore, as Pike and Capobianco (2019) have explained, to challenge the platforms, a permission-less blockchain will need to develop within its protocols an application with that functionality. If this were possible, it would remove the bottleneck, or at least the market power over that bottleneck (for the reasons described in Sect. 3.1), provided that the decentralised blockchain remains decentralised and does not become concentrated over time. Such an application might be less nimble than corporate operated platforms, due to the potentially difficult process of changing the protocols on a permission-less blockchain. However, the efficiency advantage that it derives from operating without a rate-of-return target might enable it to thrive and access the same valuable network effects that private platforms enjoy (see Wikipedia).[10]

4.2.3 The Benevolent Market Power of a Decentralised Permission-Less Blockchain

This leads us to the benevolent market power of a decentralised permission-less blockchain. What does this mean? First, that if successful on a large scale, then a blockchain will likely have market power. It has the same cross-platform network effects that have proved a blessing to digital platforms and a curse for competitive intensity in the unregulated markets in which they swim. As is familiar, we can expect that users and validators will struggle to coordinate switching to better value platforms that preserve the network effects they obtain from the dominant platform. But, for this to be of a concern would require that those that control the blockchain can in fact control (raise) its price, or reduce quality, or execute an exclusionary foreclosure strategy. If instead, the blockchain is in essence uncontrollable, then it is strategically impotent. Permission-less blockchains might then be compared to platforms holding latent significant market power, but incapable of exercising it. They might become dominant platforms that follow common carrier requirements

[10] Mason (2015).

and offer valuable network effects, and a level playing field to all at an efficient price without even a regulator to ask them to do so.

Would this not be wonderful? The perfect reflection of European competition law's desire for an entity that exercises a special responsibility in its market dominance. Moreover, might such an entity provide an antidote to our often-disappointed aspirations for our own publicly owned enterprises? A collectively controlled cooperative without the bureaucracy, and one that does not have 'do not exploit' as a disposable mantra or principle, nor as a piece of code hidden inside its proprietary algorithm, but one which is instead actually incapable of exploiting.

Should the creation of such entities not make a fine example of a genuinely new inclusive (and not reheated) industrial policy? Indeed, might their development not embody the radical possibilities envisaged under the democratising stakeholder remedies approach of Hitzig et al. (2020)?[11] For instance, the CMA sponsored the development of open banking following the market investigation that identified the market was failing to work for consumers. Might agencies sponsor the development of permission-less blockchains in other failing markets? After all, while in the UK the BBC has long been a trusted state-owned solution to what is evidently a failing news market, the appetite in many countries for state-owned social networks, search engines, or digital retailers, is quite reasonably somewhere between limited and non-existent.

Alternatively, if competition agencies decide not to lead such radical efforts to remedy these failing markets, should other parts of government do so? Should innovation or industry ministries or productivity commissions make such entities the mission for their next-generation innovation policies? In such circumstances, competition agencies would in any case have a key role to play. In particular, it would be vitally important that they become vigilant in preventing the centralisation of validation capacity. Defending the decentralised nature of systemically important permission-less blockchains would be fundamental. Where it was not possible to defend the existing blockchain, this might involve a coordinated fork to create a new one. Similarly, if decentralised permission-less blockchains were to begin to break through, incumbent platforms, or rival permissioned blockchains may seek to foreclose and stifle their adoption. Competition agencies would therefore need to be vigilant in regard to such efforts and would need the option to use interim measures in regard to potentially anticompetitive conduct in order to close the barn door before the horse has bolted.

Incumbents and permissioned rivals may also attempt to stifle the development of decentralised permission-less blockchains by lobbying for disproportionate regulation of the technology. Precisely because of their decentralized nature, permission-less blockchains are unlikely to be effective at lobbying to defend themselves from such proposals (indeed this inability to lobby is another helpful characteristic). Competition agencies can and have been effective advocates against anticompetitive regulation, and the OECD Competition Assessment Toolkit

[11] Hitzig et al. (2020).

provides a useful framework for thinking through these questions. For example, it notes that policymakers should consider potential rent-seeking strategies when developing regulations of new technologies and pro-actively consult with those that are less effective at making their voice heard. As in other areas, regulatory sandpits may prove helpful for developing the necessary and proportionate regulatory requirements for these new technologies and businesses.

4.2.4 User Control of Their Data

Finally, another potential threat to the market power of digital platforms is that blockchain might facilitate the sale of data, and thereby break the zero-price floor that has protected many digital platforms from being undercut by new entry. For example, blockchains like that of the Tide Foundation allow users to store their data and to limit access to it to those that pay for it. This allows the data to be organised and sold directly to advertising agencies that want to target their advertising, or to firms that want to train a pricing algorithm, or to firms that want to implement a pricing algorithm (the functioning of which requires personalised identifiers in order to produce a personalised price).

Moreover, consumers might use blockchains to jointly sell their data via data unions that manage and monetise the collective data that consumers create.[12] To facilitate the growth of such unions, they might be constituted as civil society organisations rather than as commercial intermediaries, and membership might be by opt-out consent. This joint selling via blockchain might allow consumers to extract the value of the large externalities created when data is combined. This externality value presently accrues as advertising revenue for those platforms that receive the data in exchange for 'free' products. However, by bypassing or collectively selling access to data to these platforms, users might obtain that income to share amongst themselves. Perhaps this income might even provide a component of a broader universal basic income.

Users may of course sell their data without a Blockchain (see for instance the Solid initiative).[13] A blockchain might however help in a number of ways. First, it might give both parties confidence in the uniqueness or exclusivity of the access to the data that is sold (or in the number of licenses to that data). It might also require any other firm that wants the data (or a piece of it) to buy permission access from the holder of the data account in exchange for a micropayment. Alternatively, the user might share the data willingly, for instance if the data was their healthcare record, and they were happy to share this with their own doctor and any doctor who might treat them. Similarly, it might allow consumers to offer compensation should they later sell additional access to the data (thereby raising the initial price). If limits can be placed on the re-use of the accessed data (e.g., it is non-duplicable and self-erases

[12] Posner and Weyl (2018).

[13] CMA (2019, pp. 6–12).

after a specified period), it might even prevent a recipient of the data from running further analysis on the data without again compensating the user (again potentially using micropayments to keep the transactions economically worthwhile).

4.3 *Innovative Remedies*

Commercial products such as those discussed above might come to market themselves. However, where market studies identify that competition is not working well in digital markets, competition agencies may consider proactively facilitating or sponsoring the development of such products in the same way that the development of Open API standards in banking has been driven by competition agencies like the CMA. As noted above (Sect. 4.2.2) this might involve facilitating the development of decentralised permission-less blockchains to provide digital platforms. However, it might also apply in a whole range of other markets.

For instance, innovative remedies might include removing regulatory barriers to the use of blockchains to set-up trusted automated (robo-) switching services. This might for example include the switching of electricity accounts when the price is no longer the best available on the market (e.g., Flipper). These are already available without blockchain technology, but are more costly to operate, and as with a price comparison website, require a user to trust that the service is effective in its monitoring of market prices, and that it automatically switches on the basis of prices and not commissions. It might also work for services that switch social networks, search engines, browsers, or music streaming website when a sufficient number of friends and family make conditional decisions to make the same switch, or when a different provider with the same functionality offers a larger payment, better privacy conditions, or any other quality-enhancement that users value.

4.4 *Ways of Working*

A final opportunity from blockchain is the potential for competition agencies to innovate in their own ways of working. For instance, the development of industry blockchains may offer an opportunity to competition agencies to improve the effectiveness and efficiency of their investigations. Agencies with access to the blockchain might, as in the case of R3's platform, receive real-time information on the market at zero marginal cost to participants.

This might allow them to monitor markets, adherence to commitments, collect data for ongoing cases, and screen for suspicious patterns, all without imposing a burden on parties to respond to extensive information requests.

For example, where firms choose to move all, or most, of a market's transactions onto a blockchain (e.g., shipping or diamonds), an agency might then be able to observe, extract and store transaction prices and volumes directly. This data might then be used when merger investigations or antitrust complaints arise in the sector without imposing any burden on parties to respond to extensive information requests. The data might also be fed into the cartel screening tools that are being developed and adopted by competition agencies around the world (see for instance Cerebro in Brazil), which might in time allow for the development of self-learning capabilities. Finally, the data may also be useful for monitoring behavioral commitments that have been made by firms in the course of competition cases, for instance adherence to providing access on fair, reasonable and non-discriminatory terms.

5 Conclusion

The possible competition risks from permissioned blockchain are increasingly well recognised,[14] but the competitive opportunities from decentralised permission-less blockchains remain under-appreciated. Moreover, the opportunity for competition agencies and policymakers to facilitate through market investigation remedies or sponsorship, the emergence of decentralised permission-less blockchains as part of a pro-competitive industrial policy is considerable. We encourage all agencies and policymakers to distinguish between the two types of blockchain, and to be pro-active and ambitious and make the most of the pro-competitive opportunity that the technology may offer.

We are therefore pleased to see agencies such as the Autorité de la Concurrence leading the way by beginning to look at blockchain issues in their fintech sector inquiry.[15] We hope this will include a full assessment of the features of the market that prevent restrict or distort competition between Blockchain-powered fintech products and their more established rivals. Meanwhile the US Department of Justice have also signaled their interest in acting to prevent abusive conduct by incumbents that might seek to exclude or suppress the disruptive innovation offered by new Blockchain-powered business models.[16] This vigilance seems likely to be particularly important in the area of merger control where we know that the early acquisition of potential rivals by large digital platforms has become an established strategy that has, thus far, largely evaded scrutiny from competition agencies.[17] We therefore welcome the European Commission's examination of the Archipels blockchain project in France and Facebook's Libra project. We also hope that the recent steps taken by competition agencies to ensure they have the necessary flexibility to investigate the acquisition of high-value low-turnover blockchain-powered firms will be successful in addressing the risk of killer acquisitions. However, we note that the uncertainties in relation to blockchain technology are such that challenging

[14] Pike and Capobianco (2019, 2020), OECD (2018).

[15] Connor (2020).

[16] Delrahim (2020).

[17] OECD (2020).

such acquisitions under the existing framework will be extremely difficult. Therefore, we would identify blockchain-related mergers as an area that would particularly benefit from the increasing calls to revise the framework for assessing potential competition.[18]

Having said all of this, we do not claim to know whether blockchain will have the disruptive effect that it might. To be clear, if it does not fulfil its promise, then the above is entirely academic, at this stage, we just do not know. All we know is that if it does deliver on its promise, then there are reasons to be cheerful for those of us that place their hope in competitive answers to the riddle of promoting shared prosperity and inclusive growth.

References

Baker J, Farrell J, Gavil A, Gaynor M, Kades M, Katz M, Kimmelman G, Melamed D, Rose N, Salop S, Scott Morton F, Shapiro C (2020) Joint Response to the House Judiciary Committee on the State of Antitrust Law and Implications for Protecting Competition in Digital Markets. https://equitablegrowth.org/wpcontent/uploads/2020/04/Joint-Response-to-the-House-Judiciary-Committee-on-the-State-ofAntitrust-Law-and-Implications-for-Protecting-Competition-in-Digital-Markets.pdf

Caro de Sousa P, Pike C (2020) How soon is now? (October 2020). Competition law and policy debate, 2020, Available at SSRN: https://ssrn.com/abstract=3706772 or https://doi.org/10.2139/ssrn.3706772

Catalini C, Tucker C (2018) Antitrust and Costless Verification: An Optimistic and a Pessimistic View of the Implications of Blockchain Technology. MIT Sloan Research Paper No. 5523-18. Available at: http://ide.mit.edu/sites/default/files/publications/SSRN-id3199453.pdf

CMA (2019) Online Platforms and Digital Advertising, Market Study Interim Report, Competition & Markets Authority. Available at: https://assets.publishing.service.gov.uk/media/5dfa0580ed915d0933009761/Interim_report.pdf

Connor C (2020) France examines blockchain and cloud storage in fintech inquiry. Glob Compet Rev, May 20, 2020, Available at: https://globalcompetitionreview.com/france-examines-blockchain-and-cloud-storage-in-fintech-inquiry

Delrahim M (2020) "Never Break the Chain": Pursuing Antifragility in Antitrust Enforcement https://www.justice.gov/opa/speech/file/1310506/download

Hitzig Z, Meagher M, Veiga A, Weyl EG (2020) Economic Democracy and Market Power, Antitrust Chronicle. Competition Policy International, April 2020

Jayachandran P (2017) The Difference between Public and Private Blockchain, Blockchain Unleashed: IBM Blockchain Blog, 31 May. www.ibm.com/blogs/blockchain/2017/05/thedifference-between-public-and-private-blockchain/

Libra (2020) White Paper, v2.0. Libra Association Members, available at: https://libra.org/en-US/wp-content/uploads/sites/23/2020/04/Libra_WhitePaperV2_April2020.pdf

Mason P (2015) PostCapitalism: a guide to our future. Allen Lane, New York

Motta M, Peitz M (2020) Big Tech Mergers. https://www.crctr224.de/en/research-output/discussion-papers/discussion-paper-archive/2020/bigtech-mergers-massimo-motta-martin-peitz

Nakamoto S (2008) A peer-to-peer electronic cash system. Bitcoin. Available at: https://bitcoin.org/bitcoin.pdf

[18] Caro de Sousa and Pike (2020), Motta and Peitz (2020), Valletti (2018) and Baker et al. (2020).

OECD (2018) Executive Summary of the hearing on Blockchain and Competition Policy. Available at: https://one.oecd.org/document/DAF/COMP/M(2018)1/ANN8/FINAL/en/pdf

OECD (2020) Start-ups, Killer Acquisitions and Merger Control – Background Note. https://one.oecd.org/document/DAF/COMP(2020)5/en/pdf

Pike C, Capobianco A (2019) Antitrust and the trust machine. Symposium: Artificial Intelligence & Blockchain. Compet Law Policy Debate 5(3)

Pike C, Capobianco A (2020) Antitrust and the Trust Machine, 2020, OECD https://papers.ssrn.com/sol3/papers.cfm?abstract_id=3940527

Posner E, Weyl EG (2018) Radical markets: uprooting capitalism and democracy for a just society. Princeton University Press

Shrier DL (2020) Basic Blockchain: what it is and how it will transform the way we work and live. Robinson, London

Stylianou, K. (2019) What can the first blockchain antitrust case teach us about the crypto economy? Harv J Law Technol Digest. Available at: https://jolt.law.harvard.edu/digest/what-can-the-first-blockchain-antitrust-case-teach-us-about-the-crypto-economy

Valletti T (2018) Après moi, le déluge! Tech Giants in the Digital Age, Presentation. https://ecp.crai.com/wp-content/uploads/2018/12/Tommaso-Valletti-2018.pdf

Vincent J (2019) Bitcoin consumes more energy than Switzerland, according to new estimate. The Verge, July 4, 2019. Available at: https://www.theverge.com/2019/7/4/20682109/bitcoin-energy-consumption-annual-calculation-cambridge-index-cbeci-country-comparison

Can Antitrust Trust Blockchain?

Giovanna Massarotto

Abstract Although blockchain is decentralized by designed, today this technology is in practice in the hands of few corporations—antitrust can be crucial in restoring blockchain's decentralization. Having provided a toolkit to navigate into the blockchain ecosystem of Distributed Ledger Technologies (DLT), Section 3 investigates the relation between competition and blockchain. *Is blockchain the real game-changer for today's centralized digital markets?* Section 3 explores the exploitation of DLT as a tool to enforce antitrust principles more efficiently in today's tech-digital economy. In particular, it will be analyzed if blockchain and DLT, in general, can be considered as revolutionary progress also in the context of antitrust. Section 4 bears the question as to whether blockchain raises antitrust concerns and how to deal with them. Technologies are not the driver of anticompetitive conduct, but forms of government surveillance, such as antitrust, are fundamental for keeping people's trust in new advanced technologies.

1 Introduction

Blockchain brings the discussion between technology and policy back. Antitrust is the first arm of government regulation. The government needs to stay ahead of technologies to be effective in today's fast-moving technological era—blockchain is the new testing ground. Antitrust needs to protect blockchain technologies from anticompetitive conduct and exploit the identical blockchain's ingenuity to be effective. The magnitude of blockchain is enormous, but it will create more harm than benefit if abused and left totally uncontrolled as any powerful tool.

Blockchain should bring a sense of wonder to people in the field of antitrust. At least, I found myself reasonably curious about this technology, as blockchain can give the edge antitrust needs. Blockchain can decentralize today's centralized

G. Massarotto (✉)
Center for Technology, Innovation and Competition (CTIC), University of Pennsylvania, Philadelphia, PA, USA
e-mail: gmassa@law.upenn.edu

A. Portuese (ed.), *Algorithmic Antitrust*, Economic Analysis of Law in European Legal Scholarship 12, https://doi.org/10.1007/978-3-030-85859-9_6

platforms governed by the so-called *Big-Tech*. On the other hand, *smart contracts* that run in an antitrust blockchain, can auto-enforce most of antitrust remedies and rules. In other words, as explored throughout the chapter, blockchain technologies can be what antitrust needs to tackle its present challenges: *Big Tech* and data-driven markets[1]. However, blockchain technology is far from being perfect. Permissioned and closed blockchains can, for example, create the perfect conditions for competitors to engage in cartels; smart contracts, on the other hand, can automatize the punishment for any cartel's deviation. Although blockchain is decentralized by designed, today this technology is in practice in the hands of few corporations—antitrust can be crucial in restoring blockchain's decentralization[2].

Having provided a toolkit to navigate into the blockchain ecosystem of Distributed Ledger Technologies (DLT), Section 3 investigates the relation between competition and blockchain. *Is blockchain the real game-changer for today's centralized digital markets?* Section 3 explores the exploitation of DLT as a tool to enforce antitrust principles more efficiently in today's tech-digital economy. In particular, it will be analyzed if blockchain and DLT, in general, can be considered as revolutionary progress also in the context of antitrust[3]. Section 4 bears the question as to whether blockchain raises antitrust concerns and how to deal with them. Technologies are not the driver of anticompetitive conduct, but forms of government surveillance, such as antitrust, are fundamental for keeping people's trust in new advanced technologies[4].

2 Distributed Ledger Technologies Toolkit

Blockchain is a technology that emerged in 2008 with the introduction of bitcoin, in a time where the bank system was facing one of the worst crises ever[5]. To recognize the potentialities and possible antitrust concerns behind this technology, it is necessary to analyze its origin, characteristics, applications, and its most recent developments. Blockchain, along with cryptocurrencies and smart contracts, is part of the so-called *Distributed Ledger Technologies* (DLT)[6] analyzed here. Section 2 starts with an overview of blockchain origin and DLT, focusing on blockchain, blockchain tokens and smart contracts. It proceeds with the investigation of the most recent developments and applications of DLT and how this technology has the potential to revolutionize markets yet again.

[1] Massarotto (2019a).

[2] Massarotto (2019b, 2020a).

[3] Id.

[4] Massarotto (2019b); Werbach (2018).

[5] Massarotto (2020b).

[6] Tasca and Tessone (2019).

2.1 Blockchain Origin

There is nothing more intriguing than studying the origin of blockchain, which dates back to the 1990s and the rise of the *Cryptoanarchy* movement[7]. The main idea that drives the Cryptoanarchy movement is that computer technology can deal with policies, such as privacy, security, and economic policies, much better than governments[8]. In 1988, Timothy C. May, who is considered the father of the Cryptoanarchy movement, wrote the "Crypto Anarchist Manifesto"[9]. In his Manifesto, May explains how cryptography hardcoded into computer protocols (*cryptographic protocols*) can completely reshape "*the nature of government regulation, the ability to tax and control economic interactions, [and] the ability to keep information secret [protecting privacy]*"[10] without any government interventions. The anarchy is here conceptualized not as total chaos or disorder, but rather as the absence of a central government[11]. Notably, the government creates and enforces rules to preserve justice and people's freedom; computer technologies can create self-enforcing rules without involving the government[12].

Another key figure in the cryptoanarchy movement is David Chaum who created e-cash, the predecessor of bitcoin. E-cash was presented in 1983 as anonymous electronic money that would enable people to spend digital money without the need of having a bank account. Privacy and security would have been protected utilizing public key cryptography, which is a cryptographic system based on pairs of keys: a private and public key. Data is encrypted and security is preserved maintaining only the private key secret. Conversely, the public key can be openly shared because only the private key owner can decrypt data and create the digital signature.

Although e-cash was a promising project, we need to wait for the bank crisis of 2008 to see the idea of using anonymous electronic money to expand. In addition to being anonymous and digital, bitcoin is decentralized and does not rely on the bank system. Bitcoin uses a peer-to-peer network called *blockchain network* as platform for bitcoin transactions, ensuring anonymity and security through the same public key cryptography adopted in e-cash. Blockchain is not the first peer-to-peer network. Notable examples are BitTorrent and Napster[13], but in addition to sharing data blockchain peer-to-peer network stores data.

[7] Wright and De Filippi (2018).

[8] May (1994).

[9] May (1988).

[10] Id.

[11] May (1994).

[12] Ou (2017).

[13] Bashir (2017).

2.2 Blockchains

2.2.1 Bitcoin Blockchain

In November 2008, an anonymous person (or group of people) under the name of Satoshi Nakamoto introduced a distributed system for electronic transactions, which included Bitcoin and blockchain[14]. Blockchain seems to be what the cryptoanarchy movement dreamt about. Blockchain is built on the idea of a fully decentralized peer-to-peer network, where no one controls the blockchain. It is a set of rules enshrined in a computer protocol that governs the blockchain network. If everybody follows the rules, everybody wins and the blockchain functions properly.

The bitcoin blockchain protocol sets a consensus mechanism known as *Proof of Work* (PoW) to transfer bitcoins. Instead of having banks that validate a transaction, the PoW requires participants in the blockchain network to resolve a computational problem. The first participant that finds the solution broadcasts it to the blockchain network. Only when the majority of participants agree on the solution is the transaction validated and stored in a block that becomes part of the chain. Thanks to public key cryptography (PKC) the parties of the transaction remain unknown. The public key, which is broadcasted to the network, is never attached to the owner's real name. The identity of Satoshi Nakamoto is still unknown, showing the validity of cryptography in protecting users' identity and privacy. Many people in the field suspect that the same cryptoanarchy movement is behind the creation of bitcoin and blockchain.

Blockchain safety is another key component of this technology. Blockchain safety is guaranteed by using a vast number of computers called nodes. A cyber-attack in a blockchain would require striking almost all copies of the ledger simultaneously (hence the blockchain network) and would cost billions of dollars[15]. In addition, as Nakamoto observed, "*[t]o modify a past block, an attacker would have to redo the proof-of-work of the block and all blocks after it and then catch up with and surpass the work of the honest nodes*"[16]. Introduced as technology to exchange bitcoins, blockchain is now adopted in a variety of industries, from cryptocurrency to social applications and consumer goods[17]. Walmart, for example, adopted blockchain in its supply chain to track goods, which enabled Walmart to do what usually was performed in 7 days in 2.2 seconds[18]. In summary, blockchain can be used to record and store financial transactions and "*virtually everything of value*"[19] bypassing third intermediaries, which in the case of bitcoins means banks. DLT eco-system now includes a plethora of different blockchains (*e.g.*, private, and

---

[14] Nakamoto (2008).

[15] Massarotto (2019b).

[16] Nakamoto (2008), p. 3.

[17] Massarotto (2020a); UCL CBT (2019).

[18] UCL CBT Supply Chain Report (2019); Hyperledger (2019).

[19] Tapscott and Tapscott (2016).

permissioned blockchains) and emerging technologies, including smart contracts and blockchain tokens explored in the following.

2.2.2 Public, Private and Permissioned Blockchains

Bitcoin blockchain is the very first blockchain, introduced in 2008. But over the years, software developers have built up a variety of different types of blockchain: the main distinction is between public and private blockchains. Bitcoin blockchain is a public blockchain. This means that it is open and free to anybody wants to participate in the blockchain network. Private blockchains, instead, are closed networks and you need to be invited to participate in the chain. Both public and private blockchains can define different permission levels for participants creating a kind of hierarchical authority[20]. For example, all participants can have read access, while only a pre-select set of nodes has the permission to write and manage the blockchain[21]. Forms of private permissioned blockchains especially attract banks, government department, and enterprises interested in implementing blockchain as a kind of internal infrastructure similar to an intranet, but that function as a decentralized database. It is common to hear that "*public blockchains are to the internet as private blockchains is to the intranet,*"[22] to exemplify the key difference.

Permissioned blockchains are not very different from traditional databases. A single organization adopts private blockchains. Conversely, a blockchain deployed across multiple organizations is called a consortium blockchain. In a consortium blockchain, pre-authorized nodes control the consensus process while the read access may be public or limited to specific participants. R3 can be a good example of a blockchain consortium. This company leads over three hundred companies engaged in developing distributed applications on the top of Corda, called CorApp for adoption across industries, including financial services, trade finance, healthcare and digital access. Corda is an open-source distributed ledger platform, which is not based on the concept of blocks containing transactions (is not correctly a blockchain) but has features of blockchain, such as consensus, authentication, validity, and immutability. Corda has been designed to perform complex transactions in the financial industry with restricted access to data[23]. Of course, private blockchains are the most flexible in terms of configuration and inherently fast as a single organization governs and hosts the network of blockchain participants. However, there is not a real decentralization in this type of blockchain, and they have been adopted for years[24]—public blockchain is the real game-changer.

[20] Tasca and Tessone (2019).

[21] European Commission (2019).

[22] Eichholz (2017).

[23] R3 (2020); Bashir (2017).

[24] Schneier (2019b).

All these types of blockchains are characterized by a blockchain platform, namely the software applied to run a blockchain, which includes: "*the blockchain client software for processing nodes, the local data store for nodes, and any alternative clients to access the blockchain network.*"[25] The client software is necessary in any blockchain to enable processing nodes to operate in the network, transmitting, for example, transactions and creating blocks.

2.2.3 Smart Contracts and Ethereum

In addition to new kinds of blockchains, new tools enriched the DLT ecosystem. Computer programs called "smart contracts" enable the blockchain to perform more sophisticated tasks than simply recording and storing data in the form of blocks on a chain[26]. Smart contracts can administer the ownership of any assets stored on a blockchain. They generally execute an order if certain conditions are met and can be employed to self-execute parts of legal contracts. However, there is an open discussion on the legality of smart contracts. I believe that smart contracts simply reflect a new form of contract. Different from an oral or written contract, in a smart contract the terms of a contract are codified into a computer program and self-executed. From a legal perspective, the main issue related to smart contracts is that the code is "*deterministic and immutable once deployed*"[27]. Thus, there is no room for interpretation or modification of the terms of the contract. However, the smart contract might set that the code will change if certain conditions occur. In any case, the more details and instructions you write in the smart contract code, the more likely it is that your automated contract properly functions.

Smart contracts are also used to connect decentralized applications (DApps) to the blockchain. Unlike traditional applications (apps) that adopt centralized servers to store and process data, DApps use decentralized peer-to-peer networks—most DApps run on a blockchain. The idea of DApps gained popularity with Ethereum, a blockchain platform focused on adopting smart contracts to perform services without requiring a third-party intermediary. Ethereum is a public blockchain—the second in popularity and value after the bitcoin blockchain—launched in 2015, that runs not just "*send and receive Bitcoin*", but a disparate set of instructions thanks to the employment of smart contracts. Ethereum has its own currency, Ether (ETH) and is a multi-services platform that adopts a public blockchain and smart contracts to offer various new decentralized applications. In November 2019, there were 2652 DApps built on Ethereum versus about 4000 DApps in total[28]. Every operation in the Ethereum platform, which can be a transaction or the performance of a smart contract, requires some amount of gas. Ethereum gas is the unit that determines

---

[25] Xu et al. (2019), p. 7.

[26] Clack et al. (2016).

[27] Xu et al. (2019), p. 7.

[28] 2019 Dapp Market Report (2020).

the amount of computational effort necessary to perform a specific operation. There is not a fixed price for the gas, but it depends on the network traffic having more transactions competing to be contained in a block.

Smart contracts can be combined to create a *Decentralized Autonomous Organization* (DAO), namely an organization entirely governed by smart contracts or a protocol discussed in Sect. 4.1[29]. In contrast to traditional companies, a DAO is not structured in a top-down manner, with various layers of management and bureaucratic processes. In a DAO, all participants agree on codified rules self-executed through smart contracts, rather than traditional legal contracts enforced by law enforcers. Some countries, for example Austria, are in favor of classifying DAOs as civil law partnerships subject to the related law. In short, in a blockchain all participants that are part of the network follow the rules self-executed by smart contracts or defined in a protocol. This enables reduced transaction costs of management, ensuring a high level of transparency. As we will explore in Sect. 3.2, smart contracts can turn out to be valuable antitrust enforcement tools.

2.2.4 Blockchain Tokens

Again, blockchain is the infrastructure that enables recording and storing "*virtually everything of value*"[30] in a cheaper and safer way thanks to a peer-to-peer network and cryptography. What you transfer in a blockchain is usually called a "*token*," hence an asset and/or right collectively controlled by a network of computers, which can be a blockchain network, or other DLT. Tokens are usually managed by smart contracts and run in a specific blockchain; they do not run across different blockchain networks. As opposed to cryptocurrencies, such as Bitcoin and Ether, tokens are usually implemented on the top of a blockchain platform through smart contracts features and not directly in the core platform of a blockchain. This means that, in contrast to tokens, cryptocurrencies are independent from a particular platform and can be used outside their native environment as a form of currency.

Usually tokens are distinguished into "*utility tokens*" or "*security tokens*." Utility tokens can include coins or user tokens that give the holder the right to utilize the network, use products or services offered by a company, or vote to take advantage of the network. A company usually launches an Initial Coin Offering (ICO), in which tokens are issued. Different from an Initial Public Offering (IPO), through an ICO you acquire tokens instead of stocks and these tokens rely on a blockchain rather than traditional backers with a centralized ledger. Security tokens is very similar to traditional security—the only differences are that security tokens' ownership is confirmed through blockchain transactions and you can have fractional ownership[31]. Security tokens is issued through a Security Token Offering (STO), which was

[29] Kolber (2018).

[30] Tapscott and Tapscott (2016).

[31] Shilov (2019).

proposed in 2017 in the United States. Security tokens are under the supervision of the Securities and Exchange Commission (SEC) to improve the protection of investors[32]. That said, the distinction between security tokens and utility tokens, as well as an ICO and an STO, is controversial. In the USA, a token that passes the so-called "*Howey Test*" falls within the definition of security token and it is subject to the SEC regulation. Many developers simply call "*utility tokens*" something that is not to escape government regulation and taxes[33].

2.2.5 Recent Developments in DLT

In 10 years the DLT ecosystem has completely changed. As outlined above, Bitcoin blockchain is only one of the numerous blockchains now in use, which is adopted to transfer potentially everything—not only cryptocurrencies. Bitcoin blockchain is considered the first generation of blockchain technology (Blockchain 1.0) used to merely transfer cryptographic currencies, such as bitcoins. Bitcoin blockchain was a breakthrough technology. However, it showed some technical limitations, especially in terms of scalability and adaptability. Bitcoin blockchain takes around 10 min to create a new block that can accommodate approximately an average of 2700 transactions. On the other hand, Visa performs an average of 24,000 transactions per second with a peak of about 50,000.

Ethereum led the second generation (Blockchain 2.0) with the exploitation of smart contracts, the development of DApps and token assets, including financial services. In other words, Blockchain 2.0 expanded the implementation of DLT applications for general industries, such as government, media, health, justice, and the arts. Although the second generation of blockchain made the DLT eco-system more sophisticated with new tools and applications, it did not resolve the main technical limitations underlying DLT. We need to look at the third generation (Blockchain 3.0) to see some real improvements in that sense.

Blockchain 3.0 is recognized as the third generation of blockchain that has tackled the challenges raised in Blockchain 1.0 and 2.0. generations: scalability and interoperability. For example, Cardano, IOTA and Nano fall within the Blockchain 3.0. Cardano uses the Proof of Stake (PoS) protocol to solve the issues of scalability and sustainability, instead of PoW, and adds interoperability among different blockchains. PoS means that the participant in the blockchain network can mine or validate a block is determined according to its wealth (stake). In other words, the "*miner*" or "*validator*" is selected based on how many coins it holds. This means that a miner is subject to a pre-approval, and there is no block reward, but the miner receives a transaction fee. PoS seems to be more energy-efficient as it does not require spending massive amounts of energy to resolve the computational problem required by the PoW. Cardano adopts PoS. Cardano is developed in two layers to

[32]Hassani et al. (2019).

[33]PwC and Crypto Valley (2019).

improve scalability and interoperability: one for the settlement of transactions (the settlement layer) and one for computing smart contracts and DApps (computational layer). This more sophisticated architecture aims to facilitate modifications on the consensus protocol without manipulating both layers.

The issue of scalability has also been addressed through the so-called *lightning network*, which is based on a payment channel to perform transactions in a blockchain platform in a faster and cheaper way[34]. In short, the lightning network creates a micropayment channel that enables one to send large amounts of money to another party in a decentralized fashion. Parties pay a fee only once and can transact back and forth without paying fees to *miners*. As Poon and Dryja observed, these channels "*are real bitcoin transactions*", not a separate "*network on top of bitcoin*"[35]. Parties sign a balance sheet that includes each transaction; once their transactions are completed, the parties pay to close the channel[36]. In summary, Blockchain 3.0 made blockchain infrastructure more efficient and flexible for multiple adoptions[37]. It is now possible to envision a new generation of blockchain, but the innovation that will bring it about is still being investigated. Having explored the origin, the main characteristics, and the applications related to DLT, you are now prepared to embark on the exploration of antitrust and competition as it relates to DLT.

3 DLT and for Competition

As outlined in Sect. 2, the diversity of DLT applications is breathtaking. From bitcoin blockchain, we now benefit from an extremely wide portfolio of DLT solutions, which compete with each other and traditional centralized platforms[38]. DLTs usually offer more efficient alternatives than centralized platforms in terms of security and costs. In blockchain, the possibility of losing information is basically zero, as information is stored on a number of computers and synchronized ledger copies. Transparency increases without compromising privacy by adopting encrypted systems, such as PKC, or more sophisticated mechanisms like confidential computing. Usually, service providers encrypt data when data is transferred and stored; data is typically not encrypted when in use. Confidential computing aims to secure data exactly when processes in memory, hence data is in use. The Confidential Consortium Framework (CCF) is an open-source project based on Microsoft Azure Engineering that builds highly secure, available and performant applications through confidential blockchain networks (Microsoft n.d.).

---

[34] Poon and Dryja (2016).

[35] Id, p. 4.

[36] What is Bitcoin's (2018).

[37] Bashir (2017).

[38] Werbach (2018).

Section 3 investigates blockchain and competition from two different perspectives. Section 3.1 explores how blockchain platforms can compete with present centralized online platforms that today raise the most critical issues in the context of antitrust. Twenty years ago, the Internet platform enabled markets to shift from physical platforms to digital platforms, reaching people worldwide by saving time, money and gaining in efficiency compared to physical infrastructures. As the Internet did 20 years ago, blockchain can change markets yet again. The shift from centralized to decentralized blockchain-based platforms is likely to bring in a new era marked by this technology—the *Blockchain Era*[39] Section 3.2 dives into the exploration of how antitrust enforcers can exploit DLT as a tool to enforce antitrust principles with a focus on data-driven markets.

3.1 From Centralized to Decentralized Platforms

3.1.1 The Internet Centralization

Today the Internet appears to be highly centralized. Large technology companies—known as *Big Tech*—found creative ways to become necessary intermediaries between the users and the Web, which is now critically centralized[40]. In 2020, Facebook reached 2.6 billion monthly active users[41], and Google Search is the undisputed leader of search engines with a worldwide market share of over eighty-seven percent[42].

Like the end of the nineteenth century when Rockefeller, a private businessperson, controlled the most valuable resource—oil—today, a few corporations are known as *Big Tech* control the data business, recalling the threat of private monopolies in crucial industries[43]. Data is the fuel that today runs machine-learning algorithms (MLA), which is the main application of Artificial Intelligence (AI), a business that all companies are now jumping into. As a result, the value of data has surpassed that of oil[44]. Consequently, the issue of *Big Tech* is increasingly relevant for antitrust agencies because the centralization of the Internet *de facto* restrains competition in today's most crucial industry[45]. In addition, we have to consider that the same *Big Tech* are now building their own Internet infrastructure and can potentially monopolize all aspects of the Internet marketplace. Google's "*Curie*"

---

[39] Massarotto (2020a).

[40] Massarotto (2019b).

[41] Statista (2020a).

[42] Statista (2020b).

[43] Massarotto (2018).

[44] Massarotto (2018); Bhageshpur (2019).

[45] Massarotto (2020b).

project is only one example[46], and blockchain relies on the Internet. To date, the U.S. and EU antitrust agencies have shown very different approaches in dealing with digital and data-driven markets. While the U.S. antitrust enforcers are criticized for being excessively lax, the EU antitrust authorities seem to be very prone to sanction large high-tech companies for monopolizing crucial digital markets[47]. The US and EU Google cases clearly show this diversity in approach and no antitrust action at all, or heavy fines seem to be an arguable solution.

An argument here is made that DLT can effectively compete with today's centralized platform by reducing the power of *Big Tech* and restoring the Web's decentralization[48]. DLTs are decentralized by design. This means that information is distributed in a decentralized ledger where anyone (in case of public blockchains), or selected participants (in case of private and permissioned blockchains) can have access and participate in the chain[49]. This is what mainly distinguishes blockchain from a traditional database (e.g., Google Drive). However, not all decentralized databases are necessarily blockchains. In 2016, for example, Sir Tim Berners Lee, the founder of the Web, introduced Solid: a project based on a decentralized platform where data of each user are stored. Through its decentralized platform, Solid promises to enable each user to have full control of his data and better protect privacy. Although decentralized, Solid is not a blockchain; data are stored in "*pods*" and there is not a consensus mechanism to govern the Solid platform. This is why some doubt that Solid is effectively a decentralized platform[50]. However, projects like Solid compete with DLT and need to be considered in the discussion of DLT and competition.

Blockchain can promote the decentralization process of the Web and bypass third intermediaries, which in case of bitcoins are banks. Thus, the adoption of blockchain potentially makes present services and goods cheaper by having the same consumers/user's part of the chain to benefit from network effects that one could not experience as a single individual. Anyone can create and participate in a decentralized public blockchain network, like anyone can create a buyer group to acquire some specific products bypassing, for example supermarkets[51]. Blockchain is known for bitcoin and cryptocurrency but can be used to store and transfer everything that has a value, for example data, bypassing any kind of intermediary, including today's centralized databases. Through a blockchain, data can be stored in multiple computers, which constitute the blockchain network, by increasing security and ensuring the same access to data to all the blockchain participants. Therefore, blockchain architecture can enable each Internet user to have the same knowledge of data transferred through the Internet and own and control potentially all its personal

[46] Submarine Cable Network (2020).

[47] Massarotto (2020c).

[48] Massarotto (2020a).

[49] Catalini and Tucker (2018); Lianos (2018).

[50] Dujmovic (2018).

[51] Massarotto (2019b).

data stored in a blockchain. Everything is tracked in a blockchain and each user can verify and control its data anytime on the Internet through the adoption of a private key. Privacy can be better protected than existing regulation by means of PKC and confidential computing solutions[52].

Theoretically, any regulators can exploit blockchain technologies to guarantee a transparent system that better ensures privacy and security to both companies and any consumers affected by the related industry and regulation[53]. In other words, DLT can both effectively regulate the data industry and tackle today's main antitrust concern—the Internet centralization and the monopoly power of *Big Tech*[54]. In addition, DLT increases transparency among blockchain users, potentially making any services and goods cheaper.

Today, corporations in any industry have successfully completed DLT projects and are constantly working on improving these technologies. Thus, DLT magnitude is expected to grow exponentially in the next few years by providing increasingly sophisticated solutions to companies, consumers, and the same institutions. However, as explored in Sect. 4, DLT need antitrust to grow and become a fundamental component of our economy. DLT are subject to anticompetitive conduct that can compromise their key characteristic—*decentralization*. DLT should not be immune from the antitrust scrutiny to prevent engagement in anticompetitive behavior to profit beyond that attainable in open and free markets. Antitrust will be crucial in marking the transition from centralized to decentralized platforms viable[55].

3.1.2 Is It the Time for a Blockchain Era?

> In a few years, men will be able to communicate more effectively through a machine than face to face—J.C.R. Licklider and Robert Taylor

This statement dates back not to the 1990s, but to 1968 when the Internet pioneers wrote "*The Computer as a Communication Device*" paper[56], which set the tone for the creation of the most critical means of communication ever. Since the 1990s, the Internet has critically changed our daily lives, impacting every economic sector and situation. Will blockchain be the next cutting-edge technology that will revolutionize our economy and daily life again?

An argument is made here that DLT has the potential to change market paradigms again, bringing us into the *Blockchain Era*. The similarities between a public blockchain and the Web are compelling and will be explored to predict the future development of the blockchain ecosystem. Again, the creation of the Internet dates

[52] Massarotto (2020a).

[53] Id.

[54] Massarotto (2020c).

[55] Massarotto (2019b).

[56] Licklider and Taylor (1968).

back 1968, but the real game-changer was the World Wide Web (Web) in the nineties. Sir Tim Berners Lee, a computer engineer of CERN, created the Web due to his frustration to switch from one computer to another to get information. Tim Berners Lee also recounts that he often had "*to learn a different program for each computer*"[57]. Interoperability is the real power of the Web[58]. In short, the Web is a set of open protocols and standards—the Hypertext Transfer Protocol (HTTP) and HyperText Markup Language (HTML)—similar to those that we have explored for blockchains. These open protocols and standards enabled a user to switch from one site to another smoothly.

Today blockchains are running on different protocols without being interconnected, similar to the Internet situation before the advent of the Web. But soon the situation might change. Like Tim Berners-Lee in 1990, someone could set open and free protocols in a public blockchain that enable interoperability among different platforms. Like the Web, these open protocols and standards defined for blockchain could set the tone for a universal open blockchain where existing and future blockchain goods and services can run[59]. The founder of the Web decided to release and make available on a royalty free-basis the code underlying the Web by recognizing that this was the reason the Web took-off. History has later confirmed his thoughts. In the mid-90s Microsoft, for example, developed Blackbird, a proprietary version of the Web, which was offered as an alternative to HTML for a brief time. Blackbird was used to run the Microsoft Network (MSN), but it was cancelled since the overwhelming adoption of the HTTP and HTML standards.

3.1.3 Blockchain Standards

The definition of blockchain standards is compelling. However, there are many issues behind the creation of these universal standards for blockchains. Ethereum, for example, created *Enterprise Ethereum Alliance (EEA)*, a member-driven standards organization connected with large corporations, including Intel, Microsoft, academics, and start-ups. EEA develops open blockchain specifications to promote harmonization and interoperability for businesses and consumers worldwide. However, there are some concerns about EEA and the development of these standards, since Ethereum does not appear to be fully decentralized[60]. As outlined in Sect. 2, the Ethereum ecosystem relies on Gas, and the decision to hard-fork the protocol in 2016 to deal with the Ethereum DAO hacker attack questions Ethereum decentralization[61]. Therefore, the issue of interoperability among different platforms would

[57] Id.

[58] Yu (2007).

[59] Massarotto (2020a).

[60] Canellis (2019).

[61] Kolber (2018); Werbach and Cornell (2019).

likely remain unchanged by means of these sorts of standards. Each platform is likely to promote its own standards.

However, the issue of standardization in the context of blockchain is undoubtedly of primary importance. Some envision the possibility of defining standard essential patents (SEPs) for blockchains subject to FRAND (*Fair Reasonable and Non-Discriminatory*) licensing obligations[62]. SEPs are defined by Standard Setting Organisations (SSOs), such as the European Telecommunications Standards Institute (ETSI) and the Institute of Electrical and Electronic Engineers (IEEE). SSOs develop worldwide standards for information and communications technologies, including Global Systems for Mobile Communications (GSM), Wideband Code Division Multiple Access (WCDMA) and the "*Wi-Fi*" technologies, namely a set of standards for wireless local area networks (W-LAN) (http://www.ieee.org/about/today/at_a_glance.html).

The GSM is also known as 2G technology and WCDMA as 3G technology. When a SSO defines a technology as a standard, the use of the related patent becomes essential, and the patent holders agree to license the standard to anyone under the FRAND terms[63]. The ambiguity of the term FRAND and its meaning raised the opportunity for companies to engage in patent "*hold-up*" often leading to costly and time-consuming litigations[64]. The Patent Assertion Entities (PAEs), which are companies that acquire patents but do not practice them by generating revenues through license fees, royalty, and damages compensations (European Commission, *Patent Assertion Entities in Europe*)[65], were often accused of "*patent hold-up*"[66]. A study conducted in 2012 revealed that Patent Assertion Entities (PAEs) litigations, which traditionally involve SEPs, corresponded to $29 billion in 2011 in the USA[67]; the situation looks quite similar in Europe. This is why we need to consider with caution the adoption of this kind of standardization process in the discussion of defining standards for blockchain. In other words, we need to balance the need for interoperability among blockchain platforms with a standardization process that can lead to the risk of patent hold-up or other forms of abuse[68].

Another way to define standards is through the creation of a consortium similar to W3C, which Tim Berners Lee built after designing the Web to develop new and improvements of the Web's standards and protocols. Today many entities, including Amazon, Apple, MIT, and Stanford University, have joined W3C in the development of Web standards, which are publicly available free of charge. However, this kind of standardization process also casts some doubts as some of the largest Silicon

---

[62] Sung (2018).

[63] Sidak (2013).

[64] Blair and Sokol (2017).

[65] Thumm and Gabison (2016).

[66] Massarotto (2016).

[67] Bessen and Meurer (2014); Bharadwaj et al. (2018).

[68] Lianos (2018).

Valley corporations, including Google and Microsoft, joined the consortium by recommending debatable standards, such as the EME[69].

Standardization is usually developed when a technology reaches a mature stadium to decrease switching costs. In its third generation we can confidently argue that today, blockchain is a mature technology. The issue of blockchain standards will certainly be one of the most critical in the development of DLT. Antitrust enforcers should oversee the standardization process, providing any feedback. Many antitrust cases related to information technology (IT), such as Microsoft and Intel, concerned the issue of interoperability and patent licensing. There is much to learn that we can use from previous IT antitrust cases in the development of blockchain. Blockchain can revolutionize our daily life like the Internet did 20 years ago. Alternatively, as Prof. Werback observed, blockchain will be "*just the way that all organizations eventually do what they do more efficiently*".

3.2 DLT as Antitrust Tool

DLT, in particular blockchain and smart contracts, can turn out to be a valuable tool to enforce antitrust law by improving the antitrust enforcement from various aspects. For example, one of the primary antitrust concerns is related to the costs associated with monitoring companies' compliance with antitrust remedies. These remedies, which most of the time are enshrined in antitrust consent decisions, can be automated by means of smart contracts[70]. Not all antitrust remedies need to or can necessarily be automated, but certainly many of them do. For example, in August 2010 the Federal Trade Commission (FTC) settled the Intel case with a consent decree[71], which imposed on Intel to:

- "*extend Via's x86 licensing agreement for five years*" which would have otherwise expired in 2013;
- "*maintain a key interface, known as the PCI Express Bus, for at least six years in a way that will not limit the performance of graphics processing chips*"[72].

These remedies can be easily translated in a computer code that is enforced by a program. A smart contract can automatize the companies' compliance with antitrust remedies by automatically punishing the company's deviation from compliance[73]. This would significantly decrease the costs incurred by the antitrust agency in monitoring the remedies imposed. Moreover, antitrust agencies can better monitor

---

[69] Halpin (2017).

[70] Massarotto (2019a); OECD (2018).

[71] FTC (2010).

[72] Id.

[73] Massarotto (2019a).

companies' compliance with antitrust remedies by releasing the company from filing extensive Reports to the agency, which are usually required for companies every 6 months or so. Perhaps, a wide adoption of smart contracts would raise the risk of bugs and hacker attacks, and this is certainly something that the enforcers need to consider in adopting smart contracts[74]. Smart contracts could also be implemented in advance to ensure blockchain compliance with antitrust and any other affected regulations.

As I suggested in my book "*Antitrust Settlements: How a Simple Agreement Can Drive the Economy*" these smart contracts can run in an antitrust blockchain made up by antitrust officers, where potentially, each officer or division/department represents a node. This antitrust blockchain could be built for one specific or multiple agencies. For example, a European antitrust blockchain network might be ideal to enhance communication and harmonize the enforcement of competition principles among the European Member States. Each European agency might have its own blockchain connected to the European Antitrust Blockchain. In practice, what antitrust authorities could explore is the adoption of smart contracts that run on a blockchain network base, for example, on the Hyperledger Fabric DLT platform. The antitrust agency's smart contracts would require privileged access to all transactions on the ledger, monitor all transactions, and produce compliance reports. Companies may be granted read-only access to those aspects of the reports related to their activities.

Antitrust agencies may also require companies that raise antitrust concerns to adopt pro-competitive remedies, including the implementation of a blockchain to track the data flow and enable the antitrust agency to oversee the company's use of data[75]. In summary, antitrust discipline can find various situations and ways to exploit DLT in enforcing antitrust principles in any market. The adoption of innovative technologies in the context of antitrust is not merely recommended, but it seems to be essential to ensure effective antitrust enforcement in today's tech-economy.

3.3 Conclusions

In the context of antitrust and in any field, and a variety of opportunities for antitrust enforcers. As explored in this section, DLT seems to be all that antitrust dreams about a tool to effectively decentralize today's consolidated platforms on the Web and regulate data by ensuring privacy in a more efficient way than existing regulations. Antitrust enforcers should not miss the opportunities that these innovative technologies offer to face its present challenges in the tech economy. There is essentially no chance that an antitrust agency can effectively face today's challenges

[74] Dingman et al. (2019).

[75] Massarotto (2020c).

in increasingly dynamic and high-sophisticated markets without exploiting the same *Big-tech* ingenuity[76].

4 Do Blockchain Raise Antitrust Concerns?

Antitrust practices are present in blockchain and can seriously compromise the key component of blockchain—*decentralization*. Similar to the Web, blockchain originated as a decentralized and open network, but anticompetitive conduct can lead to centralize blockchain's governance, jeopardizing blockchain's future development. In this section, we will explore:

1. the meaning of trust in trustless technologies;
2. what kind of entity blockchain is;
3. forms of collusion;
4. the issue of market concentration;
5. exclusionary conduct.

All these issues are fundamental and need to be considered in the development of blockchain. If decentralization is compromised through collusion and market concentration and exclusionary conduct, blockchain will become only another centralized platform adding no tangible extra value to the existing platforms.

4.1 Anti-trust in Trustless Technologies

The word *trust* appears frequently in the context of blockchain. We often hear that blockchain is a trustless technology. But the meaning of trust in the blockchain ecosystem seems to be controversial. The issue dealing with antitrust is particularly intriguing, as this discipline centers around the word *trust*. This section investigates the meaning of *trust* exploring whether the so-called trustless blockchain technology should be immune from the antitrust scrutiny. In contrast to centralized platforms, in public blockchain you do not need to trust a third-party intermediary (e.g., banks) by using a blockchain. In his white paper, Satoshi Nakamoto claimed to have introduced "*a system for electronic transaction without relying on trust,*" potentially making bitcoin and blockchain immune from the antitrust scrutiny[77]. Thus, at the first glance someone could argue that blockchain is exempted from antitrust surveillance.

However, Satoshi Nakamoto's claim is not entirely true. The peer-to-peer network bypasses centralized platforms, but its functioning relies on the network of

[76] Massarotto (2020c).

[77] Nakamoto (2008).

participants in the chain, which (as explained in Sect. 2.2) is governed by a protocol. In other words, you need to trust the technology and who set the protocol, instead of an intermediary[78]. The success of blockchain relies on the trust of people in this modern technology: blockchain and DLT in general is not an exception to this fundamental economic principle[79]. The truth is that the agreed algorithm protocol establishes mutual trust among the participants in the network by validating transactions based on a peer-to-peer mechanism[80]. This means lowering the costs of checking digital information, though the cost of verifying offline information remains the same. Professor Kevin Werback observed that bitcoin and blockchain do not eliminate *trust*, but they introduced a new form of *trust* by inverting the problem. People "make payments confidently with a decentralized digital currency" because they "*pay people with it*"[81]. Professor Werback defined a fourth structure of trust in blockchain.

I believe that *trust* is always the same *trust*, from cryptocurrencies to the context of antitrust. What does change is the context where this term is employed that can significantly change its meaning. Rather than trusting your competitor from not competing with you, or the government and judges for correctly enforcing the rules, or a bank for keeping your money safe, you trust the technology—the protocol[82]. This brings us back to the cryptoanarchy movement. You adopt a blockchain and you buy bitcoins because you trust a computer protocol more than the bank system and the government's regulation. If something goes wrong, bitcoin protocol enables most of the network to create a fork to reverse the consequences of hacking or bugs. The possibility to fork a blockchain keeps blockchains constantly under competitive pressure. In case a fork "*offers better governance or is more competitive, it will quickly gather users and developers since switching costs are extremely low*"[83]. This does not occur in private and permissioned blockchains, where there is no real decentralized platform; they are remarkably similar to traditional databases.

Up until May 2020, there were three hard forks in the bitcoin network (Bitcoin XT, Bitcoin Classic and Bitcoin Unlimited), but none reached the consensus, namely the majority of hash power. In 2016, a hard fork succeeded in Ethereum to repair the failure of '*The DAO*' launched in Ethereum platform. At that time, the world seemed to be ready for a venture capital firm entirely self-governed by a smart contract running on a blockchain—Ethereum. The enthusiasm was so high that DAO raised $150 million in only a few months. Unfortunately, a project aimed to be remained in history for proving the validity of DAO, is now the symbol of a massive failure. A bug in its smart contract enabled a hacker to drain about $50 million. Some blockchain purists argued that this was part of the game and the hacker just

[78] Schneier (2019b).

[79] Massarotto (2020a).

[80] Puthal et al. (2018).

[81] Werbach (2018).

[82] Schneier (2019b).

[83] Catalini and Tucker (2018), p. 8.

performed something that the computer code permitted[84]. However, Ethereum opted to fork its blockchain, and the fork successfully created Ethereum classic, which maintains the original blockchain, and the new Ethereum with the theft reversed[85].

This episode indeed led many to distrust DAO, and DLT, confirming that these technologies are not immune from the economic principle of *trust*. In the history of bitcoin and blockchain, *The DAO* of 2016 is not the only episode that discouraged people from investing in DLT. Silkroad and BitInstant are other two symbolic examples of how these technologies can be used to commit or incentivize crimes, such as money laundering, selling drugs, and other illegal goods and services on the Web[86]. These episodes seriously affected the reputation of bitcoin and the DLT ecosystem. The price of Bitcoin, for example, dropped from 140$ to 110$ after the FBI shouted Silk Road, the website for selling drugs administered by Ross Ulbrich, where all transactions were conducted using bitcoins[87]. Likewise, DLT is not trustless from an antitrust perspective. As explored in the following Sect. 4, some types of blockchain may create the perfect conditions for companies to collude. Moreover, as previously observed, participants need to trust each other, raising the issue of whether this might imply some sort of collusive conduct among blockchain participants relevant to antitrust scrutiny.

In summary, the magnitude of DLT is enormous. Still, like any promising technology, DLT can be used for enabling people and markets to do what they do more efficiently or creating more harm than benefit. DLT requires trust to increase its reputation and attract business. We live in a reputation-based system—today, the economic principle of *trust* is even more relevant. We commonly hear the slogan: "*Don't trust anyone with more money that their reputation is worth*"[88]. Reputation will be far more important in dealing than ever the credit ranking now[89]—blockchain marketplace is the next testing ground.

Antitrust and effective forms of regulation will be critical to increase the reputation of the market and build—*trust*—in DLT and any markets[90]. On the other hand, the adoption of blockchain technologies by the same government agencies might increase cryptoanarchy purists' trust in government's regulation. In any case, antitrust and DLT should play in the same team by pursuing an identical goal: increasing consumer welfare by advancing markets through innovative technologies. They can only benefit from mutual assistance[91].

[84] Kolber (2018).

[85] Leising (2017).

[86] Planet Compliance (n.d.).

[87] Hern (2013); BBC (2013).

[88] Schneier (2019a).

[89] Schneier (2019a).

[90] Zak (2017); Massarotto (2020a).

[91] Massarotto (2020a).

4.2 What Kind of Entity Is Blockchain?

Before exploring possible antitrust concerns, it is worth investigating blockchain's identity to verify if this entity can be personally liable for antitrust violations. Antitrust presumes a defined entity or a set of entities that aim to market power, which in case of monopolization, conduct or agreements in restraint of trade, can be investigated. Otherwise, as Professors Catalini and Tucker observed, it is impossible to prosecute antitrust conduct in the context of blockchain.[92] Should blockchain be considered as a firm, or a network that enables people and companies to interact or something different? The decentralized nature of blockchain can, as we have seen, help antitrust agencies in preserving competition in today's centralized platforms. On the other hand, the inherent decentralization of blockchain brings new challenges for antitrust enforcers in terms of defining blockchain's identity. Like the nineteenth century, where society created corporations to separate people from entities devoted to business, a decade ago it introduced a new decentralized entity/infrastructure to operate. Unlike traditional corporations, in decentralized blockchains, people participate and interact with the blockchain network through a digital identity.

Digital identity can be identified as "*the digital data corpus being built by users and digital systems*"[93] that enable people and any other entity to access computers and interact with computer networks. Blockchain is a decentralized computer network and in public blockchain, such as bitcoin blockchain, people's digital identity is characterized by pseudonyms to protect privacy. The same creator of bitcoin is still known under the pseudonym of Satoshi Nakamoto, no one was able to reveal his real identity. Satoshi Nakamoto is likely to be only one of the several pseudonyms that the founder of bitcoin uses to interact on the Internet. There is often the wrong assumption that we have only a digital identity that follows us everywhere; but this is not true. Every day, we create, for example, several email and social media accounts. Digital identity is different from our passport or social security number, and it is naïve to think that we should have only one digital identity[94]. Like corporations that were created as a separate entity from its owners, digital identity is something separate (although related) to its creator.

In other words, blockchain creates a network made up by blockchain participants who interact with each other by using digital identities. Blockchain is the platform that enables people to interact to do much of their regular work more efficiently bypassing intermediaries. Like a buyer group, as we have seen, participants in the blockchain group/network are basically users who leverage their force of acting together to get goods and services that are usually provided through intermediaries. Thus, what kind of entity is blockchain? A deeper inquiry is necessary, but as any group such as associations, consortiums or networks, blockchain does not appear immune from antitrust scrutiny. By considering the US and EU competition law,

[92] Catalini and Tucker (2018); Lianos (2018).

[93] Fehér (2019).

[94] Ou (2017).

which are the leading antitrust jurisdictions, we can observe that antitrust law is giving an increasing importance to the economic effects of practices in the affected markets, rather than formalistic legal definitions of entities relevant for antitrust legislation. The US antitrust law clearly emphasizes this point as under Section 7 of the Sherman Act, antitrust law is applicable to potentially any "*person*," including "*corporations and associations existing under or authorized by the laws*" (Section 7 of the Sherman Act). In Europe, Article 101 and 102 of the TFEU applies to undertakings and associations, which exercise an economic activity[95]. Therefore, blockchain can easily fall into both the US and EU antitrust jurisdictions. As outlined above, a set of rules set into a protocol governs the blockchain network. But a group of people wrote the protocol and is leading the blockchain growth. The fact that these people are using digital identities does not make them less liable.

4.3 *Forms of Collusion*

In the context of blockchain, one of the main antitrust issues entails collusive practices among participants or different blockchain networks. If this concern takes place, the subsequent issue is whether antitrust agencies should prosecute blockchains and in which way. First, in this discussion, it is necessary to treat private, permissioned, and public blockchains separately.

4.3.1 Private and Consortium Blockchains

Private blockchains are not so different from traditional databases; for these reasons, some scholars considered them "*100 percent uninteresting*"[96] because they have been used for years. They are closed networks; blockchain participants need to be invited and are only known to each other[97]. In other words, participation occurs by invitation only, and everything that happens within is totally private. As outlined in Sect. 2, while usually singular organizations take part in private blockchains, consortium/federated blockchains include multiple selected organizations. Suppose a blockchain consortium is built among competitors to exchange sensitive information, such as prices. In that case, they are dangerous in terms of competition as much as any other consortium/organization associated with that scope. Decisions are taken through a voting or multi-party consensus algorithm whose rules rely on the participants' agreement in the protocol that governs the blockchain network. For example, a consortium of fifty organizations could rule that a transaction is only added to the blockchain if more than thirty-five organizations part of the consortium

[95] Lianos (2018).

[96] Schneier (2019b).

[97] Jacobs (2018).

have validated the transaction. The main differences between a traditional consortium and a blockchain consortium are adopting infrastructure to communicate and the possibility to automate tasks with the use of smart contracts, which might be adopted to detect and punish a cartel deviation, making the cartel more effective.

However, if the antitrust agency wants to participate in the blockchain process to verify the lawful compliance of participants, the possibility that the agency would detect any forms of collusion is extremely high as everything is tracked in a blockchain and immutable[98]. Thus, if on the one hand, companies can engage in collusive conduct more efficiently by adopting smart contracts, on the other hand, any forms of collusion can be easily proved. As I have written in my paper "*From Digital to Blockchain Markets—What Role for Antitrust and Regulation,*" antitrust agencies or regulators might think of setting some standard rules or conditions hardcoded in *smart contracts* to punish forms of collusion automatically. *Smart contracts* have the potential to become a remarkable legal and antitrust tool. In summary, blockchain and smart contracts seem to be a double-edged sword for companies that want to collude with each other. A natural question is whether a company should use blockchain to collude when the proof of collusion would become easy to get for antitrust enforcers. Even today, meeting in a restaurant or hotel rooms seems to be the most effective and convenient ways for companies to engage in cartels and collusive practices. Especially, if antitrust agencies start adopting the same blockchain technologies to do what they regularly do.

4.3.2 Public Blockchain

The discussion of collusion in public blockchains is much more compelling. Public blockchains are intellectually stimulating because they resolved the so-called *Byzantine Generals' Problem* related to distributed networks. Computer scientists studied for years how to reach a consensus among different computers in distributed systems by because some computers might not tell the truth. Until the advent of blockchain, no viable solutions were found to resolve such a problem. When the 2008 Satoshi Nakamoto white paper was announced, the entire computer science community was amazed.

The ingenuity of blockchain was to define a consensus algorithm according to which participants in the network need to agree to a set of protocols and rules to achieve the consensus. Like a game, the consensus mechanism works as long as most participants in the network follow the rules hardcoded into a protocol. If everybody follows the rules, everybody wins. As explored in Sect. 2, bitcoin blockchain adopts the PoW to reach the consensus in the network and validate the transaction, while for example Cardano uses the PoS.

[98] Massarotto (2019b).

Professors Lin William Cong and Zhiguo He observed that "*achieving [the] consensus requires sufficiently distributing information for verification;*"[99] this increases transparency potentially leading to collusive practices. However, as the Organisation for Economic Co-operation and Development (OECD) observed, the transparency of price information can increase consumer welfare[100]. For example, the ride sharing company Uber developed a pricing algorithm that matches drivers to consumers seeking rides by employing a real-time pricing algorithm. A study estimated that this algorithm generated a consumer surplus of $2.9 billion in four U.S. cities[101]. In addition, everybody sees everything in a public blockchain, which is open to any person interested in joining the network. This implies that forms of cartel among blockchain participants do not seem to be an issue as the secrecy of a cartel here fails and the number of blockchain participants is subject to change constantly. The genuine antitrust concern in public blockchains is mining pools, hence participants that pool together their computing power to resolve the puzzle required in PoW and increase the possibility of adding a block and be rewarded. If the block is successfully mined, the pool manager distributes the coinbase transaction to reward the group of miners who participated in forging the block[102]. Usually, each participant receives a flat fee, or the award is based on the amount of computing resources used to solve the hash problem[103].

There are also mining services contracts that you can purchase though easy-to-use web interface or the cloud[104]. You buy, for example, some share of mining power from cloud mining and you profit along with the pool without the need of owning mining hardware. The two main types of cloud mining are: hardware leasing and hashing power leasing. In the first type you rent their miner for a determinate amount of time, while hashing leasing means renting a specific amount of processing power. Cloud mining diverges from mining pools because in cloud mining, you pay a service provider that mines for you to get the rewards. In mining pools, miners share their computational power to mine blocks and gain rewards. However, also cloud mining can give rise to antitrust concerns as they imply a concentration of power in a single cloud. In summary, mining pools and cloud mining can *de facto* lead to anticompetitive practices as they are becoming increasingly popular in the context of blockchain. A study determined that within 4 months the percentage of pool-mined blocks "*increased from 49.91% to 91.12%*" in Bitcoin and "*from 76.9% to 92.2%*"[105] in Ethereum.

In other words, mining pools hold more than ninety percent of the entire blocks production in the two largest blockchain. In addition, mining pools might be

[99] Cong and He (2019), p. 1755.

[100] OECD (2018).

[101] Cohen et al. (2016).

[102] Ren and Ward (2019).

[103] Bashir (2017); Cong et al. (2018).

[104] Bashir (2017).

[105] Ren and Ward (2019).

attempted to collude and engage in cartels acting as a monopoly pool that controls the blockchain network. In May 2019, four mining pools were controlling more than fifty percent of the hash rate of the Bitcoin blockchain, by implying that if they get together these mining pools could successfully perform fifty-one percent attacks of the Bitcoin network (Medium 2019). The hash rate is "*the measuring unit of the processing power of the Bitcoin network,*" (Bitcoin.org) Antpool alone holds about fifteen percent of the entire hash rate of all Bitcoin mining pools used to mine Bitcoin (Blockchain.com). Bitmain Technologies Ltd. (Bitmain), which is the largest Bitcoin hardware manufacturer worldwide, runs Antpool. In 2018, United American Corp. sued Bitmain for antitrust violations before the U.S. Court of South of Florida (*Case No. 1-18-cv-25106 (S.D. Fla)*).

4.3.3 United American Corp v. Bitmain

United American Corp. v. Bitmain is the first antitrust blockchain dispute in the context of blockchain.[106] Although up to the writing of this chapter the case is still pending, it is interesting to examine the potential antitrust issues involved and the United American Corp. (UnitedCorp) allegations. In November 2018, Bitcoin Cash, which is one of the varieties of permission less cryptocurrencies, was forked into Bitcoin SV and Bitcoin ABC. According to UnitedCorp, Bitmain colluded with a number of investors and mining pools to get enough miners to support Bitcoin ABC over the Bitcoin SV version of Bitcoin Cash. By doing so, Bitmain would have "centralized what is intended to be a decentralized transactional system enabling the corruption of the democratic and neutral principles of the Bitcoin Cash network" (*United American Corp. v. Bitmain, Inc.*, 2018). This would have compromised the value of both forks of Bitcoin Cash, which fell below the value of united Bitcoin Cash before the forking by causing financial harm to investors. In particular, United Corp's investments in Bitcoin Cash were seriously compromised due to the manipulation of the cryptocurrency market for Bitcoin Cash. The first question we should ask is whether the alleged conduct directly harmed United Corp. United Corp did not specify in its complaint whether it was harmed as an investor, a miner or as a spender of Bitcoin Cash.

The complaint appears quite vague also with respect to the antitrust injury that United Corp would have suffered. Bitcoin Cash's devaluation seems to be the only possible valid allegations that could effectively harm consumers. But, in that case it seems unlikely that a judge recognizes a direct harm of UnitedCorp. In sum, from an antitrust perspective, the case at hand seems to be weak on many levels. Although cryptocurrencies and blockchains are based on the concept of decentralization, there is nothing that goes against possible agreements among participants to pool their computational power or stakes, for example, to attack the blockchain and create a fork.

[106] Stylianou (2019).

Conversely, the possibility to fork a blockchain increases competition by keeping blockchains constantly under competitive pressure[107]. Again, a public blockchain like Bitcoin Cash is based on a consensus mechanism that requires that the majority of blockchain participants agree on a standard solution before adding a new block. This means that *bad participant(s)* or '*traitors*' of the related blockchain network to succeed in an attack need the consensus of fifty-one percent of the participants in the network. The US cryptographer and legal scholar Nick Szabo calls this '*democracy in action*,'[108] rather than an attack and he is probably right.

In addition, we need to consider that the mining pool itself does not necessarily own the hash power needed to mine for example Bitcoin or Bitcoin Cash. Bitcoin miners can easily switch mining pools by routing their hash power towards a different mining pool. This means that the market share of mining pools is subject to change constantly[109]. Mining pools, such as Antpool, are open and free; thus, anyone can join and leave the mining pool anytime. In summary, *UnitedCorp v. Bitmain* is certainly an antitrust case of primary importance for the entire blockchain and cryptocurrency's community. However, on February 5th the Southern District Court of Florida dismissed the case without prejudice allowing the plaintiff to amend the complaint by no later than February 28, 2020[110]. United American Corp.'s amended complaint continues to claim the violation of the Sherman Act, but abandoned all five of its state laws claims and it will be compelling to see the judge's ruling. This case has the potential to set the tone for future blockchain and cryptocurrencies antitrust issues.

4.3.4 Delegate Proof of Stake (DPS)

In the context of public blockchains, forms of collusion and cartels were identified in blockchains that adopted the delegate proof of stake (DPS) consensus algorithm. As previously discussed, over the last 10 years blockchain engineers developed new consensus mechanisms to tackle technical challenges raised by the PoW, particularly the issue of blockchain scalability and the speed in processing transactions. A blockchain engineer designed the DPS consensus mechanism, where blockchain participants vote the validator nodes (delegates) that will forge blocks for the chain. Each participant holds at least a token, and one token corresponds to one vote. In theory, the DPS should encourage competition because users vote for people they trust more. However, in practice, this consensus mechanism led in some situations to clear forms of collusion and cartels. The most notable case is probably *Lisk*, where two cartels ran the blockchain by producing eighty-five percent of blocks[111].

[107] Catalini and Tucker (2018).

[108] Szabo (2017).

[109] Tuwiner (2020).

[110] Baker (2020).

[111] Günther (2018).

Similarly, EOS, which adopts a DPS consensus mechanism, was accused of collusion and to be controlled by a "*Chinese oligarchy*"[112]. In conclusion, forms of collusion are present in the context of blockchain and need to be prevented in order to enable blockchain to maintain its key characteristic—*decentralization*. Antitrust surveillance will be increasingly crucial and necessary in the blockchain ecosystem, not only to prevent forms of collusion, but also any forms of re-centralization and exclusionary conduct.

4.4 Blockchain Concentration

Blockchain is decentralized by design, implying that a number of computers (the so-called validating nodes) constitute the blockchain network. The same Blockchain's creator requires that no single entity shall control more than fifty-one percent of global computational power for Bitcoins to function appropriately[113]. In principle, anyone can create and participate in a decentralized public blockchain network; the more validating nodes a blockchain has, the more securer a blockchain is[114]. As previously discussed, this peer-to-peer network has the potential to become universally adopted, as the Internet (more accurately the Web) is today (Lee n.d.). However, blockchain is far from being perfect.

4.4.1 ASICs

The risk of centralization, as we have seen, is effective. Today, mining bitcoins is basically impossible for a single desktop computer[115], because the increase in value of bitcoins let to the development of more powerful hashing hardware. Powerful hardware called Application Specific Integrated Circuits (ASICs) can execute billions of hashes per second. There are professional mining centers that today adopt thousands of ASIC units in parallel giving to users the possibility to contract with them to perform mining on their behalf[116]. Today, the attempt to mine without an ASIC is unprofitable and led to the formation of the so-called *mining farms* that are usually run by corporations based in Countries with access to low-cost electricity, such as China. The same crypto purists recognized that ASIC Mining farms can lead to re-centralize the blockchain network because people cannot compete individually with ASIC farms in the mining competition[117]. In addition, this has created a

---

[112] Dale (2019).

[113] Nakamoto (2008).

[114] Orcutt (2018).

[115] Lianos (2018).

[116] Bashir (2017).

[117] Beikverdi and Song (2015).

dependency on Bitmain, a dominant chip/ASICs manufacturer, which became a kind of third-party intermediary. This clearly goes against the same concept of a decentralized trustless technology created exactly to bypass intermediaries.

The blockchain community have created ASIC-resistant proof-of-work (PoW) algorithms that alter the required extra memory-based computing effort in response to the ASIC's threat. Ethereum, for example, introduced Ethash, the ASIC-resistant PoW. However, it has not resolved the problem in concrete terms since "chipmakers seem to be increasingly designing ASICs worthless again"[118]. In April 2018, Bitmain announced the first ASIC miners for Ethash. Bran Cohen, the author of the peer-to-peer BitTorrent protocol recognized that "*ASIC resistance just creates more centralization around manufacture when it inevitably fails,*"[119] and it makes more sense to be ASIC-friendly. ASICs advance security thanks to their efficient hashing power that makes a potential "*fifty-percent attacker*" more challenging. In other words, ASICs are not entirely negative but they *de facto* increase the hash rate concentration raising antitrust concerns[120]. The same blockchain community widely recognizes that the hash rate is extremely centralized, and this is one of the main challenges for the development of the blockchain ecosystem[121]. P2Pool is a decentralized Bitcoin mining pool devised to tackle the problem of centralized mining. Similarly, Stratum V2 is a protocol for pooled mining that aims to improve decentralization through a system that enables miners to choose their own transaction sets by means of a negotiation process with pools. However, mining pools like P2Pool and Stratum V2 protocol are small realities compared with AntPool or F2Pool. In addition, P2Pool and Stratum V2 protocols are not simple tasks for non-technical users to learn.

4.4.2 Vertical Concentration

In the discussion of blockchain concentration, we need to consider possible vertical concentration along the value chain of bitcoin mining[122]. Bitmain, as we have seen, runs Antpool one of the largest bitcoin mining pools, in addition to being the largest worldwide Bitcoin hardware manufacturer. Companies like Bitmain risks to monopolize all aspects of the Bitcoin marketplace: antitrust agencies should consider such risks. About eighty percent of cryptocurrencies users use intermediaries, such as Coinbase, to custody their cryptocurrencies[123]. Coinbase is another example of centralization as it is the most successful Bitcoin wallet that has a clear centralized

[118]Casey (2018).

[119]Cant (2019).

[120]Cong et al. (2018).

[121]Corallo (2019).

[122]Cong et al. (2018).

[123]Werbach (2018).

structure[124]. Coinbase is remarkably similar to payment platforms, such as PayPal, that controls your information with the possibility to block a client that does not follow its rules. Blockchains, such as Cardano, are also criticized for being centralized as few participants hold more than seventy percent of all Cardano coin ADA's total supply[125]. In summary, blockchain's re-centralization and concentration phenomena are effective and lead to both antitrust and security issues. Moreover, if the decentralization fails, there are not many reasons why someone should prefer blockchain from any other database.

4.5 Exclusionary Conduct

In case blockchain platforms become dominant and deliver essential goods or services for other blockchains or services, we have to consider the performance of possible exclusionary conduct relevant for antitrust. Exclusionary practices include refusal to deal, tying or bundling, loyalty discounts, predatory practices. Exclusionary behaviors do not seem to be an issue in public blockchains, which are open to anybody. In contrast, exclusionary conduct can represent an effective threat in closed blockchains where participation is by invitation only. In case a closed blockchain abuses its dominant position in a market, the antitrust agency might think of imposing remedies to tackle exclusionary behaviors. The antitrust agency, for example, might require the blockchain to break up into various parts. Or, somewhat, similar to the context of standard essential patents (SEP), antitrust agencies could require the blockchain to open its membership for non-participants on fair, reasonable, and non-discriminatory conditions (FRAND terms)[126]. In previous antitrust cases related to exclusionary conduct, the agency prevented, for example, the company from entering into a specific business or engaged in loyalty discounts. In *Intel*, which is a leading case on exclusionary conduct, the Federal Trade Commission[127] required Intel to:

1. 'modify its intellectual property agreements with AMD, Nvidia, and Via [three of its major competitors] so that those companies have more freedom to consider mergers or joint ventures with other companies, without the threat of being sued by Intel for patent infringement;'
2. 'extend Via's x86 licensing agreement for 5 years, which would have otherwise expired in 2013;'
3. 'maintain a key interface (PCI Express bus) for 6 years in a way that would not limit the performance of geographic processing chips;'

---

[124] Beikverdi and Song (2015).

[125] Medium (2019).

[126] Nazzini (2018); Finney (2018).

[127] FTC (2010).

4. 'disclose to software developers that Intel computer compilers discriminate between Intel chips and non-Intel chips, and that they may not register all the features of non-Intel chips.'

In IBM *unbundling decision*, the Department of Justice (DOJ) required IBM to sell its hardware and software separately, allowing software development companies to enter the operating systems and compete with IBM[128]. At that time, IBM held seventy-four percent of the market of general-purpose digital computers. The IBM unbundling decision led to creating the operating systems market; a start-up called Microsoft became in the 1980s IBM main supplier[129]. At this moment it might be difficult to elaborate specific remedies for exclusionary conduct in blockchains that we cannot even envisage, but past antitrust cases can certainly be used as a useful model of reference to anticipate future antitrust remedies in the context of blockchain. Antitrust agencies could also provide some guidance to markets to prevent possible exclusionary conduct and any other anticompetitive practices in the context of blockchain[130]. Companies are typically risk-adverse. "*[T]he best of all monopoly profits is a quiet life*" John Hicks wisely observed[131]; thus, especially large blockchains would benefit from government guidance.

5 Conclusions

In the 1990s, May admitted that "*a lot of work remains*"[132] but the cryptoanarchy movement will soon colonize cyberspace. A question we should ask is whether blockchain will make this possible. According to the cryptoanarchy movement, when you have an idea just put into place, not wait for regulatory feedback as regulation would always limit/delay innovation (cf. Napster or BiTorrent and the same bitcoin). When a technology becomes widespread it is basically impossible for the regulator to impede its entry in the market and development. Due to network effects, a successful technology would take off with no chance to turn it down. However, there are examples like Napster or Facebook original project of Libra that show the contrary. In June 2019, Facebook in partnership with a variety of relevant partners, such as PayPal and Visa, launched its cryptocurrency Libra that has never taken off. The current Facebook Libra project is nothing more than a version of PayPal for cryptocurrency[133]. Similarly, Telegram has to drop Telegram Open

---

[128] Lopatka (2000).

[129] Massarotto (2020a).

[130] Massarotto (2019b).

[131] Hicks (1935).

[132] May (1994).

[133] Popper and Isaac (2020).

Network (TON) blockchain project after the U.S. Securities and Exchange Commission (SEC) won the injunction to prevent Telegram blockchain launch[134].

In summary, DLT is not immune from government forms of regulation, including antitrust. The lack of considering antitrust and other forms of regulation can make a project illegal, therefore unsalable, in the market before it is launched. Antitrust is the first arm of government regulation that anyone needs to consider before entering into the blockchain business since this discipline is applied to any industries and situations[135]. Blockchain needs antitrust to succeed and antitrust needs to embrace blockchain technologies to be effective in today's data economy. The anarchy movement is only partially correct. Technologies can undoubtedly deal with some issues in a more efficient way than present regulations, but we cannot leave humans entirely out of the equation. The re-centralization of the blockchain phenomenon is only one symbolic example.

Neither overregulation nor self-regulation (anarchy) seems to be ideal. As the "*security guru*" Professor Bruce Schrneir observed, "*markets don't take society into account*" and "*can't resolve collective problems*"[136]. The government does. Antitrust has consumer welfare and the increase of market efficiency as primary goals. But technologies run faster than policies. Embracing frontier technologies like blockchain is not only encouraged, but also necessary if the government wants to protect society by fostering innovation. Otherwise, it will only be a matter of time for the cryptoanarchy movement to reach the right momentum.

References

2019 Dapp Market Report (2020) Dapp review. Retrieved from https://dapp.review/article/238/2019-Dapp-Market-Report

Baker P (2020, February 5) US Judge dismisses Bitcoin cash 'Hijack' lawsuit against Bit main, Kraken. Coindesk. Retrieved from https://www.coindesk.com/us-judge-dismisses-bitcoin-cash-hijack-lawsuit-against-bitmain-kraken

Bashir I (2017) Mastering blockchain distributed ledgers, decentralization and smart contracts explained. Packt, Birmingham

BBC (2013) Bitcoin value drops after FBI shuts Silk Road drugs site. BBC News, 3 October 2013. Available at https://www.bbc.com/news/technology-24381847

Beikverdi A, Song J (2015) Trend of centralization in Bitcoin's distributed network. IEEE. Retrieved from https://ieeexplore.ieee.org/document/7176229

Bessen J, Meurer MJ (2014) The direct costs from NPE disputes. Cornell Law Rev 99(2):387–424. Retrieved from http://scholarship.law.cornell.edu/clr/vol99/iss2/3

Bhageshpur K (2019, November 15) Data is the new oil -- and that's a good thing. Forbes. Retrieved from https://www.forbes.com/sites/forbestechcouncil/2019/11/15/data-is-the-new-oil-and-thats-a-good-thing/#298c5d127304

[134] Frankel (2020).

[135] Massarotto (2018).

[136] Schneier (2019a).

Bharadwaj A, Devaiah VH, Gupta I (2018) Complications and quandaries in the ICT sector: standard essential patents. Springer

Bitcoin.org (n.d.) Vocabulary, hash rate. Retrieved from May 26, 2020 https://bitcoin.org/en/vocabulary#hash-rate

Blair RD, Sokol DD (2017) Antitrust intellectual property, and high tech. Cambridge University Press

Blockchain.com (n.d.) Hashrate distribution. Retrieved from https://www.blockchain.com/charts/pools

Canellis D (2019) More than 60% of Ethereum nodes run in the cloud, mostly on Amazon Web Services. Is this decentralisation? The Next Web, 23 September 2019. Available at https://thenextweb.com/hardfork/2019/09/23/ethereum-nodes-cloud-services-amazon-web-services-blockchain-hosted-decentralization/

Cant J (2019, November 16) BitTorrent creator calls Vitalik's ASIC-resistant proof-of-work "A Pipe Dream and a Bad Idea." Cointelegraph. Retrieved from https://cointelegraph.com/news/bittorrent-creator-calls-vitaliks-asic-resistant-proof-of-work-a-pipe-dream-and-a-bad-idea

Casey MJ (2018, May 1) Crypto needs more than code to beat the ASIC mining threat. Coindesk. Retrieved from https://www.coindesk.com/bitcoin-code-defend-against-asic-mining-threat

Catalini C, Tucker C (2018) Antitrust and costless verification: an optimistic and a pessimistic view of the implications of blockchain technology. Retrieved from http://ide.mit.edu/sites/default/files/publications/SSRN-id3199453.pdf

Clack CD, Bakshi VA, Braine L (2016) Smart contract templates: foundations, design landscape and research directions. Retrieved from https://arxiv.org/pdf/1608.00771v3.pdf

Cohen P, Hahn R, Hall J (2016, August 30) Using big data to estimate consumer surplus: the case of Uber. Retrieved from https://www.ftc.gov/system/files/documents/public_comments/2018/08/ftc-2018-0048-d-0124-155312.pdf

Cong LW, He Z (2019) Blockchain disruption and smart contracts. Rev Financ Stud 32 (5):1754–1797

Cong LW, He Z, Li J (2018) Decentralized mining in centralized pools. Retrieved from http://www.law.nyu.edu/sites/default/files/upload_documents/SSRN-id3160046_1.pdf

Corallo M (2019, June 24) Mining: no good, the bad, and the ugly [Video file]. Retrieved from https://www.youtube.com/watch?v=k_z-FBAil6k

Dale B (2019, September 19) Everyone's worst fears about EOS are proving true. Coindesk. Retrieved from https://www.coindesk.com/everyones-worst-fears-about-eos-are-proving-true

Dingman W, Cohen A, Ferrara N, Lynch A, Jasinski P, Black PE, Deng L (2019) Defects and vulnerabilities in smart contracts, a classification using the NIST bugs framework. Int J Networked Distrib Comput 7(3):121–132

Dujmovic J (2018, October 15) The good and the bad of Tim Berners-Lee's new project on data privacy. MarketWatch. Retrieved from https://www.marketwatch.com/story/the-good-and-the-bad-of-tim-berners-lees-new-project-on-data-privacy-2018-10-12

Eichholz L (2017, August 25) Private blockchains! =intranets. Retrieved from https://medium.com/@liesleichholz/private-blockchains-intranets-eeb8066240af

European Commission (2019) Blockchain now and tomorrow. Retrieved from https://ec.europa.eu/jrc/en/publication/eur-scientific-and-technical-research-reports/blockchain-now-and-tomorrow

Federal Trade Commission (FTC) (2010, August 4) FTC settles charges of anticompetitive conduct against Intel. Press Release. Retrieved from http://www.ftc.gov/news-events/press-releases/2010/08/ftc-settles-charges-anticompetitive-conduct-against-intel

Fehér K (2019) Digital identity and the online self: footprint strategies – an exploratory and comparative research study. J Inf Sci 1. Retrieved from https://journals.sagepub.com/doi/10.1177/0165551519879702

Finney B (2018) Blockchain and antitrust: new tech meets old regs. Trans Tennessee J Bus Law 19:709–736

Frankel A (2020, March 25) SEC wins injunction against Telegram blockchain launch in key ICO case. Reuters. Retrieved from https://www.reuters.com/article/legal-us-otc-telegram/sec-wins-injunction-against-telegram-blockchain-launch-in-key-ico-case-idUSKBN21C3N0

Günther S (2018, June 1) Lisk—the mafia blockchain [Blog Post]. Retrieved from https://medium.com/coinmonks/lisk-the-mafia-blockchain-47248915ae2f

Halpin H (2017) The crisis of standardizing DRM: the case of W3C encrypted media extensions. Retrieved from https://hal.inria.fr/hal-01673296/document

Hassani H, Huang X, Silva ES (2019) Fusing big data, blockchain and cryptocurrency. Springer

Hern A (2013, October 3) Bitcoin price plummets after Silk Road closure. The Guardian. Retrieved from https://www.theguardian.com/technology/2013/oct/03/bitcoin-price-silk-road-ulbricht-value

Hicks SR (1935) Annual survey of economic theory: the theory of monopoly. Econometrica 3:1–8

Hyperledger (2019) Case study: how Walmart brought unprecedented transparency to the food supply chain with Hyperledger Fabric. Retrieved from https://www.hyperledger.org/learn/publications/walmart-case-study

Jacobs R (2018, February 12) The good and bad of blockchain. Chicago Booth Review. Retrieved from http://review.chicagobooth.edu/finance/2018/article/good-and-bad-blockchain

Kolber AJ (2018) Not-so-smart blockchain contracts and artificial responsibility. Stanf Technol Law Rev 21(2):198–234

Lee TB (n.d.) Frequently asked questions. Retrieved from https://www.w3.org/People/Berners-Lee/FAQ.html. Last visited 19 Nov 2015

Leising M (2017, June 13) Ether thief remains mystery year after $55 million heist. Blomberg News. Retrieved from https://www.bloomberg.com/features/2017-the-ether-thief/

Lianos I (2018) Blockchain competition. Retrieved from https://www.ucl.ac.uk/cles/sites/cles/files/cles_8-2018.pdf

Licklider JCR, Taylor R (1968) The computer as a communication device. Retrieved from https://www.ais.org/~jrh/licklider/computer-as-communications-device.html

Lopatka JE (2000) United States v. IBM: a monument of arrogance. Antitrust Law J 68(1):145–162

Massarotto G (2016) Open-source paradigm: beyond the solution to the software patentability debate. John Marshall Rev Intellect Prop Law 15:647–675

Massarotto G (2018) From standard oil to Google: how the role of antitrust has changed. World Competition 41(3):395–418

Massarotto G (2019a) Antitrust settlements: how a simple agreement can drive the economy, 1st edn. Wolters Kluwer

Massarotto G (2019b) From digital to blockchain markets: what role for antitrust and regulation. Retrieved from https://papers.ssrn.com/sol3/papers.cfm?abstract_id=3323420

Massarotto G (2020a) Antitrust in the blockchain era. Notre Dame J Emerging Technol 2 (1):253–279

Massarotto G (2020b) Can blockchain be the key to compete in today's digital era? [Kluwer Competition Law Blog Post]. Retrieved from http://competitionlawblog.kluwercompetitionlaw.com/2020/05/19/can-blockchain-be-the-key-to-compete-in-todays-digital-economy/?doing_wp_cron=1589904976.2744710445404052734375

Massarotto G (2020c, February 24) Grasping the meaning of big-tech antitrust consent. Competition Policy International. Retrieved from https://www.competitionpolicyinternational.com/grasping-the-meaning-of-big-tech-antitrust-consent/

May TC (1988) The crypto anarchist manifesto. Retrieved from http://groups.csail.mit.edu/mac/classes/6.805/articles/crypto/cypherpunks/may-crypto-manifesto.html

May TC (1994) Crypto anarchy and virtual communities. Retrieved from http://groups.csail.mit.edu/mac/classes/6.805/articles/crypto/cypherpunks/may-virtual-comm.html

Medium, Cryptocurrency (2019, May 2) How decentralized is Cardano? [Blog Post]. Retrieved from https://medium.com/@undersearcher/how-decentralized-is-cardano-d3a47f985ce1

Microsoft (n.d.) Confidential Consortium Framework. Retrieved from https://www.microsoft.com/en-us/research/project/confidential-consortium-framework/

Nakamoto S (2008) Bitcoin: a peer-to-peer electronic cash system 3, https://bitcoin.org/bitcoin.pdf
Nazzini (2018) The blockchain (R)evolution and the role of antitrust. King's College London Law School Research Paper No. 2019–20. Available at SSRN: https://ssrn.com/abstract=3256728
Orcutt M (2018, April 25) How secure is blockchain really? MIT Technology Review. Retrieved from https://www.technologyreview.com/2018/04/25/143246/how-secure-is-blockchain-really/
Organisation for Economic Co-operation and Development (OECD) (2018, November 28) Personalized pricing in the digital era. Retrieved from http://www.oecd.org/officialdocuments/publicdisplaydocumentpdf/?cote=DAF/COMP(2018)13&docLanguage=En
Ou E (2017) A hundred of years of crypto anarchy. Retrieved from https://elaineou.com/2017/08/03/a-hundred-years-of-crypto-anarchy/
Planet Compliance (n.d.) Innovation & regulation in finance. Retrieved from https://www.planetcompliance.com/2017/05/10/top-10-scandals-rocked-blockchain-world/
Poon J, Dryja T (2016) The Bitcoin Lightning Network: scalable off-chain instant payments. Retrieved from http://lightning.network/lightning-network-paper.pdf
Popper N, Isaac M (2020, April 16) Facebook-backed Libra cryptocurrency project is scaled back. New York Times. Retrieved from https://www.nytimes.com/2020/04/16/technology/facebook-libra-cryptocurrency.html
PricewaterhouseCoopers (PwC) & Crypto Valley (2019, March) 4th ICO/STO Report. Retrieved from https://cryptovalley.swiss/wp-content/uploads/ch-20190308-strategyand-ico-sto-report-q1-2019.pdf
Puthal D, Malik N, Mohanty SP, Kougianos E, Yang C (2018) The blockchain as a decentralized security framework. IEEE Consumer Electron Mag 7(2):18–21
R3 (2020) Retrieved June 3, 2020, from https://www.r3.com/
Ren L, Ward PAS (2019) Pooled mining is driving blockchains toward centralized systems. IEE
Schneier B (2019a) "Click Here to Kill Everybody" talks at Google [Video file]. Retrieved from https://www.youtube.com/watch?v=GkJCI3_jbtg
Schneier B (2019b, January 22) Keynote: security, trust, and blockchain-Bruce Schneier [Video file]. Retrieved from https://www.linuxfoundation.org/blog/2019/01/how-blockchain-changes-the-nature-of-trust/
Shilov K (2019, July 12) Programmable ownership: what security tokens mean for individuals. Hackernoon. Retrieved from https://medium.com/hackernoon/programmable-ownership-what-security-tokens-mean-for-individuals-d18a7f56e088
Sidak GJ (2013) The meaning of FRAND. J Competition Law Econ 9(4):931–1055
Statista (2020a) Number of monthly active Facebook users worldwide as of 1st quarter 2020. Retrieved from https://www.statista.com/statistics/264810/number-of-monthly-active-facebook-users-worldwide/
Statista (2020b) Worldwide desktop market share of leading search engines from January 2010 to January 2020. Retrieved from https://www.statista.com/statistics/216573/worldwide-market-share-of-search-engines/
Stylianou K (2019, April 26) What can the first blockchain antitrust case teach us about the crypto-economy? Retrieved from https://jolt.law.harvard.edu/digest/what-can-the-first-blockchain-antitrust-case-teach-us-about-the-crypto-economy
Submarine Cable Networks. Curie. Retrieved from June 1, 2020. https://www.submarinenetworks.com/en/systems/brazil-us/curie
Sung HC (2018) When open-source software encounters patents: blockchain as an example to explore the dilemma and solutions. J Marshall Rev Intellect Prop Law 18:55–82
Szabo N (2017, February 9) Enumerated [Blog Post]. Retrieved from http://unenumerated.blogspot.com/2017/02/money-blockchains-and-social-scalability.html
Tapscott D, Tapscott A (2016) Blockchain revolution. How the technology behind bitcoin and other cryptocurrencies is changing the world. Penguin Random House
Tasca P, Tessone CJ (2019) A taxonomy of blockchain technologies: principles of identification and classification. Ledger, 4. https://doi.org/10.5195/ledger.2019.140

Thumm N, Gabison G (2016) Patent assertion entities in Europe: their impact on innovation and knowledge transfer in ICT markets. JRC Working Papers JRC103321. Retrieved from https://ideas.repec.org/p/ipt/iptwpa/jrc103321.html

Tuwiner J (2020 March 12). Bitcoin mining pools. Buy Bitcoin Worldwide. Retrieved from https://www.buybitcoinworldwide.com/mining/pools/

UCL CBT (2019) DLT in the supply chain report. Retrieved from http://blockchain.cs.ucl.ac.uk/dlt-in-the-supply-chain-report/

UCL CBT Supply Chain (2019) DLT on supply chain. Retrieved from http://blockchain.cs.ucl.ac.uk/dlt-in-the-supply-chain-report/

United American Corp. v. Bitmain, Inc. 2018 1:2018cv25106 (D.C. Flo.)

Werbach K (2018) The blockchain and the new architecture of trust, 1st edn. MIT Press

Werbach K, Cornell N (2019) Contracts Ex Machina. Duke Law J 67:313–382

What is Bitcoin's Lightning Network? (2018, February 23) Coindesk. Retrieved from https://www.coindesk.com/learn/bitcoin-101/what-is-the-lightning-network

Wright A, De Filippi P (2018) Blockchain and the law. The rule of code, 1st edn. Harvard University Press

Xu X, Weber I, Staples M (2019) Architecture for blockchain applications. Springer

Yu PK (2007) Intellectual property and information wealth: issues and practices in the digital age. Praeger, Westport

Zak PZ (2017) The neuroscience of trust. Harvard Business Review. Retrieved from https://hbr.org/2017/01/the-neuroscience-of-trust

The Technology Innovation Time Gap in Competition Law Enforcement: Assessing the European Commission's Approach

Pierre Kirch

Abstract In this Chapter, it will be demonstrated that, over the years, a competition enforcement discrepancy (or "technology innovation time gap") has emerged. It has become apparent that old regulatory tools, such as the Vertical Block Exemption Regulation (and its accompanying Commission Guidelines) respond to past phenomena without being a means to anticipate upon and regulate not only future and unknown technological change, but also those technological innovations, such as Blockchain, which are too "young" to have any enforcement precedent which would provide an analytical background for the needs of block exemptions and the guidance which defines their application in practical terms. This will be analyzed in Section I below. Second, new tools are created to allow the Commission to react virtually immediately to new technological phenomena that introduce disruptive features into competition in certain markets, and this, with less and less procedural constraints. And this will be analyzed in Section II below.

1 Introduction

The question of the *time gap* between the introduction of new technological tools and the emergence of laws to regulate their use is a fascinating topic, especially in times of antitrust upheavals as we know today. If the emergence of a new tool using innovative technology were to engender new laws to regulate it, this would logically involve a generalized societal reaction to the tool, which would render lawmaking necessary. The time gap between technological innovation and regulation of the technology and its effect *is* a measurable quantity. For any innovative technology, we can seek out the laws which addressed it. For instance, the Gutenberg's invention of the print has caused any generalized movement to an immediate need for legal protection. However, one could argue that the emergence of copyright and

P. Kirch (✉)
Paul Hastings (Europe) LLP, Paris and Brussels Bars, Catholic University of Paris, Paris, France
e-mail: pierrekirch@paulhastings.com

A. Portuese (ed.), *Algorithmic Antitrust*, Economic Analysis of Law in European Legal Scholarship 12, https://doi.org/10.1007/978-3-030-85859-9_7

defamation laws, centuries later, in particular, resulted in some way from the existence of reproduction of written works derived, at its origin, from the use of printing machines. Inevitably, the time gap delta derives not only from the emergence of innovative technology and its influence on societal organization and behavior but political and societal pressure to regulate.

Historically, the most telling example of the time gap is undoubtedly the numerous decades it took for the law to catch up with the industrial revolution technology. For instance, in England in 1833, about a hundred years after the debut of the industrial revolution in England, the government passed a Factory Act to protect young children, who could be legally employed in factories as from 9 years of age. In Germany, labor unions started to emerge in the 1890s (some 150 years after the advent of the industrial revolution in Europe). In France, trade unions were prohibited by a law of 21 March 1884 at a critical turning point in the Industrial Revolution (electricity and the dawn of automobiles). It was only in 1936 (more than 200 years after the start of the Industrial Revolution in Europe) that the right to form unions was established, as well as other rights such as paid vacations. One may even be led to think that the law has still not fully caught up with the successive waves of the industrial revolution or is still a work in progress.

Coming now to the present and its challenges, the time gap phenomenon has now become critically acute in EU competition law enforcement. Technology, in recent years, has conspicuously accelerated in its rapidity of the change via an increased pace of innovation pa. For at least the first 40 years of the existence of EU competition law, from the time of the entry into force of the Treaty of Rome on 1 January 1958, it would be reasonable to argue that the time gap was not a specific issue. The pace of technological innovations followed a manageable rhythm, and the volume of phenomena were manageable as well. Subsequent technological innovations started to change that even-paced evolution, in particular the introduction and generalization of the use of personal computers and their integrated software in the late 1980s and 1990s (IBM/Microsoft, Apple), the introduction of the World Wide Web and then the Internet on a general public basis, in the mid-1990s. We know the rest of the story where the founding of Apple in 1976, Microsoft in 1981, Amazon in 1996, of Google in 1998, Facebook in 2002, just to limit the references of technological change to the "GAFAM" (Google, Apple, Facebook, Amazon, Microsoft), took place.

New algorithmic tools and considerable advances in data processing power have led to the production of heretofore unheard-of quantities of Big Data. Their exploitation, starting in around 2010, just 10 years ago as of this writing: a whole new game for competition regulators (Big Data, along with exponential advances in computing power, being the fuel used to trigger the development of many advances of Artificial Intelligence tools, in particular). And at the same time, in around 2010, the public has become aware of the invention of Blockchain, by the still unidentified creator of Bitcoins, "Satoshi Nakomoto". Bitcoins constitute, of course, the most celebrated use of Blockchain technology. More on Blockchain, below.

Increasingly, over the past 20 years or so, since the beginning of this century, it has been a challenge for the European Commission, as a competition enforcer, to react in a time-efficient way to the continually increasingly rapid flow of technological change. The issue of a time gap between technology advances and antitrust enforcement is quite recent, perhaps starting with the groundbreaking *Microsoft* case at the turn of the century. In a speech given in Brussels on 17 January 2019, the head of the European Commission Directorate-General for Competition opined in favor of the *status quo* to deal with technological changes: "*The fundamental EU Competition rules as embodied in the treaties have shown over their first 60 years of existence that they can capture changing realities and new phenomena*", whereas, 18 months later, the European Commissioner in charge of competition, Margrethe Vestager, was explaining the reasons for which she was proposing a "New Competition Tool": "*This new tool would let us deal with structural problems with competition, when we can't do that with the powers that we already have (...)*".[1]

In this Chapter, it will be demonstrated that, over the years, a competition enforcement discrepancy (or "technology innovation time gap") has emerged. It has become apparent that old regulatory tools, such as the Vertical Block Exemption Regulation (and its accompanying Commission Guidelines) respond to past phenomena without being a means to anticipate upon and regulate not only future and unknown technological change, but also those technological innovations, such as Blockchain, which are too "young" to have any enforcement precedent which would provide an analytical background for the needs of block exemptions and the guidance which defines their application in practical terms. This will be analyzed in Section I below. Suppose old tools are inadequate, at least in their traditional format and intended use (such as the block exemption) to address technological change. What recourse is available to the European Commission to deal with rapid technological innovation? Over the last few years, the Commissioner in charge of Competition, Margrethe Vestager, and the top officials of the Commission's Competition Directorate—General ("DG Competition"), have come back to this issue, repeatedly, fixatedly, in the policy speeches which the Commission systematically publishes on dedicated websites. The response is straightforward, in two points. First, where necessary, apply existing rules in new ways, by way of adaptation, including the resurrection of tools that were not used in the recent past, such as the recourse to interim measures which the Commission rediscovered in 2019 with regard to Broadcom, after an 18-year enforcement hiatus. Second, emerging in 2019 and into 2020, new tools are created to allow the Commission to react virtually immediately to new technological phenomena that introduce disruptive features into competition in certain markets, and this, with less and less procedural constraints. And this will be analyzed in Section II below.

[1] Laitenberger (2019); Vestager (2020).

2 Why The Vertical Block Exemption and Vertical Guidelines are Inadequate to Respond to the Technology Time Gap

It would be possible to take any of the various EU block exemptions to illustrate inadequacy in addressing the time gap between technological innovation and the tools of competition enforcement. However, the Vertical Block Exchange Regulation ("VBER")[2] and the European Commission's accompanying Guidelines (the "Vertical Guidelines")[3] are particularly *à propos,* in that the current texts, introduced in 2010, expire on May 31, 2022, and must be renewed, replaced, or left to lapse by that date. The issue is most current regarding the VBER and Vertical Guidelines, as the review process is more advanced than for other instruments, such as the horizontal block exemption and guidelines. Although the European Commission has a triple-option as to the solution that it may adopt, in what follows, we will analyze issues with the expectation that the Commission will follow the path of the inevitable and replace the current VBER by a new VBER and new Guidance before the May 31, 2022 deadline.

Indeed, what is striking about the current Vertical Guidelines, which set out the Commission's policy position on the application of the rather bare-bones text that is the VBER, is its concentration upon "bricks and mortar" distribution scenarios with scant reference being made to the various vertical antitrust issues which find their origin in the online world. The Vertical Guidelines encompass 229 paragraphs, of which only seven (paragraphs 51–54/56–58) include a specific policy position regarding distribution over the Internet, which is to say online distribution. The rest of the Guidelines follow traditional brick and mortar vertical analysis (much of that analysis is, of course, transposable, *mutatis mutandis*, to the online world, but the Commission's text does not try: the parties concerned must make a self-analysis of how to transpose bricks and mortar language to the virtual world).

And these seven paragraphs concerning online distribution are concentrated, in essence, on just one legal point: the application of Articles 4 (b) and 4 (c) of the VBER, which defines as a "hardcore restriction" leading to the inapplicability of the safe harbor of the block exemption, of any vertical covenant which restricts *"the territory into which, or of the customers to whom, a buyer party to the agreement (...) may sell the contract goods on services"* with several exceptions to that prohibition, and most notably, in the first instance *"the restriction of active sales into exclusive territory or to an exclusive customer group reserved to the supplier or allocated by the supplier to another buyer, where such a restriction does not limit by the customers of the buyer (...)".*

[2]Commission Regulation (EU) No 330/2010 of 20 April 2010, On the application of Article 101 (3) of the Treaty on the Functioning of the European Union to categories of vertical agreements and concerted practices, OJEU 2010, n°L 102/1.

[3]European Commission, Guidelines on Vertical Restraints, OJEU 2010, n°C 130/1.

At the time of the last review, more than 10 years ago now, via the Vertical Guidelines, the Commission considered necessary to delineate the distinctions between active and passive sales in the on-line world, where physical territories do not exist. This was a significant issue at the time (it has now become banal). The analysis is based on a definition of "passive sales" which is straightforward, as set out at par. 51 of the Vertical Guidelines: *"Passive sales mean responding to unsolicited requests from individual customers, including delivery of goods or services to such customers. General advertising or promotions that reaches customers in other distributors' exclusive territories or customer groups but which is reasonable way to reach customers outside those territories or customers groups, corollary to that rule, established by Commission policy and the case law, is that, although the protection in favor of an exclusive distributor against active sales into the territory is valid, a prohibition against passive sales into the territory is not... instance to reach customers in one's own territory, are considered passive selling (...)"*.

The Commission goes on to analyze the consequences of recourse to internet sales (Para. 52: *"The internet is a powerful tool to reach a greater number and variety of customers than by more traditional sales methods"*) concerning the application of Article 4 (b) (i) VBER, which deprives from the benefit of the block exemption *"the restriction of active sales into the exclusive territory or to an exclusive customer group reserved to the supplier or allocated by the supplier to another [exclusive] buyer (...)*". It establishes the following guidance (para. 52–54):

- As a general principle, *"Every distributor must be allowed to use the internet to sell products."*
- The simple use of a website is considered, as a general principle, to constitute a *"form of passive selling"* (any effects into another distributor's exclusive territory result *from "the technology allowing easy access from everywhere: if a customer visits the website of a distributor and contacts the distributor and if such contact leads to a sale, including delivery, then that is considered passive selling (...) offering different language options in the website does not, of itself, change the passive characters of such selling").*
- A restriction on a distributor's use of the internet for sales is valid and thus compatible with the VBER to the extent that promotion on the internet or use of the internet would tend to active sales into another exclusive distributor's territory. This would be the case of online advertisements addressed specifically to the other exclusive distributor's customers. Banners that would specifically identify the other distributor's exclusive territory would qualify as active sales.
- As for selective distribution, a supplier may require that the use of an internet site by selective distributors correspond to quality standards, in the same way that the supplier may require the same of brick-and-mortar stores to ensure that the act of sale correspond to the luxury brand image or technical sophistication of the product. The same requirements may be imposed where sales are made through a third-party platform, to maintain brand image. In addition, the suppliers may require that the selective distributor before having recourse to internet sales, have

created "*one or more brick and mortar shops or showrooms as a condition for becoming a member of the distribution system*."

- In sales performance between off-line and online sales, any difference in treatment must be grounded in objectively justified differences in performance criteria as imposed by the supplier.

In June 2020, the European Commission published an independent study prepared by a consortium of economic consultancies and institutes, entitled "*Evaluation support study on the EU competition rules applicable to vertical agreements in the VBER and the Guidelines*" (the "VBER Support Study").[4] In this respect, the Commission is working well in advance of its deadline (31 May 2022), to renew, replace or allow to lapse the current block exemption. Already, in 2019, the Commission had conducted a public consultation and in August 2019, it had published a summary of the results of the public consultation. Over hundreds and hundreds of pages, the VBER Support Study seems to constitute the major source of analysis based on data in pointing towards a draft of a new VBER and Commission Guidelines.

The VBER Support Study relies on several analytical tools: (i) the results of the public consultation (which the Commission finished in mid-2019), (ii) a review of the 392 cases before national competition authorities and Courts identified and cataloged by the authors of the study whose decisions were based on the VBER, (iii) detailed business model case studies (Zalando, Uber, Amazon) undertaken by the authors; (iv) interviews and CATI ("Computer Assisted Telephone Interviews") questionnaires; (v) review of academic and non-academic research and literature; (vi) empirical study of consumer online behavior; (vii) econometric analysis; (viii) stakeholders workshop. With the annexes, the VBER Support Study is more than 500 pages long.

Now that the European Commission has this study, it has begun to integrate it into its thinking. On 8 September 2020, the Commission published a "Staff Working Document Evaluation of the Vertical Block Exemption Regulation".[5] Once again, a voluminous contribution (232 pages). The purpose of it is to set out an evaluation of the VBER, "*based on evidence gathered from various sources*", including (i) the public consultation (responses from 164 stakeholders), (ii) a targeted consultation of EU Member State NCAs (20 responses), (iii) a stakeholder workshop, (iv) the VBER Support Study and (v) "*evidence gathered in the context of other Commission initiatives*" such as its e-commerce sector inquiry and enforcement experiences.[6] As a general observation about this document, what is of particular interest is the Commission's acknowledgement of the inability of the 2010 version of the VBER and the Vertical Guidelines to bridge the technological gap in a workable way: "*The main concern that arises from the evaluation is the fact that the VBER and the*

[4]European Commission (2020a).

[5]Commission Staff Working Document Evaluation of the Vertical Block Exemption Regulation, (SWD (2020) 173 Final).

[6]Id, p. 88.

Vertical Guidelines are not well adapted to the market developments that took place since the adoption of the rules, notably the growth of online sales and of new market players such as online platforms".[7]

And this conclusion as to the possible need for a change in method: "*(...) The evaluation has shown that market developments that take place after the adoption of the rules can have an impact not just on the relevance but also on the effectiveness and efficiency of the rules. Future market developments are of course hard to predict, and it is therefore challenging to design a set of rules that allows such developments to be taken into account. Nevertheless, this suggests that there is a need for rules which are, to the extent possible, future proof. This means that they should not only address known issues but also contain bright-line principles that can cater for possible new types of vertical agreements and restrictions*".[8]

The Commission's logical next step will be to proceed to an impact assessment and the drafting of a proposal (presuming that it opts to replace the existing VBER by a new VBER), which we are anticipating for 2021. The VBER Support Study is dense. It represents a colossal enterprise by four economic consultancies working together, with additional individual contributions: a total of about twenty persons as authors.

The case studies alone (Zalando, Uber, Amazon) make for fascinating reading, which we recommend for background on how the most advanced internet platforms operate, in specific terms, for both goods and services. However, for this analysis, we would like to concentrate on three other points developed in the study, on a more general basis.

The *first* point is the general attempt to catch up with over 10 years of technological change, barely dealt with in the Vertical Guidelines. As noted above, the VBER exercise (and that of EU block exemptions in general), is a backwards-looking exercise. In the current, 2010 version of the Vertical Guidelines, and as noted above, the internet, which was at the time of preparation of the current VBER and Vertical Guidelines in full development for electronic platform-based distribution (one need only think of Amazon, already a fully generalized online sales platform in 2010), was analyzed in only seven of 219 paragraphs of European Commission guidance. The VBER Support Study just released in 2020, comes out, indeed, as a *backward-looking* analysis of internet vertical phenomena, but totally ignores the effects of other tools of *forward-looking* technological change, such as the use of algorithms and blockchain in vertical relationships. The VBER Support Study makes the demonstration on the relevance of internet platforms in the period leading up to the 2010 issuance of the current VBER and Vertical Guidelines through its case study of Amazon. The case study notes that already in 2007, Amazon had launched Amazon Pay, and that by 2009, its services had extended from its retail business (that is to say vertical distribution) basics such as books ("content") and self-manufactured electronic devices (tablets, streaming devices,

[7] Id, p. 92.

[8] Id, p. 93.

e-book readers (Kindle)), etc, to a broader offering including products such as notebook cases, batteries or computer and audio/video cables under private labels, including, the Amazon Basics brand.[9]

The purpose of the VBER Support Study, as stated by the authors, is to "provide evidence-based grounds for a possible revision of the VBER and the Vertical Guidelines, through identification *and analysis of provisions which may no longer be up to date with the latest market developments and business practices, and/or overlay with other provisions or give rise to possible inconsistencies*".[10] As a general conclusion, the authors conclude that "*there is potentially room for improvement of the VBER and the Guidelines.*"[11] The study relies heavily on interviews with market players. In general, these opined that "*the VBER and the Guidelines do not sufficiently reflect the market changes and e-commerce developments, especially the increased importance of e-commerce leading to reduced relevance and effectiveness of the VBER and Vertical Guidelines (. . .).*"[12]

It can be anticipated that the new future Vertical Guidelines which will accompany the new VBER (presuming, on a logical basis, that the Commission will decide to replace the current VBER by a new one before the deadline of 31 May 2022), will be a somewhat internet-concentric guidance document. Already in its market consultation, the Commission inferred that it would be working in catch-up made on that point. Indeed, in launching its public consultation on the VBER and Vertical Guidelines in May 2019, the Commission had to admit that its gathering of evidence on the functioning of the VBER, would need to be made "*in light of the new market developments since their adoption in 2010, notably the increased importance of on-line sales and the emergence of new market players such as online platforms*".[13]

The Commission's consultation questionnaire was heavily weighted towards an understanding of online phenomena. The consultation was held between 4 February 2019 and 27 May 2019. Some five hundred companies and stakeholders responded. Once the Commission had digested that input from the market, it organized, on 14 and 15 November 2019, a vast "stakeholder workshop" at Autoworld, Parc du Cinquantenaire, in Brussels. The interest of the exercise: the workshop thematics corresponded, logically, to the Commission's perception in 2019 of issues arising from the public consultations. These have been summarized in a Commission document, post-workshop, entitled "*Summary of the stakeholders workshop on the evaluation of the Vertical Block Exemption Regulation (EU) n°330/2010*".[14] Indeed, as narrated by the Commission, during the course of the workshop "*four roundtable discussions covered different issues in relation to the treatment of online sales in the current rules such as (i) restrictions on the use of third party online platforms, price*

[9]European Commission (2020a).

[10]Id., Section 1.3 ("Objectives of the Study").

[11]Ibid, Section 4.1 ("Types of Vertical Restraints").

[12]Ibid, Section 4.1.2 ("Legal certainty (. . .)").

[13]European Commission (2018a).

[14]European Commission (2018b).

companies, tools and search origins, (ii) dual pricing and (iii) more generally, how to protect investments against free-riding by online distributors."[15]

As noted above (Amazon case study, in particular), online sales were fully developed in 2010: the Commission could have dealt with these three fundamental issues as listed above at the time of preparation of the 2010 version of the VBER and the Commission Guidelines. It has been the case because of the absence of experience on the issues in real life circumstances. As noted above, the preparation of a block exemption is a backward-looking exercise, not a forward-looking exercise, and the Commission looks to have firsthand experience in antitrust issues before it commits to a policy option in safe-harbor guidelines. Hence, the relative silence of the Commission in the Vertical Guidelines: only 7 of 219 paragraphs dedicated to online vertical antitrust issues in the 2010 version of the Vertical Guidelines.

At present, thanks to the research of the team which put together the VBER Support Study, the Commission has an abundance of precedent to work with: 392 cases from EU Member State competition authorities and courts. Given that the VBER and the Commission's Vertical Guidelines—as with any block exemption exercise—are backward-looking for purposes of consolidating the enforcement of the relevant antitrust rules at a specific point in time (on this case, that point in time will be set at 31 May 2022), it is to be expected that the Commission will exploit, to the extent logically possible, the lessons learned in the 392 cases of application of the VBER/Vertical Guidelines by EU national competition authorities and national courts, to extract from them revised vertical principles, to the extent possible and necessary. The authors of the Vertical Support Study have prepared the way. The 392 precedents over a 10-year period have been classified and analyzed, by EU Member State and issue category.

Of the 392 cases, fifty-two come from the Austrian competition authority, forty-one from the Slovak authority, thirty-two from the French *Autorité de la Concurrence*, thirty-one from the German authority (*Bundeskartellamt*), thirty from the UK Competition and Markets Authority (CMA). Most of the cases (222 out of 392) concerned price restrictions (resale price maintenance/maximum resale price/ recommended resale price), sixty-four selective distribution issues, thirty-seven exclusive distributors, twenty "Most Favored Nation" ("MFN") arrangements, with other cases concerning diverse antitrust issues such as single branding and franchising.[16]

During the 10 years of the current VBER, the most significant case at the EU level was a preliminary reference case to the European Court of Justice in Case C-230/16 Coty Germany GmbH Oberlandesgericht Frankfurt. The issue was, precisely, the interpretation of Articles 4(b) and 4(c) of the VBER, provisions that were the subject of guidance in the Vertical Guidelines.[17] The preliminary reference request was

---

[15] Ibid, p. 6.

[16] European Commission (2020a).

[17] European Court of Justice, judgment of 6 December 2017, Coty Germany GmbH, Case C-230/ 16, EU: C: 2017.

submitted in the context of a dispute between Coty Germany, a supplier of luxury cosmetics, and Parfümeric Akzente GmbH, an authorized distributor of those goods, under a standard selective distribution contract between Coty Germany and its authorized distributors. The dispute centered around Akzente's recourse to third party electronic platforms for internet sales. It should be recalled that certain restrictions are deprived of the VBER's safe harbor under Article 4, and in particular (i) "*the restriction of the territory into which, or of the customers to whom, a buyer party to the agreement, without prejudice to a restriction as its place of establishment may sell the contract goods or services (...)*" (Article 4(b)) and "*the restriction of active or passive sales to end users by members of a selective distribution system operating at the retail level of trade (...)*". In the facts of the case, Akzente, the selective distributor, distributed Coty Germany goods via both its brick-and-mortar locations and over the internet, partly through its own online store and partly via the electronic platform amazon.de.

The selective distribution agreement binding the parties included the following provision: "*The character of Coty Prestige's brands requires selective distribution in order to support the luxury image of these brands*" and included requirements as to the "luxury character" of Façade, interior furnishings and floor covering types of walls, ceilings, furniture, sales space, and lighting ("as well as an overall clean and orderly appearance"). Sales through a non-authorized third party were prohibited. At the time of entry into force of the VBER in 2010, Coty Germany had revised the standard selective distribution agreement to allow for sale of its products on the internet, provided however the internet sales activity is conducted through an electronic shop window of the authorized store and the luxury character of the products is preserved.[18] Akzente refused to sign the modified contract and Coty brought action before the German Courts to seek an order prohibiting the sale of its products via amazon.de.

Established EU case law sets selective distributors outside of the prohibition of Article 101(1) TFEU provided that (i) the characteristics of the products concerned necessitate a selective distribution network in order to preserve "*quality*" and ensure "*proper use*" and (ii) the selection of resellers is based upon objective and qualitative criteria, limited to what is necessary, applied uniformity and, in a non-discriminatory fashion.[19] With regard to luxury goods, the Court stated that the reference to quality included not only "*material characteristics*" but also "*the allure and prestigious image which bestow on them an aura of luxury, that aura is essential in that it enables consumers to distinguish them from similar goods and that therefore an impairment to that aura of luxury is likely to affect the actual quality of those goods*".[20] The Court decided that, subject to factual inquiries to be made by the referring court, the prohibition on sales via third party platforms was lawful

[18] Id, para. 9–16.

[19] Id, para. 24 cf. European Court of Justice, judgment of 13 October 2011, Pierre Fabre, Dermo-Cosmétique, Case C-439/09, EU: C: 2011: 649, para. 49.

[20] Id, para. 25.

concerning Article 101(1) TFEU (rendering the issue of the VBER safe harbor a moot point). The Court pointed to the absence of a contract between the supplier and the third-party platform, the risk of deterioration of the luxury image (potentially unbeknownst to the supplier), and the fact that such prohibition did not go beyond what was strictly necessary, since a Commission study had shown that the main channel of online distribution was constituted by distributors' own online shops (not third-party channels such as amazon.de).[21]

The reasoning of the Court in *Coty* is elegant and relies on a deepened interpretation of its prior case law (*Copad*, judgment of 23 April 2009 Case C-59-08 and *Pierre Fabre Dermo-Cosmétique*, judgment of 13 October 2011, Case 439/09). What is most noteworthy, however, is the absence of any reference whatsoever to the Vertical Guidelines. Indeed, in 2010, the year in which the VBER and the Vertical Guidelines entered into force, the internet and internet sales, including via platforms such as amazon.de, was a considerable technological phenomenon. According to Internet World Stats, in June 2010, almost two billion people in the world were using the Internet (in June 2020, the figure has grown to 4.65 billion about 60% of the world population). The reason for so little guidance concerning the Internet in 2010 lays on the lack of experience. The Commission tends to avoid speculations in its block exemption guidance on-hands, real-life.

Prior to the entry into force of the VBER in 2010, the Commission had apparently, no practical experience of internet distribution to draw upon for the Vertical Guidelines. Hence, seven spare paragraphs out of 219 which refer to internet in its vertical aspects, and in those seven paragraphs, no citations to precedent. Now, in drawing upon a revised version of the VBER for 2022, and new Vertical Guidelines, the Commission will benefit from 392 precedent cases at national level (many of which involve, logically, although this was not a categorical criterion for analysis internet distribution), as well as the *Coty* judgment and the many hundreds of pages of analysis in the VBER Support Study published in June 2020 and the stakeholders' comments submitted as published a year earlier.

In the run-up, by 31 May 2022, to what will be, logically, a new VBER and a significantly revised and modernized version of the Vertical Guidelines, it may be anticipated that considerations of internet distribution will be given a key role in the analysis. Sales via internet platforms represent, in 2020, a major chunk of economic activity in Europe. Internet represents a mature distribution channel. Amazon is one of the world's biggest companies in terms of revenues (around USD 300 billion). On the other hand, in the current state of things, the new texts will probably remain silent on the more recent technology which will likely mark in a unique way both horizontal and vertical markets over the next 15 years, during the period of validity of the next version of the VBER and Commission Guidelines and that is Blockchain.

It should be emphasized that, from the point of view of market players, *Coty* seems to have engendered a whole new series of issues that the Commission is expected to deal with in the latest version of the Vertical Guidelines. *"The*

[21] Id, para. 49–58.

roundtable participants also pointed to the current lack of guidance on the Coty ruling, notably with regard to its scope and the product categories covered".[22] The preliminary reference ruling in *Coty* was made in specific reference to a supplier selling luxury brand products (and the Court went to lengths to establish that it was reasoning concerning luxury products): *quid* of all the other platforms out there which fall outside of the "luxury" definition? Quid of other restrictions that can emerge from internet platforms such as prohibitions using comparison tools or restrictions on distributors bidding for supplier-brand-related keywords in auctions conducted by a platform operator (such as Google Adwords) in cases in which the supplier would want to retain for itself bidding rights? There are many questions extant, and the issue will arise whether the VBER Support Study, in particular, will bring to the Commission the confidence to deal with such issues where it has no case precedent to rely upon.

What is striking in this block exemption exercise is the absence of any forward-looking guidance in connection with present and future technology breakthroughs. The most crying example is that of Blockchain. There is no antitrust precedent regarding Blockchain at this writing at this writing, at least not within the European Union. There is no reference to Blockchain in all the European Commission documentation relating to the new VBER. The absence of reference to Blockchain can only be explained by the will of the European Commission to conduct a backward-looking exercise by which it would bring the VEBR up to date on the basis of past precedent (the 392 national cases and *Coty*) and other *past* analyses, interviews, and scholarly writing and the VBER Support Study, but not speculate on innovative technologies. And yet, such silence on Blockchain, reflects, logically, a policy choice by the Commission, to avoid exploring such future phenomena, in cases where future phenomena have no case precedents within the EU, nothing but educated speculation to rely on.

Blockchain has been a major technological breakthrough in a way similar to the Internet, and this only over the past decade. It is an emerging technology, which is becoming increasingly mainstream, with a variety of uses. Even the banking establishment has begun to embrace Blockchain as a means of diversification into digital money: for instance, over the past year, Société Générale has issued bonds in a digital money of the Banque de France, and secured the emission through Blockchain technology (the bonds are materialized via security tokens on a blockchain register).[23] Blockchain is, of course, a peer-to-peer electronic ledger, which operates via a computer network and which has four characteristics in comparison with other technologies: (i) decentralized control amongst users, (ii) consensus mechanisms via unstoppable code, (iii) user pseudonimity due to access via electronic keys private and (in private and some permissioned networks, identity must be established), (iv) immutability of recorded information and transactions, once verification via the consensus mechanism has taken place.

[22] European Commission (2018b).

[23] Feat (2020).

In recent years, Blockchain has attracted a lot of attention from an antitrust perspective, essentially from a horizontal approach, spanning public and private/permissioned networks. Schrepel sets out a clear delineation of these risks in his article, "Collusion by Blockchain and Smart Contracts," published in 2019 in the *Harvard Journal of Law & Technology*.[24] The analysis is forward-looking in that there is no precedent to be cited. For Schrepel, Blockchain can facilitate the creation of two types of collusive agreements: (i) "*agreements that directly concern the conditions of access, use and/or exit from the blockchain*" and (ii) agreements that "*are created outside the blockchain which use the technology to make the agreements more efficient*." A characteristic of Blockchain is the availability of information to all users: could this be a means of coordination between competitors? Will price transparency amongst competitors within a blockchain network stifle competition due to reducing market uncertainty (all operators disposing of the same market information via the blockchain)? And then there is the issue of whether an enterprise (or enterprises, collectively) in dominant position which has created a private or permissioned blockchain (this being the sole provider of the technology) were to exclude a market competitor, and thus abuse of a dominant position within the meaning of Article 102 TFEU.[25]

This being said, little or no attention has been given in the specialist *legal* literature to antitrust *vertical* issues deriving from the use of Blockchain. In contrast, non-legal Blockchain specialists see Blockchain as a tool to revolutionize, *inter alia*, supply chain management.[26] Simply put, Blockchain ensures the traceability, transparency, and immutability of every aspect of a supply chain which is managed through it.

This is when the fact that the VBER and the Vertical Guidelines are backward-looking, not forward-looking legal instruments comes into play once again. In its VBER consultation document in 2019, no reference was made to Blockchain by the Commission. In the VBER Support Study published in June 2020, no reference was made to Blockchain (over more than five hundred pages of analysis). It seems highly probable that the new VBER and new Vertical Guidelines which will predictably enter into force in mid-2022 and remain applicable through to 2032 or 2034 will be devoid of any reference, any guidance whatsoever, with regard to Blockchain. And yet, the Commission as an *institution* has considerable expertise in Blockchain issues, through the EU Blockchain Observatory and Forum. On 27 September 2019, it published a thematic report entitled "*Legal and Regulatory Framework of Blockchains and Smart Contracts*" which states: "*If the blockchain will indeed become the catalyst for innovation, jobs and economic growth in the EU that many hopes, there is no doubt that a key element will be a predictable legal and regulatory framework for blockchains and smart contracts*".[27]

---

[24] Schrepel (2019, p. 118).

[25] Ibid, pp. 128–134.

[26] Brody (2017).

[27] EU Blockchain Observatory & Forum (2019).

The report includes a section entitled "*Risk to Fair Competition*," which concentrates on risks of collusive conduct and abuse of dominance, without any specific reference to vertical issues. The report refers to the issue of information exchange. It identifies the case where guidance would be helpful: "*The increased transparency advanced by blockchains could pose competition law infringement risks linked to information exchange. Seeing as information exchange on a blockchain can generate inefficiencies by improving contractability, its incompatibility with Article 101 TFEU needs to be evaluated on a case-by-case basis*".[28] Any guidance today on antitrust issues and Blockchain is necessarily forward-looking and block exemptions instruments such as the VBER and the Commission Guidelines are backward-looking. Where, then, will the guidance come from regarding new technological tools such as Blockchain?

3 The Commission's New Tools for Bridging the Technological Time Gap

The VBER and the Commission's Vertical Guidelines, as well as the other block exemptions and their guidelines, are manifestly useful instruments for purposes of enforcement and adjudication: as set out in the VBER Support Study, there were 392 cases of recourse to the VBER as an adjudicatory or regulatory tool in the Member States over an approximate 10-year period 2010-2020. This constitutes, manifestly, a corpus of precedent which can be analyzed for purposes of a new, revised VBER as from 1 June 2022. This said, the EU block exemption system is old law. It is, as an antitrust practitioner has said, "*a vestige of the pre-modernisation era*" (Jean-François Bellis) which has continued to function in the era of antitrust modernization, as practiced over the last 20 years, approximately. The EU block exemption system is unique. Non-EU antitrust lawyers, who are familiar with the US-style "*rule of reason*" approach, can have difficulty in grasping its concepts. It is "backward-looking," not "forward-looking."

In 2010, the contemporary example was the inability of the new VBER and Vertical Guidelines to capture the true importance of internet distribution as a technological tool in full break-through mode at the time (as shown by Amazon's concurrent explosive growth): the VBER was not a forward-looking tool. In 2020, the new contemporary example is Blockchain, which is a tool of today well-known to the European Commission as an institution (creation of the Blockchain Observatory and Forum in 2018), but which represents a total blank for the Competition Commissioner, Margrethe Vestager and DG Competition up to the present. And yet, as noted above, Blockchain will continue to develop, perhaps exponentially, as a technologically disruptive instrument over the coming years, having both horizontal and vertical market effects. By recourse to standard search engines and

---

[28] Id, pp. 20–21.

keywords, it has not been possible to identify any statements by the EU Competition Commission (Margrethe Vestager) or senior staff at DG Competition, which consider Blockchain as a horizontal or vertical antitrust phenomenon. This is due to an obvious reason: there have not (yet) been any cases. But, as the use of Blockchain becomes more general (and it is in the process of doing so), there will, logically, be cases (both horizontal and vertical cases).

Meanwhile, the text of the new VBER and new Vertical Guidelines will be set non varietur for 10 or 12 years, up to 2032? 2034? 2035? When the cases do come, it seems likely (based on the current approach) that the current and future VBER and Vertical Guidelines will not include any particular approach or insight towards the application of the EU competition rules to vertical Blockchain relationships. During the last 10 years or so, as the rhythm and nature of technological change became more acute, the European Commission insisted that the basic principles had stood the test of time, due to their "stability and flexibility." In a speech in Brussels on 1 March 2018, Johannes Laitenberger, at the time Director-General for Competition, addressed the issue of "whether disruptive competition disrupts competition enforcement." He said:

> Change is undeniable. In our practice at DG Competition, we see it every day. Scientific and technological innovation sparks new business models and makes others increasingly obsolete (...). We must make sure today – as our predecessors had to make sure 60 years ago, when the EU competition rules were first enacted in the EU Treaties – that markets remain open and contestable; that consumers are not harmed by distortions of the competitive process, by anti-competitive agreements (...). This mandate, this remit, is a beacon that guides us through disruptive change. And this is so because it is a lesson distilled out of disruptive change (...). This is why EU competition law has been historically resilient. Business, the economy, and society have changed beyond recognition since EU competition rules came into effect 60 years ago. But our basic principles have stood the test of time (...). Our ground rules were designed to be future-proof – in the EEC at first and later in the EU – precisely so that they can accompany an economy in there (...). The Treaties' competition rules have remained unchanged, relevant and effective over time because they were designed to be applicable to a wide range of developments, They are not a static implementation program.[29]

That was in 2018. By the turn of the decade into 2020, the European Commission had changed the discourse, in favor of *new tools*. On 9 December 2019, Margrethe Vestager, the EU's Competition Commissioner, told an audience at the Chillin' Competition Conference in Brussels, that "*The challenges we're facing, at the start of this new decade, mean that we need to look again at the tools we use to enforce the competition rules*".[30] The next day, on 10 December 2019, at another conference, the Acting Director-General for Competition, Cecilio Madero, stated: "*Today's digital markets in particular often present issues that we have analysed in practice but not set out in an updated notice, such as how to deal with zero-price products/services and the consideration of digital ecosystems in our analysis. So perhaps the question*

[29] Laitenberger (2018).

[30] Vestager (2019).

is not really whether we have the right tools to intervene, but how to ensure that intervention is timely enough to prevent irreparable harm in fast-moving markets."[31]

The Commission announced a series of measures to address technological change in a rapid way. *First*, it resurrected the legal tool of interim measures (which had not been used over the previous 18 years), in a case in which it ordered Broadcom to stop enforcing customer contracts including exclusivity of chips supply temporarily.[32] *Secondly*, it announced a plan to revamp its market definition guidance, to reflect more recent cases and, in particular, digital markets: "*(. . .) How to deal with zero-price products/services and the consideration of digital ecosystems in our analysis*."[33] Thirdly, the Commission launched a public consultation on platform-specific ex-ante regulation. On other fronts relating to technological change the Commission published, *inter alia*, in February 2020, its White Paper on artificial intelligence (trust-based AI ecosystem)[34] and in May 2020, it launched a public consultation on a Digital Services Act. As Ms. Vestager acknowledged in a speech at the ASCOLA Annual Conference on 26 June 2020. "*(. . .) There's no one, simple solution. We need a mix of approaches. That includes new regulations, and new competition powers. But it also means making full use of the ones we already have*."[35] This has led Mrs. Vestager, on behalf of the Commission, to introduce, on 2 June 2020, a new tool which would allow the Commission to intervene directly in markets where the "*very structure of a market can create problems for competition" and to "carry out market investigations and impose remedies to fix any competition problems they find (. . .) by imposing obligations that would protect competition*".[36] This is the (appropriately named) "New Competition Tool" and, along with the recent announcement of its creation, the Commission launched a concomitant public consultation.[37]

The New Competition Tool reflects a whole innovative approach to EU antitrust enforcement, totally removed from the "*pre-modernisation*" concept of self-assessment block exemption regulations, such as the VBER. The Commission will logically keep the VBER and the Vertical Guidelines (as well as the other block exemption instruments) in its toolbox as these traditional self-assessment mechanisms do provide a means of some legal comfort or even legal "security" to market operators as based on past experience. But the Commission seems to point to a future of freehold interventionist tools, with a certain dose of legal "discomfort," from unpredictability, for operators. Under the New Competition Tool, the Commission could intervene directly in markets where it has identified competition concerns, with a minimum of procedure. Not to impose fines for infringements, but rather to impose behavioral and structural remedies. Although digital markets inspired the

---

[31] Madero (2019).

[32] European Commission (2019).

[33] Madero (2019).

[34] European Commission (2020b).

[35] Vestager (2019).

[36] Id.

[37] European Commission (2020c).

creation of the tool, its use is intended to span all industrial and services markets. In practical terms, the Commission could use the tool to reshape an entire industry, at least for its operations in the European Union. The Commission motivates the need for a New Competition Tool by reference to the concept that digital markets may involve anti-competitive characteristics which extend beyond the reach of current EU antitrust tools. The New Competition Tool is intended to be resolutely forward-looking. It is not intended to regulate as based upon past market characteristics (as the new VBER will do, for instance), but to intervene in market change *as it happens*, when such change engenders real-time competition concerns, in line with four "use" scenarios identified by the Commission:

- *Option 1*: A dominance-based competition tool with a horizontal scope (unilateral conduct by dominant companies: any markets)
- *Option 2*: A dominance-based competition tool with limited scope (unilateral conduct by dominant companies, but limited to problematic sectors only, and in particular digital or digitally enabled markets)
- *Option 3*: A market structure- based competition tool with a horizontal scope: intervention in accordance with test based structural risk for competition/structural lack of competition.
- *Option 4*: A market structure-based competition tool with a limited scope (use of tool restricted to problematic sectors only: certain digital or digitally enabled markets, or other sectors prone to similar concerns).

As for Blockchain, its relevance as a vertical tool (supply chain, but not only) will almost certainly be absent from the new VBER and Vertical Guidelines. Which means that it will be exposed to the Commission's new forward-looking method to deal with technological change, consisting of ad-hoc enforcement issues, within a (relatively) brief-lapse of time as soon as there is perception of a need. Regarding Blockchain, there are signs that the seeds of the "need" are already in the process of being nurtured. As noted above, although the EU Competition Commissioner, Margrethe Vestager, and DG Competition officials have made no public pronouncements about Blockchain, the Commission, as an *institution* has, indirectly, through the recently published report of the EU Blockchain Observatory and Forum, taken some initiatives on proposing, in general terms, a competition law approach to Blockchain. In the thematic report referenced above, *Legal and Regulatory Framework of Blockchains and Smart Contracts*, the Observatory not only takes note of certain issues around a "*Risk to Fair Competition*," but also the potential for new competition rules to deal specifically with Blockchain: "*Whether Competition policy would need to develop new norms or tools will depend on the nature and effects of the economic activity transacted on Blockchains. No two cases are likely to be identical and a competition law assessment will depend entirely on the particular circumstances of a given Blockchain and the relevant market.*" At the same time, the Observatory notes that permissioned blockchains would need to be attentive to ensuring that Blockchain code is compatible with the competition law framework under the "*self-assessment*" method of EU Competition law (replicated in national laws of Member States).

One final thought, inspired by the report of the EU Blockchain Observatory: the idea that regulators, themselves, could "*make use of Blockchain as a regulatory tool.*" This is the final recommendation of the report: "*Last but not least, we think an excellent way for regulators to help monitor and regulate the industry is to get involved themselves, (…) as an indirect method of regulation through helping to shape the ecosystem. Blockchain also offers potentially powerful new regulatory tools. For example, regulators could plug themselves into new Blockchain-based platforms as they come online, unleashing new opportunities to improve the efficacy but also efficiency of their operations – including potentially with real-time regulatory monitoring and intervention capabilities.*"

Perhaps there are plans within DG Competition of the European Commission to participate directly, as suggested, in the eco-system of technological innovation. If so, such plans are not yet public. But there is at least one competition authority which seems to have caught the basic idea of getting directly involved in technological innovation, and that is the French Competition Authority (*l'Autorité de la Concurrence).* On 19 February 2020, it published a "contribution" to the discussion around competition policy and digitalization, in which it included specifically Blockchain amongst the new technologies, at the origin of its reflections (along with the use of algorithms and Artificial Intelligence and cloud computing).[38] Without going into the detail of the contribution, it should be noted that the French Competition Authority clearly indicates that Blockchain is at the heart of emerging new technologies that are the subject of its analysis. More telling information comes from a communiqué from the same Authority, issued at about the same time, showing its willingness to "*get its hands dirty*" by not only working towards competition enforcement tools for purposes of addressing these innovative technologies, but, as the EU Blockchain Observatory recommends, "*to get involved themselves*" through actual plug-in and direct use. On 9 January 2020, the French Competition Authority announced the creation of a new digital unit, tasked with "*developing in-depth expertise in all digital areas*": "*This unit will take part in the Authority's discussions and sector-specific inquiries on new issues related to the development of digital technology, in line with those already carried out on big data, online advertising and algorithms. It will thus be able to contribute to on-going studies on payments, blockchain platforms and technologies, as well as to changes to physical retail brought about by digital technology ("phygital" study)*" including - and this is what is truly noteworthy - the development and use of "*new digital investigation tools based in particular on algorithmic technology, big data and artificial intelligence (…) to effectively crack down on anticompetitive effects on competition (…)*".[39] The germinal idea seems to be there: in order to regulate the use of algorithms and other new technological tools such as Blockchain when instrumental to the market behavior of companies, the Authority must be prepared to develop its own matching

[38] French Competition Authority (2020a).

[39] French Competition Authority (2020b).

technological tools. On a forward-looking basis, some of antitrust enforcement seems to be evolving towards an "*our tools versus yours*" set-up.

4 Conclusion

There is, today, considerable pressure on the European Commission and other competition regulators to intervene quickly in markets. The current review procedure of the VBER and the Vertical Guidelines has allowed to understand that old, traditional tools, with their backward-looking approach, do not seem to constitute sufficient means to bridge technological time gaps. Old regulatory tools respond to past phenomena without being a means to anticipate future market developments deriving from technological change. The Commission has recognized that it is difficult to predict future market developments. It has been acknowledged that it would be challenging to design a set of rules, such as the future version of the VBER, which would allow for such developments to be considered in the rules. For the European Commission, the solution seems to be in developing new, variable tools, based on broad rights of market intervention.

References

Brody P (2017) Paul Brody, "How blockchain is revolutionizing supply chain management", Digitalist Magazine by SAP, August 23, 2017, available at: https://www.ey.com/Publication/vwLUAssets/ey-blockchain-and-the-supply-chain-three/$FILE/ey-blockchain-and-the-supply-chain-three.pdf

EU Blockchain Forum (2019) Legal and Regulatory Framework of Blockchains and Smart Contracts, Report published on 27 September 2019, available at: https://www.eublockchainforum.eu/sites/default/files/reports/report_legal_v1.0.pdf

European Commission (2018a) Consultation strategy for the evaluation of the Vertical Block Exemption Regulation, available at: https://ec.europa.eu/competition/consultations/2018_vber/consultation_strategy.pdf

European Commission (2018b) Summary of the stakeholder workshop on the evaluation of the Vertical Block Exemption Regulation (EU) No330/2010, available at: https://ec.europa.eu/competition/consultations/2018_vber/workshop_summary.pdf

European Commission (2019) Antitrust: Commission imposes interim measures on Broadcom in TV and modem chipset markets. Presse Release, 16 October 2019, available at: https://ec.europa.eu/commission/presscorner/detail/en/IP_19_6109

European Commission (2020a) Support studies for the evaluation of the VBER (final report), prepared by Valdani Vicari & Associates, Economics & Policy, LE Europe, WIFO, WIK Consult, with contributions from Dawid Ustowski, Charles Seidenberg, Michel Boeheim, Luxembourg: Publications Office of the European Union, 2020 (the "VBER Support Study"), available at: https://ec.europa.eu/competition/publications/reports/kd0420219enn.pdf

European Commission (2020b) White Paper On Artificial Intelligence – A European approach to excellence and trust, COM(2020) 65 final, 19 February 2020. Available at: https://ec.europa.eu/info/sites/info/files/commission-white-paper-artificial-intelligencefeb2020_en.pdf

European Commission (2020c) Antitrust: Commission consults stakeholders on a possible new competition tool. Press Release, 2 June 2020, available at: https://ec.europa.eu/commission/presscorner/detail/en/ip_20_977

Feat T (2020) Blockchain: Société Générale et la Banque de France innovent, Option Finance, 12 June 2020, available at: https://www.optionfinance.fr/entreprises-finance/financement-des-entreprises-et-tresorerie/blockchain-societe-generale-et-la-banque-de-france-innovent.html

French Competition Authority (2020a) Contribution de l'Autorité de la Concurrence au débat sur la politique de la concurrence et les enjeux numériques 14 February 2020, available at: https://www.autoritedelaconcurrence.fr/sites/default/files/2020-02/2020.02.28_contribution_adlc_enjeux_num.pdf

French Competition Authority (2020b) L'Autorité crée un service de l'économique numérique, 9 January 2020, available at: https://www.autoritedelaconcurrence.fr/fr/communiques-de-presse/lautorite-cree-un-service-de-leconomie-numerique

Laitenberger J (2018), Speech, W@Competition Conference, 1 March 2018, "Enforcing EU Competition Law in a Time of Change: Is Disruptive Competition Disrupting Competition Enforcement?" available at https://ec.europa.eu/competition/speeches/text/sp2018_03_en.pdf

Laitenberger J (2019) Closing Remarks at the "Shaping Competition Policy in the Era of Digitisation, Speech, 17 January 2019, conference https://ec.europa.eu/competition/speeches/text/sp2019_01_en.pdf

Madero CV (2019) Antitrust in times of upheaval, *Speech at the 2019 CRA Conference,* Brussels, 10 December 2019, available at: https://ec.europa.eu/competition/speeches/text/sp2019_13_en.pdf

Schrepel T (2019) Collusion by blockchain and smart contracts. Harv J Law Technol. 33, n° 1, Fall 2019. https://jolt.law.harvard.edu/assets/articlePDFs/v33/03-Schrepel.pdf

Vestager M (2019) Defining marks in a new age, Vestager, Margrethe (2019) Defining marks in a new age, Speech at Chillin' Competition Conference, Brussels, 9 December 2019, available at: https://ec.europa.eu/commission/commissioners/2019-2024/vestager/announcements/defining-markets-new-age_en

Vestager M (2020) Competition in a Digital Age: Changing Enforcement for Changing Times, 26 June 2020, ASCOLA Annual Conference, Speech available at: https://ec.europa.eu/commission/commissioners/2019-2024/vestager/announcements/competition-digital-age-changing-enforcement-changing-times_en

Epilogue: Algorithmic Antitrust—A Questioning

Aurelien Portuese

Abstract What have we learned from the competition analysis applied to algorithm-driven companies? First, the interest by enforcement agencies and the complexity of the antitrust implications of algorithms suggest that a new area of antitrust inquiry has emerged – namely, what we coin as "algorithmic antitrust". Second, contrary to early treatments of algorithmic antitrust, the experience of algorithms on competition both reveals considerable innovation benefits of algorithms and limited anticompetitive concerns. As algorithms increasingly become technologies adopted by every company in any given industry, the competitive advantage of algorithms over non-algorithmic competitive shrinks. As algorithmic innovation quickly becomes commonly used, algorithmic competition intensifies, and allegedly anticompetitive conduct becomes common business practices. In other words, more than strong assertions, algorithmic antitrust raises many questions and more questioning than gloomy predictions of algorithm-driven anticompetitive conduct. As companies compete via algorithmic innovations, antitrust enforcement ought to reconsider their overall pessimistic conclusions about algorithmic antitrust and rather ensure that companies embrace algorithms as an innovative way to compete.

Algorithmic antitrust—an expression we coined, scrutinized and tried to unwrap the mystics. The journey we have embarked on leaves us with perhaps more questions than answers.

To be sure, the brilliant contributors of this book have indeed conveyed a more positivistic approach to technological innovation and its impact on competition. Without naivety, the contributors have developed a coherent and convincing view beyond the mere techlash or a precautionary approach to technological innovations. The authors may not fully agree with one another, and yet they share the willingness to develop a rationale, lucid, and not catastrophic view of technological innovation.

A. Portuese (✉)
The Schumpeter Project on Competition Policy, Information Technology and Innovation Foundation, Washington, DC, USA
e-mail: aportuese@itif.org

A. Portuese (ed.), *Algorithmic Antitrust*, Economic Analysis of Law in European Legal Scholarship 12, https://doi.org/10.1007/978-3-030-85859-9_8

Evidence matters, so too innovation. Mere speculations should not be the banal exercise of lawyers, even less of regulators. Innovation, and the capacity of our society to progress, are at stake.

Algorithmic antitrust remains in its infancy. We may have delineated the contours of the study of algorithms for antitrust purposes, more researches are needed, and numerous questions abound yet. First, the final judgments in the leading cases (Google Shopping, Amazon,. . .) would determine the direction European algorithmic antitrust takes. Would judges be willing to deep dive into the algorithms as a criterion for anticompetitive conduct, or would they prefer to stay outside the black box? Second, as European algorithmic antitrust develops, how do the American antitrust authorities would react and develop their practices: would the ocean widen up or be filled up with standard practices and shared information? Third, as new European regulations on algorithms developed at the time of writing these few lines,[1] would algorithms be regulated through antitrust exclusively or with a mixture of antitrust and sectoral regulations? How would these regulations and antitrust enforcement function in practice so that innovation in Europe is not stifled? Fourth, what is the relevance of the regulation of European algorithmic antitrust with the rise of blockchain technologies that disrupt digital platforms?

We may have deciphered some of the complexities about algorithmic antitrust, but many other areas needing clarification require both time and further research. We believe nevertheless that this book provided valuable insights for an ever-evolving area of enforcement. As we consume products and services increasingly via algorithms, the relevance of these debates may certainly not wane out.

References

European Commission (2020) Europe fit for the Digital Age: Commission proposes new rules for digital platforms, Press Release, December 15, 2020

European Commission (2021) Europe fit for the Digital Age: Commission proposes new rules and actions for excellence and trust in Artificial Intelligence, Press Release, April 21, 2021

[1] European Commission (2020, 2021).